SOCIALIST SOCIETY AND
FREE ENTERPRISE POLITICS

SOCIALIST SOCIETY AND
FREE ENTERPRISE POLITICS

A Study of Voluntary Associations in Urban India

Robert G. Wirs ng

WITHDRAWN

CAROLINA ACADEMIC PRESS
Durham, North Carolina

Published in the United States by

CAROLINA ACADEMIC PRESS
2206 Chapel Hill Road
Box 8791 Forest Hills Station
Durham, N.C. 27707

ISBN 0-89089-066-8

Library of Congress Catalog Card No. 76-6775

Printed in India

To Nancy and Aaron

Preface

Democratic politics mandates the sharing of power. The mandate to share in power does not, however, describe the precise institutional mix through which the sharing is to be done. Neither does it set clear limits on the amounts of power to be held by those sharing in it, identify the groups entitled to more (or less) of it, provide for ironclad checks on its abuse or, for that matter, make any promises (or give any instructions) about its intelligent use. Share power. That is all it commands.

Democratic India has bowed to the mandate. Power sharing devices abound from top to bottom in the political system. Most of them are familiar enough to citizens of other democracies. One of the most familiar is the voluntary association. India's voluntary associations are prolific, diverse and, like many of their counterparts elsewhere, politically involved. They are part of the institutional mix generated in independent and democratic India to preside over the sharing process. Their part of the mix is not uniform in all places. Neither is their share in power. They are found in rural as well as urban areas. This book is about voluntary associations—some powerful, some powerless—in one city of central India.

It is more than that, however. It is a book about political accountability, about the bonds between local politicians and their urban constituents, and about the institutionalizing of these bonds through the medium of voluntary associations. It is an inquiry into both the process and the meaning of power sharing in urban India.

India is an important area in which to study the development of voluntary associations and the political relationships that grow within them, not only because its political system has entered upon a "time of troubles" with unforeseeable consequences for the future of democracy itself, but because in virtually no other developing country has the democratic mandate been hitherto so avidly applied to the task of mass social mobilization. Rightly or wrongly, mass voluntary action has been presumed intrinsic to and a catalyst of the processes of social and economic development. India's voluntary associations are in great measure the deliberate offspring of government policy, the annointed local executors of social change. How well they function in this capacity, and with what consequences for the political system, are matters of concern far beyond the borders of India.

This study is based most importantly on a series of interviews conducted in Nagpur, in the state of Maharashtra, between January 1969 and March 1970. Roughly 300 persons were formally interviewed in sessions lasting generally from one to two hours, though in some cases single interviews spanned as many as four separate sessions. Most of the respondents were active in connection with the municipal election of 16 March 1969, Nagpur's fourth post-independence municipal contest. Of the 543 candidates who contested the election, 187 (34 per per cent) were interviewed, 136 (25 per cent) as part of a systematic random sampling and the remaining 51 to fill various gaps in knowledge uncovered in the course of research. Interviews were held, additionally, with 73 campaign workers, fleshing out the grassroots perspective of the study, as well as with over 32 local political party leaders and office bearers, government bureaucrats, academics, leaders of trade union organizations, cooperatives, and other associations. Interviewing was carried out principally in the eleven months following the election.

Uniform social and political background data were collected on all the 543 candidates. This was accomplished in part through direct interviews, in part through resort to questioning of alternative but informed sources within each of the city's seventy-five wards. The amount of data collected varied considerably, having been most comprehensively gathered for the 136 candidates in the random sampling, less so for the 75 winning candidates, and least thoroughly for the 543 candidates as a whole. I chose not to administer a formal questionnaire. I did ask a uniform set of basic questions of all respondents, but the interviews were otherwise open-ended, guided by my perception of the respondent's knowledge and experience. The core questions, apart from personal and social background, related to voluntary associational affiliations. These were aimed at elucidating the types and extent of the respondent's active involvement in a given voluntary association, and included questions pertinent to the activities of the associations themselves, ranging from size of membership to sources of financial support. In an effort to spot the points at which politics crossed paths with associational activity, questions were raised, for example, concerning the mechanics of building political support from associational networks, and concerning the uses of voluntary associations in mounting a campaign strategy. The interviews were, moreover, a rich source of information on local political history, community composition of the wards, and patterns of political rivalry. Respondents were asked in most cases to comment on their opponents' associational involvements, a useful doublecheck on the veracity of informants.

The interviews varied considerably in quality, and the reliability of data gathered through them is not and could not be uniformly high. Every effort was made to obtain multiple confirmation of statements made in interviews from different types of sources. In analyzing and reporting the data, care has been taken to weigh the circumstances under which collection occurred. Where facts were of dubious validity, they have either not been reported at all or have been appropriately qualified in the text. Interviews were consciously guided along the pathway of experienced phenomena rather than opinion, avoiding, whereever possible, questions of motive either of the respondents' or their opponents' behavior.

Most of the interviews with campaign workers, party leaders, bureaucrats and so on, dealt with particular facets of voluntary associational activity. Though originally conceived to be merely supportive of the general survey, these case studies came to assume central importance. Whether concerned with a branch of the cooperative movement, with a local education society, with a particular politician's background, or with an election contest, they enabled a concentration of attention for which the survey of candidates by itself was ill-suited. Nonetheless, the study is dependent for its persuasiveness on the extent to which the results of the survey dovetail with those of the case studies.

In addition to the interviews, considerable useful information was obtained from locally published books, government documents, newspapers, and other printed material, translated when necessary with the aid of linguists of Nagpur University. Daily reading of two of the more prominent local newspapers (both English-medium publications), the *Nagpur Times* and the *Hitavada*, helped in gaining perspective on the city's political life. Their reports on local politics were supplemented by translated material from the local vernacular press, especially the Marathi-medium *Tarun Bharat* and the Hindi-medium *Navbharat*.

Next to the interviews, perhaps of greatest importance in developing a realistic appreciation of the texture of local politics was the deliberate effort to repeatedly visit the city's seventy-five wards, to tour them when possible with local political leaders, to explore neighborhood associations, and to observe political personalities interacting with each other and with the public. With respect to the election period itself, there was abundant opportunity to observe its various aspects, to attend rallies, to accompany candidates on their canvassing rounds and, in general, to witness the spectacle of a local election.

While I have followed the practice of using real names of persons and places in the text, identities have been concealed whenever their revelation might have tended to place individuals in an unfavorable light or where non-attribution was specifically requested. This was necessary in only a few cases, permitting the great bulk of data to be reported essentially as originally communicated. Purely decorative professional language has been avoided. Hindi and Marathi words, whenever employed, have been spelled in accord with conventional local usage. Since transliteration from these languages into English is a matter where people may reasonably differ, I have occasionally had to insert my own preferences in spelling governed by the rule of consistency.

I have received invaluable assistance from numerous persons in the course of preparing this book. My greatest debt of gratitude is owed to those hundreds of Nagpur politicians whose generosity with me and candor about themselves can never really be repaid. For friendship and sound counsel throughout my stay in Nagpur, special thanks are due to Professor N. G. S. Kini, Dr Ramprakash Ahuja, Dayaram S. Nikose, Braham Dutt, M. B. Karangale, and Prabhakar Khedkar. I relied heavily on the interpreting skills of Ulhas G. Deshmukh and Pratoo N. Chaudhari. Sudhakar M. Joshi and Kamal H. Dafre invested endless hours in the patient translation of books and documents. Though they go unnamed, my gratitude is no less to the many others in India who helped me in small ways and large.

The research for this book was accomplished originally for a doctoral dissertation supervised by Professor David H. Bayley of the University of Denver. His guidance and constant encouragement were helpful at all stages. A number of persons assisted along the way by reading parts or all of the manuscript. Of these, my special thanks are due to Professor Donald B. Rosenthal who made valuable suggestions on the final draft. Philip Oldenburg provided me with a copy of his M.A. thesis, an earlier study of Nagpur municipal politics, and some of his findings are included in the present text.

Field research in India was supported by a fellowship grant from the American Institute of Indian Studies. Writing of the original version was assisted by financial support from the Graduate School of International Studies of the University of Denver. The Department of Government and International Studies and the Institute of International Studies of the University of South Carolina, where I have been teaching since 1971, have provided typing assistance at crucial points of the book's preparation.

Two articles based on materials gathered in the course of this study have previously been published: "Associational 'Micro-Arenas' in Indian Urban Politics," *Asian Survey* (April 1973); and "Strategies of Political Bargaining in Indian City Politics," a chapter in *The City in Indian Politics*, Donald B. Rosenthal, editor (New Delhi: Thomson Press, Ltd., 1976). While some of the same materials are discussed at various points in the present volume, they are exploited in ways substantially different from these articles.

My wife Nancy has been a slave to this book as long as I. Her patient and intelligent reading of each successive draft has made the book appreciably more comprehensible than it would otherwise have been. For this and for much else, this book is affectionately dedicated to her and to our son Aaron.

ROBERT G. WIRSING
Associate Professor
University of South Carolina

Postscript

This book was completed during the period of emergency rule, which extended for twenty-one months, from June 1975 to March 1977. The abridgment of civil liberties and constitutional rule which occurred during that period seemed to betray a weakening commitment to democratic institutions on the part of India's leaders. My apprehensions in this regard appear from time to time in the pages that follow. The emergency is at an end as this book goes to press. In the last days of March, in India's sixth general election, the ruling Congress party was swept from power, defeated by a coalition of non-communist opposition parties. Ironically, Indira Gandhi, who had confidently called the election to vindicate her assumption of emergency powers, turned out to be its chief political casualty. Happily, this study of India's democratic political process is now not only of historical interest.

R.G.W.

May 1977

List of Tables

Contents

1

Introduction

In the late hours of 14 August 1947, on the solemn occasion of the transfer of power to a free India, the new prime minister, Jawaharlal Nehru, eloquently captured the majesty of the moment in his famous "tryst with destiny" speech to the constituent assembly. India, he announced, had awakened to life and freedom. "A moment comes," said Nehru, "which comes but rarely in history, when we step out from the old to the new, when an age ends, and when the soul of a nation, long suppressed, finds utterance."[1] Almost three decades have passed since that historic hour. Nehru's impassioned words remain as stirring as ever; but with the passage of time their innocence has been exposed to the vicissitudes of a society destined not only to life and freedom, but to widespread impoverishment, uncontrolled population growth, bitter communal strife, recurring warfare and—with the declaration of an unprecedented state of emergency in late June 1975—the shattering realization of its political frailty. Indeed, with the departure of the British, an age had ended. But we have been reminded many times since that the release of the soul of India promised a good deal less than a golden new age.

In terms of political achievement, the record of the past several decades is certainly open to controversy. In spite of repeated and severe threats to its political institutions, India remains a parliamentary democracy. Indeed, if the *endurance* of parliamentary institutions is an acceptable measure of success, then India has better claim to it than most

[1]Quoted in Michael Brecher, *Nehru: A Political Biography* (Boston: Beacon Press, 1962), p. 137.

new states. In a succession of five major national elections and a far greater number of state and local contests, India's political system has proven itself a tenacious and almost solitary counterexample to the innumerable cases of collapsed democracy in the post-colonial world. After a temporary lapse in the wake of the electoral setback of 1967, the ruling Congress party was restored to one-party dominance at the national level and in most of the states in the 1971-72 elections. Confounding the many prophecies of disintegration, India began the decade of the 1970s not only with a rejuvenated Congress and the stunning defeat of its arch rival Pakistan, but with its democratic institutions essentially intact.

Endurance is, of course, not the only or even the best measure of a system's performance. It has long been apparent that for many of India's millions hunger, disease, inflation and joblessness were far more salient criteria by which to judge their country's progress. No system could merit popular confidence if it failed decade after decade to remove the most elemental and stark forms of oppression and misery from the backs of its people.

Endurance is more than ever a questionable measure in India today. The arrest and detention in summer 1975 of thousands of members of the non-communist political opposition, the quick passage of constitutional amendments undermining judicial checks on the authority of the executive branch, the postponement of national elections, and the vesting of almost unlimited emergency powers in the hands of Prime Minister Indira Gandhi have sent India lurching ahead on an unfamiliar and unpredictable course. But even before the curtailment of political freedoms in 1975, gathering economic and political crises had already persuaded many that Indian democracy had at last reached a threshold beyond which continuing failure to cope with mounting demands would imperil the very survival of its political institutions.[2]

Clearly, however, endurance may not be the only achievement of the Indian political system. While the calamitous aspects of India's post-independence history have perhaps made enigmatic the persistence of its political institutions, they have also obscured whatever other virtues the system may possess. This is understandable. Crises attract attention; and India's crises have been many and spectacular. They have diverted attention from the routine events and transactions that comprise

[2]See, for example, Ram Joshi, "India 1974: Growing Political Crisis," *Asian Survey*, XV (February 1975), 85-95.

the great bulk of political activity and, in making the system's survival seem the greatest of anachronisms, have magnified the virtue of endurance. But Indian politics is not merely the sum of its crises, and no estimate confined to the system's ability to manage (or mismanage) them can capture the full import of political democracy in Indian life. In fact, so brief has been the duration of democracy in India and so problematic is its future that endurance, the most obvious of its virtues, may turn out to be the least of its accomplishments.

This being the case, it is essential to ask: Of what else does Indian politics consist? And is some of this to be reckoned among India's achievements, along with the system's survival? These questions underlie this study. To answer them attention has been drawn away from the catastrophic in order to bring into sharper focus the commonplace events, rude institutions and unpolished politicians in whose mundane universe may be obtained an alternative and perhaps more reliable (or at least more impartial) measure of India's political development. This study searches for this measure in the politics of one city—Nagpur, in the central Indian state of Maharashtra.[3] More precisely, it explores

---

[3]Indian urban politics has been the subject of considerable research. Among the more valuable studies are those of Donald B. Rosenthal, whose writings chiefly concern the cities of Agra and Poona. See, for example, his "Functions of Urban Political Systems: Comparative Analysis and the Indian Case," in *Community Structure and Decision-Making: Comparative Analyses*, Terry N. Clark, editor (San Francisco: Chandler Publishing Company, 1968), pp. 269-303; "Deurbanization, Elite Displacement, and Political Change in India," *Comparative Politics*, II (January 1970), 169-201; "Factions and Alliances in Indian City Politics," *Midwest Journal of Political Science*, X (August 1966), 320-349; "Administrative Politics in Two Indian Cities," *Asian Survey*, VI (April 1966), 201-215; "Friendship and Deference Patterns in Two Indian Municipal Councils," *Social Forces*, XLV (December 1966), 178-192; "Local Power and Comparative Politics: Notes Toward the Study of Comparative Local Politics," unpublished paper prepared for delivery at the annual meeting of the American Political Science Association, Washington, D.C., 5-9 September 1972; and *The Limited Elite: Politics and Government in Two Indian Cities* (Chicago: The University of Chicago Press, 1970). A major study of state government penetration of urban affairs, focused on Indore, is Rodney W. Jones, *Urban Politics in India: Area, Power, and Policy in a Penetrated System* (Berkeley: University of California Press, 1974). For a recent broad discussion of Indian city politics, see the contributions of Robert Wirsing, Mary Katzenstein, Peter Mayer, and Roderick Church in "Symposium on Indian Urban Politics," *Asian Survey*, XIII (April 1973), 380-438. Older but still useful studies include B.A.V. Sharma and R.T. Jangam,

the politics of voluntary associations—cooperatives, education societies, social and religious organizations, and the like—in that city.

There are several compelling reasons for concentrating on voluntary associations. The simplest, perhaps, is that there is an enormous amount of political activity evident within them. This is a virtually inevitable consequence of the essentially decentralized and mass participatory strategy of social and economic development adopted by the Indian government. The strategy encourages the creation of voluntary associations in such areas as housing, education and credit, makes various kinds of public assistance available to them and, in doing so, assures competition for their control. Concerned with the satisfaction of basic social needs, voluntary associations are inescapably politicized. It could hardly be otherwise in a society where the very survival of many depends on the assiduous use of every means (the organized influence of voluntary associations is one) to obtain the bare necessities of life. Voluntary associations do not exercise exclusively political functions (e.g., education societies manage schools, religious groups arrange local festivals, sports societies sponsor athletic events). But this study verifies,

---

The Bombay Municipal Corporation: An Election Study (Bombay: Popular Book Depot, 1962); V.M. Sirsikar's study of elections in Poona, Political Behavior in India: A Case Study of the 1962 General Elections (Bombay: Manaktalas, 1965); Henry C. Hart, "Bombay Politics: Pluralism or Polarization?" Journal of Asian Studies, XX (May 1961), 267-274; S.P. Verma and C.P. Bhambhri, editors, Elections and Political Consciousness in India (Meerut: Meenakshi Prakashan, 1967), which contains a study of a legislative constituency in Jaipur; R. Srinivasan and B.A.V. Sharma's study of the corporations of Bombay, Delhi, Calcutta and Madras, "Politics in Urban India: A Study of Four Corporations," in Studies in Indian Democracy, S.P. Aiyar and R. Srinivasan, editors (Bombay: Allied Publishers, 1965), pp. 467-514; several urban-related studies in Indian Voting Behavior, Myron Weiner and Rajni Kothari, editors (Calcutta: Firma K.L. Mukhopadhyay, 1965); Robert T. Norman, "Urban Political Development: India," and Philip Oldenburg, "Indian Urban Politics: Citizen, Administrator, and Councilor in Delhi," both unpublished papers prepared for delivery at the annual meeting of the American Political Science Association, Chicago, 7-11 September 1971. The only prior studies of Nagpur politics are Philip K. Oldenburg, "Indian Urban Politics, With Particular Reference to the Nagpur Corporation" (unpublished Master's thesis, Department of Political Science, University of Chicago, 1968); and the series of studies of the 1967 general elections in Nagpur, currently in preparation by N.G.S. Kini and other members of the political science faculty of Nagpur University.

as have others,[4] that they are major arenas of political activity and, hence, vital to an appreciation of Indian politics.

The relevance of voluntary associations to the study of Indian politics goes beyond internal struggles for control of them. Associational politics occurs in the broader context of city (and state) politics, and is an integral part of it. Nagpur's voluntary associations were examined in connection with the March 1969 municipal election campaign, in which 543 candidates contested for 75 seats in the municipal council (corporation).[5] A striking number of the candidates was found to be actively involved in voluntary associations, often exploiting them as a means for obtaining public political office. The associations are staging grounds for political campaigns, and frequently mirror the power rivalries of the larger municipal arena. The politics of the city is, in significant ways, the politics of voluntary associations. A central purpose of this study is to illuminate the linkages between them. Accordingly, attention is on ways in which voluntary associations have affected the criteria of successful political leadership, to the relationship between voluntary associations and political party and factional organization, and to the role associations play in the calculation of political strategy.

There are additional important reasons for studying voluntary associations. Any assessment of India's political development must confront the question of the quality of its democracy. The Indian constitution extends the franchise to all citizens enabling them, theoretically, to hold their leaders accountable for their actions. But how much of this promise has been realized? Much has been written casting doubt on the ability of the masses to use the vote as intended. A common theme is that India's traditional hierarchical pattern of social authority, sanctioned by custom and reinforced by gross inequalities in status, wealth and power, continues to handicap the growth of attitudes and behaviors

---

[4]In his study of Congress party recruitment for the 1967 general election in Bihar and Maharashtra, W.H. Morris-Jones reported "the outstanding importance of two areas of public life—education and cooperatives" among the applicants for Congress nominations. "Political Recruitment and Political Development," in *Politics and Change in Developing Countries*, Colin Leys, editor (London: Cambridge University Press, 1969), p. 132.

[5]As of 1961, some twenty-four of India's larger cities bore the designation of corporation, a distinction based mainly on population, but also on political status, size of revenue and commercial importance. Nagpur gained corporation status in 1951. Historical background and details of urban government may be found in *Local Government in India*, M. Venkatarangaiya and M. Pattabhiram, editors (Bombay: Allied Publishers, 1969).

essential to the practice of genuine democracy. It has been claimed, for
example, that the pattern of relations between elite and mass in India
is characteristically one of deference, dependence and sublimation of
individual drives for autonomy. "The traditional Indian peasant," writes
Phyllis Arora,

> is conditioned to feel a strong obligation to offer obedience and res-
> pect—usually in a formal, highly stylized manner—to teachers,
> elders, and heads of groups into which he has been born. He is
> socialized to accept not merely the authority of a recognized leader,
> but the collective authority of the group upon whose behalf the
> leader exercises his will and prerogative.[6]

The effects of such ingrained habits of deference to traditional authorities allegedly pervade the political process. According to Arora, India's
peasant population typically relegates the responsibility for political
decision-making to group leaders; and defiance of their decisions is
a path open ordinarily only to those possessed of high social status,
economic autonomy, or education. Even if the individual peasant were
so motivated, the monopoly of political knowledge by a narrow stratum
of the population, and the ability of this group to inflict costly reprisals
on the economically dependent peasant, pose almost insuperable barriers
to the assertion of political independence. The legitimacy of authority
is upheld by personal intimacy; the peasant's world is a universe closed
to penetration by the impersonal and goal-oriented associations of modern political systems. In these circumstances, direct communication
between political outsiders and peasant villagers is difficult to establish;
whatever communication there is, is likely to be conveyed through (and
filtered by) the traditional indigenous leadership.[7]

The combination of fear, helplessness, ignorance and deep-seated
emotional acceptance of submissive roles prevent, Arora contends,
the development of attitudes and behaviors requisite to a democratic
system. The response to political authority necessary in political democracies depends on the citizen's assumption that his participation is

[6]"Patterns of Political Response in Indian Peasant Society," in *Asian Political
Processes*, Henry S. Albinski, editor (Boston: Allyn and Bacon, Inc., 1971),
pp. 33-34.
[7]*Ibid.*, pp. 34-38. For a recent systematic attempt to define the political traits
of traditional societies, see Monte Palmer, *Dilemmas of Political Development*
(Itasca, Illinois: F.E. Peacock Publishers, Inc., 1973), pp. 10-38.

legitimate, that he is more or less equal to those holding or aspiring to power, and that independent choice and conflict are natural and even desirable components of the political process. Accordingly, democracy relies on the individual's effective conduct of the role of bargainer, in which he is competent to exchange votes for benefits, and to hold the powerful accountable for their actions in responding to his demands.[8]

In probing leader-follower relationships in the context of urban voluntary associations, we will be dealing with a set of variables remote in many respects from those influencing the narrow universe of village society. While Nagpur, a relatively small and only marginally industrialized city of the hinterland, is likely to contain a type of politics different from that of the sprawling and highly industrialized conurbations of Bombay, Madras, Calcutta, or Delhi, it is even more likely that its politics, affected by such factors as the spatial proximity of large numbers of people, occupational mobility, higher rates of literacy, the presence of a substantial middle class, and the influx of large numbers of uprooted rural migrants, will differ in substance from that of agrarian society. On the other hand, it cannot be assumed that the patterns of authority characteristic of traditional village India have evaporated entirely, or even substantially, in the urban environment. There are a number of studies indicating that behavioral traits associated with rural society persist in spite of urbanization.[9] Nagpur's voluntary associations provide a concrete setting both for assessing the extent of the persistence of traditional political values and for tracing their influence on political relationships.

If deference and dependence far surpass equality and reciprocity in the relations between political leaders and their voting clientele, then we are led to expect voluntary associations (regardless of their stated intentions) to perform merely as traditional agencies in modern garb—that is, to protect and enrich the privileged, to exploit, manipulate and hold subservient the poor. If the poor "do not even perceive their own plight very clearly [and] believe their inferior status is ordained by heaven,"[10] then they are unlikely to use voluntary associations to press their demands for a fairer distribution of social goods.

[8]"Patterns of Political Response in Indian Peasant Society," *op. cit.*, pp. 44–46.

[9]See, for example, Joan M. Nelson, *Migrants, Urban Poverty, and Instability in Developing Nations*, Occasional Papers in International Affairs No. 22 (Cambridge: Center for International Affairs, Harvard University, 1969).

[10]Gunnar Myrdal, *Asian Drama: An Inquiry into the Poverty of Nations*, II (Middlesex, England: The Penguin Press, 1968), p. 767.

How substantially social change, in company with the exercise of the franchise, has eroded traditional obligations to authority may be answered, in part, by our examination of voluntary associations. The associations are certainly well positioned to articulate voter interests. But do associational leaders respond, in fact, to broad-based popular demands? Do the associations provide real opportunity for hitherto subordinate strata of the urban population to gain positions of power and to influence the allocation of public resources? What governs the distribution of associational patronage? Who dispenses? And who receives? In brief, do we encounter in the voluntary associations conditions favorable to the emergence of participant values, that is, values consistent with the development of relations of accountability between the leaders and the led?

The study of voluntary associations is equally illuminating in regard to another and closely related characteristic of Indian society—its extreme cultural fragmentation. By virtually any definition, India ranks as one of the world's most culturally heterogeneous societies—a fact of enormous importance in evaluating the development of its democratic institutions.[11] The very birth of independent India was attended by communal rivalry of unprecedented dimensions; and its history since then has been replete with examples of cultural self-assertion ranging from the conflict over the linguistic reorganization of states to the demands of hill tribes for greater autonomy or even independence.

The persistence and the strength of these cultural loyalties have been the object of much attention by students of the Indian political system, and the cause of considerable pessimism among them. The priority attached to the building of a national value consensus has led many scholars to equate political modernization with national integration,[12] and to question whether India and other ascriptively plural societies of the Third World can successfully foster democratic processes in the face of the seemingly irrational primordial and sectarian attitudes of the masses. Selig Harrison was among the first to draw widespread atten-

[11]The best recent discussion of India's cultural cleavages is Paul R. Brass, *Language, Religion and Politics in North India* (London: Cambridge University Press, 1974). For a wide-ranging exploration of ethnic conflict, consult Cynthia H. Enloe, *Ethnic Conflict and Political Development* (Boston: Little, Brown and Company, 1973). See also Walker Connor, "Ethnology and the Peace of South Asia," *World Politics*, XXII (October 1969), 51-85.

[12]Lucian W. Pye, *Aspects of Political Development* (Boston: Little, Brown and Company, 1966), p. 38.

tion to this matter in reference to Indian politics; like many others since, he gloomily forecast a resurgence of such traditional loyalties as to caste, language and religious community in the struggle for scarce resources. Unity, he judged, was likely to be maintained against these centrifugal forces only through resort to authoritarian forms of government.[13] In another seminal piece, Clifford Geertz wrote that the less developed states were "abnormally susceptible to serious disaffection based on primordial sentiments" such as ties of blood, race, language, region, religion or custom.[14] These ties, extraordinarily potent in such countries as India, do not yield to arguments or programs couched in the vernacular of rational self-interest, for their essence, in Geertz's opinion, is neither temporal nor material.[15]

More recently, in one of the most emphatically pessimistic investigations of the politics of multi-ethnic states to appear thus far, Alvin Rabushka and Kenneth Shepsle arrive at the conclusion that the resolution of intense but conflicting preferences in culturally plural societies is rarely, if ever, compatible with a democratic framework.[16] In a sophisticated analysis, illustrated with case study materials from eighteen culturally plural societies, they strive to demonstrate that government intervention in the allocation of social goods, when coupled with democratic institutions, almost inevitably "ethnicizes" the political process; that is, it makes ethnicity the most salient issue in public political arenas. Accordingly, ethnic differentiation in plural societies is frequently the most convenient and exploitable condition governing access of groups to collectively provided goods. State intervention in development invites group contention over resources in public arenas; and political democracy facilitates the generation of isolated and non-negotiable demands by separate cultural communities. Political entrepreneurs, concerned foremost with winning elections, naturally forge coalitions on the basis of the most intensely felt preferences of the voters. Since the intensity of ethnic preferences is constantly enlarged by the

[13] *India: The Most Dangerous Decades* (Princeton: Princeton University Press, 1960), p. 4.

[14] "The Integrative Revolution: Primordial Sentiments and Civil Politics in the New States," in *Old Societies and New States: The Quest for Modernity in Asia and Africa,* Clifford Geertz, editor (New York: The Free Press of Glencoe; 1963), p. 109.

[15] *Ibid.,* pp. 109-110.

[16] *Politics in Rural Societies: A Theory of Democratic Instability* (Columbus: Charles E. Merrill Publishing Company, 1972), p. 217.

real or fancied discriminatory distribution of public goods, politicians are drawn to manipulate or exploit ethnic rather than alternative issues. Democracy thus breeds ethnic discontent, inhibits the aggregation of interests, and in the end produces political instability.[17]

The "ethnic pessimists" have a worldwide pool of persuasive evidence upon which to draw. There is no doubt that in India, as in other countries, cultural pluralism results in *political* as well as *social* divisiveness, handicapping the development of functionally oriented and socially aggregative interest groups, attaching a parochial definition to leadership responsibilities, and interfering with pragmatic bargaining—all potentially injurious to the practice of democracy.

Such facts should not be ignored. But it remains essential that we ask whether, in the microcosm of an Indian city, the fragmented cultural fabric does indeed result in the generation of political demands irreconcilable within the framework of political democracy. Since Nagpur's voluntary associations are important media of interest articulation and often manage the local distribution of public resources, they are a natural setting in which to observe the ways in which group identities permeate the political process. In the course of this study, therefore, much attention is paid to the community affiliations of political participants and, in particular, to the influence of cultural identifications on the goals, membership and functions of voluntary associations

Some of Nagpur's voluntary associations (e.g.., the caste associations) are explicitly communal in orientation. Others (e.g., credit cooperatives) are not. Cultural loyalties impinge, no doubt, on the motives and operational style of virtually all associational activists: the pervasiveness of communal identities is no less apparent in Nagpur than elsewhere in India. But we must seek to establish whether such identities preclude the emergence of alternative grounds for group allegiance, or merely modify them. The vulnerability of local voluntary associations to cultural divisiveness is clear enough—they are a product, in some measure, of democratic decentralization and a focal point of increased public intervention in the provision of social goods, logical grounds for ethnic collision. Less clear is the extent to which cultural criteria do in fact influence their goals and activities and, in particular, determine popular expectations of them and their managers. What needs clarification is the role,

[17] *Ibid.* The authors' conception of politics in plural societies is developed in pp. 1-92.

if any, voluntary associations are playing as catalysts of a secular style of politics, freed somewhat of the encumbrances of cultural identification and allegiance, and responding to popular claims cast in the language of material rather than primordial gratification. In brief, this study questions the *content* of the bond that links political leaders with voters in the voluntary associations of Nagpur.

Thus far, the objectives of this study have been described almost exclusively in terms of the *political* relevance of voluntary associations. Since an important *economic* mission has been entrusted to many of them, note must be taken of the role they play in implementing the nation's development plans. Voluntary associations may be contributing significantly to the realization of India's democratic aspirations; but not without economic costs—costs claimed by many to be far too great for India.

With few exceptions, India's ruling elites are committed to the rapid industrialization and modernization of Indian society. While the more blatantly coercive measures of the modernizing oligarchies of the Soviet Union and the Peoples Republic of China have been foresworn, the texture of central policy-making over the past several decades (e.g., the centralized plans and the proliferation of planning agencies at all levels; the constitutional allocation of major responsibility for development to the public sector in such areas as heavy industries, power and transport; and, more recently, the nationalization of the domestic banking system) eloquently testifies to the intention of India's leaders to intervene in order to bring about the desired transition to modernity.

Their commitment to a "socialist" pattern of development is markedly schizophrenic, however. Whereas the central organs of government may take credit for *initiating* developmental programs in India, the actual *conduct* of development administration is essentially voluntaristic, the product of a decision to promote mass participation in decision-making at regional and local levels of the polity. The decision must be acknowledged to have been a risky one. The decentralizing of authority over such critical matters as the planning and implementation of development programs could provoke social indiscipline, discourge saving for capital investment, and thwart the achievement of social and economic objectives deemed mandatory by the central leadership. Nonetheless, commitment to the decision is everywhere apparent: in the rural sector it is enshrined in the system of *panchayati raj*, a three-tiered legislative cum administrative structure reaching up from village to district and now established in virtually all Indian states; in the urban sector it is implanted in the authority of the municipal councils,[11] and in both rural and urban sectors it is manifest not only in the formally empowered state legislative assemblies but, perhaps more importantly, in the deliberate sponsorship of a mammoth system of voluntary associations—most especially the cooperatives—entrusted with the implementation of development projects authored from above.

This mating of a mildly socialist program of development with a distinctly laissez-faire brand of democracy has contributed materially to the attractions of local politics, not only for the politicians (who can now exercise some control over the allocation of externally supplied developmental resources), but for the voters (whose reasons for holding local political leaders accountable for the satisfaction of popular demands are now sharply increased). But it has inspired, at the same time, a considerable amount of despair among those who consider the evolving pattern of decentralized authority compatible neither with India's political nor its economic needs. In the publication of Gunnar Myrdal's monumental *Asian Drama* in 1968, we have perhaps the most explicit and emphatic statement of disillusion. Myrdal's distaste for South Asian "permissiveness" and the inchoate premises of its leaders' developmental ambitions are a recurrent theme throughout his study. In contrast to South Asia, he points out, the West European countries entertained universal suffrage and the concept of the welfare state well

[18]It is true, as several observers have commented, that India's larger cities have technically been bypassed in the process of democratic decentralization. There is no urban self-governing structure comparable in scope and function to the system of *panchayati raj* in rural areas. In Nagpur, as in other cities, ultimate executive authority continues to lie with the state, and the policy-making role of the municipal legislature is clearly minimal. The distinction drawn between degrees of political autonomy between town and country is somewhat arbitrary, however, for it holds true only so long as we compare merely *formal* structures of government. The commitment to democratic decentralization permeates the entire range of relationships between state and city, not only those encompassed within the relatively impotent municipal legislature. If the presence of state governance in the cities is overwhelming, as observers tend to agree, it is certainly not in the form of a *diktat*. Though Donald B. Rosenthal takes the position that "the process of democratization of administration has not funneled down to lower levels of government," he acknowledges that "the presence of an administrative authority with little formal responsibility to elected members . . . does not prevent restraints from being placed upon his activities through informal mechanisms in the local political system, some of which flow from the operations of democracy at other levels of government." "Administrative Politics in Two Indian Cities," *op. cit.*, 201-204.

after attaining consolidated nation-states and social orders secure in the consensual rule of law.[19] But Myrdal's ire is aroused not simply by the presence of politically democratic forms of government (his argument is cast against *all* South Asian states), but by excessive voluntarism. In his discussion of democratic planning, for example, he castigates the South Asian governments for their uniform desire "to avoid compulsion and to work exclusively by means of persuasion and incentives." India, he asserts, has followed this course

to an extent that must seem extraordinary to a foreign observer, whether from a Western or Communist country. The other countries in South Asia have made a similar choice. There is in all respects extreme laxity, and government policy is continually trying to do things by using the carrot rather than the stick.[20]

With many other observers,[21] Myrdal rejects the assumption (explicitly endorsed by the Indian system of political democracy) that social and economic development requires the *voluntary* participation of the masses. To the contrary, modernization appears threatened by

[19]*Asian Drama*, II, p. 774.

[20]*Ibid.*, II, pp. 893-894. Essentially the same theme is developed more recently by Barrie M. Morrison, "Asian Drama, Act II: Development Prospects in South Asia," *Pacific Affairs*, 48 (Spring 1975), 5-26. Some of Myrdal's assumptions about South Asian behavior have met with stern objection from some of his reviewers. For example, see Kusum Nair, "Asian Drama—A Critique," *Economic Development and Cultural Change*, XVII (July 1969), 449-459.

[21]Among the more important theoretical works evincing skepticism of Third World democracy are Samuel P. Huntington, "Political Development and Political Decay," *World Politics*, XVII (April 1965), 386-430; Samuel N. Eisenstadt, "Breakdowns of Modernization," *Economic Development and Cultural Change*, XII (July 1964), 345-367; and Lucian W. Pye, *Aspects of Political Development*, especially pp. 71-88. Pye concludes "that it will be a slow difficult process to achieve the substance of democratic life in most of the new states. There is much truth in the often cynically advanced generalization that these societies are 'unprepared' for democracy. This is a disturbing conclusion for many people in the West who share a basic sympathy for the struggles of the new states because personally they are committed to the democratic spirit and are naturally inclined to identify with the weak, the poor, and the disadvantaged." The skepticism appears to be shared by many Third World bureaucrats. On this, see Warren F. Ilchman, Alice Stone Ilchman and Philip K. Hastings, *The New Men of Knowledge and the Developing Nations*, Studies in Comparative Administration No. 1 (Berkeley: Institute of Governmental Studies, University of California, 1968).

the ascendance of a political order based squarely on this assumption. From Myrdal's perspective, the spread of modernizing values essential for the mere survival of the polity is substantially retarded by indulgence in a form of politics which sanctions, indeed subsidizes, the mobilization of insatiable demands while at the same time minimizing the capacity for developmental performance essential for their ultimate satisfaction. Paradoxically, the more the masses are permitted the luxury of spontaneously pursuing modernity, the less likely is its attainment.

Nagpur's voluntary associations have been spawned in large measure by decentralization. Indeed, their vitality springs from the curious mix of governmental penetration with expectations of local voluntarism which we have described. Does their vitality, as Myrdal's argument would imply, severely handicap public developmental policy? Does their *political* role result in the prostitution of their *economic* mission and the squandering of scarce developmental resources? While this study cannot provide conclusive answers to these questions, it does seek to illuminate the developmental role of the city's voluntary associations and to trace their operational impact on development programs. It asks: What are the developmental incentives that have led to the appearance of these associations? How are the associations employed in the local distribution of public developmental resources? And how much influence do they exercise on the implementation of developmental programs?

SUMMARY

This chapter has set forth a number of reasons why the study of voluntary associations is important to an understanding of India's political development: (i) the high level of political activity within the associations themselves; (ii) the interconnectedness of associational and municipal politics; (iii) the opportunity present in voluntary associations for the encouragement of participant values and strengthened relations of accountability between politicians and voters; (iv) the capacity of voluntary associations to manage the political demands of culturally divided groups; and (v) the potential influence of voluntary associations on public developmental policy. It has been pointed out that there are formidable barriers that may interfere with the development of voluntary associations into effective political institutions: The decentralization of political and bureaucratic structures does risk the loosening of central controls over the course of development and may encourage social indiscipline incompatible with the needs of an impoverished society. The persistence of caste and community loyalties may ethnicize the associations and result in irreconcilable conflict within and among them. And a response to leadership rooted in traditional habits of obedience and acquiescence may resist the growth of voluntary associations into institutions reliant on more participatory and egalitarian modes of behavior.

But how formidable are these barriers? The fact remains that for several decades India managed to avoid succumbing to the political disorder so characteristic of developing states; and it did so within the framework of decentralized political and administrative institutions, extreme cultural pluralism, and a social structure grounded essentially in hierarchical relations of authority. Whatever may have motivated Prime Minister Indira Gandhi to declare a state of emergency in 1975, it was clearly *not* the breakdown of political institutions, most certainly not *local* political institutions. These institutions may not survive the emergency, at least not in the form described in these pages. But their ultimate fate may depend less on their intrinsic merit than on the loss of confidence in representative democracy occurring among the nation's leadership. Whether local political institutions functioned well or badly over the past several decades is an important and legitimate question; but it should be asked independently of the national political crisis, whatever its outcome. The empirical model of urban associational politics depicted in this study does not provide an unambiguous solution to the riddle of India's "unstable stability."[22] Nor does it remove all doubt of the practicability of democracy under Indian conditions. But it presumes from the outset that the character of political relationships at the local level must figure in any fair assessment. For it is at the base of the pyramid of India's political institutions where that country's citizens most often encounter the tangible results of Nehru's "tryst with destiny," and where the mating of modern political forms with a unique and ancient cultural tradition has experienced its rudest and yet most fundamental trial.

Chapter 2 provides an overview of Nagpur politics—its party system, its community groups, and its voluntary associations. Chapter 3 details

---

[22]The phrase is borrowed from Hugh Tinker, "South Asia: The Colonial Backlash," in *The Study of International Affairs*, Roger Morgan, editor (New York: Oxford University Press, for The Royal Institute of International Affairs, 1972), p. 270.

the scope and functions of various types of voluntary associations in the city, and examines the reasons for their local political appeal. Chapters 4, 5, 6 and 7 trace the effects of associational politics on local leadership recruitment criteria on factional and party organization, and on campaign strategy. All chapters are concerned with discovering the nature of the encounter between local political leaders and their followers, specifically by taking a measure of the obligations that tie politicians to voters, voters to politicians. Voluntary associations are the point of contact in which these obligations are examined. A municipal election is the principal focus of events.

The Pattern of Urban Politics

Two things may be said with confidence about the local politics of India: (i) popular identification with political parties and with formally organized functional interest groups is relatively weak (hence, relatively unimportant in local politics); and (ii) popular identification with political factions and with ascriptive social groups is relatively strong (and correspondingly important in local politics). With neither of these statements will this study take issue; there exists an enormous amount of research to document their authenticity.[1]

[1]In the Indian context, wrote F. G. Bailey, "the creation of widespread groups, held together by a sense of moral dedication to a common purpose, is a task quite beyond the resources of the politicians *and* sometimes beyond their imagination." *Politics and Social Change: Orissa in 1959* (Berkeley: University of California Press, 1963), p. 141. "The absence of party loyalties," claimed Paul Brass in his study of Congress factionalism, "is the most fundamental fact of contemporary politics in Uttar Pradesh." *Factional Politics in an Indian State: The Congress Party in Uttar Pradesh* (Berkeley: University of California Press, 1965), p. 114. No less emphatically, Myron Weiner pointed out that "those who join a political party in India invariably become members of a faction." *Party Politics in India: The Development of a Multi-Party System*(Princeton: Princeton University Press, 1957), p. 237. Elsewhere Weiner has asserted that durable multi-caste, multi-occupational factions "are the units of political action both within parties and within villages, and that the relationship between party faction and village faction is the single most important variable affecting the outcome of many (but not all) elections." *Party Building in a New Nation: The Indian National Congress* (Chicago: The University of Chicago Press, 1967), p. 134. For a sophisticated analysis of factionalism within the Maharashtrian Congress, see Mary C. Carras, *The Dynamics of Indian Political Factions* (London: Cambridge University Press, 1972). On factionalism in an urban context, see Donald B. Rosenthal, "Factions

With equal confidence it may be said that these statements do not exhaust the entire inventory of politically relevant behavior; even less do they assist in plotting the often obscure and subtle *changes* in political behavior which the Indian electorate is undoubtedly undergoing.[2]

It is in reference to such changes that scrutiny of voluntary associational activity in India seems especially pertinent. The voluntary associations are a relatively new phenomenon, they are already very numerous, and their numbers are mounting rapidly. They are responsible for the introduction of a whole new "vocabulary" of local political action. Indeed, they cannot easily be described in the conventional terminology of party, faction, ascriptive group and functional interest. They preoccupy the energies of many local politicians, giving a new character to political leadership, organization and strategy. In their potentially far-reaching consequences for the legitimacy of Indian political institutions, they deserve more attention than they have thus far received.[3]

---

and Alliances in Indian City Politics," *Midwest Journal of Political Science*, X (August 1966), 320-349. The evanescent quality of party loyalties has not impeded considerable investigation into Indian politics using the party as the basic unit of analysis. Among the more important of such studies, in addition to Weiner's, are Stanley A. Kochanek, *The Congress Party of India* (Princeton: Princeton University Press,1968); Howard L. Erdman, *The Swatantra Party and Indian Conservatism* (London: Cambridge University Press, 1967); Angela S. Burger, *Opposition in a Dominant-Party System: A Study of the Jana Sangh, the Praja Socialist Party, and the Socialist Party in Uttar Pradesh, India* (Berkeley: University of California Press, 1969); Richard Sisson, *The Congress Party in Rajasthan* (Berkeley: University of California Press, 1972); and Craig Baxter, *The Jana Sangh: A Biography of an Indian Political Party* (Philadelphia: University of Pennsylvania Press, 1969). Discussion of caste and community permeates virtually all studies of Indian politics. For a good introduction, consult Rajni Kothari, editor, *Caste in Indian Politics* (New Delhi: Orient Longman Ltd., 1970).

[2]See, for example, the illuminating discussion of increasing political differentiation within castes by A. H. Somjee, "Caste and the Decline of Political Homogeneity," *American Political Science Review*, LXVII (September 1973), 799-816.

[3]The only comprehensive effort, thus far, to tackle associational politics in India is Myron Weiner's *The Politics of Scarcity: Public Pressure and Political Response in India* (Chicago: The University of Chicago Press, 1962). Though Weiner makes it plain, here and elsewhere, that he recognizes the political utility of such associations as cooperatives, his analysis is pitched largely at the level of regional or national organizations (trade unions, business associations, student groups, agrarian movements and ethnic associations) which in form and function

Precisely what role local voluntary associations play in urban politics is the subject of this research. While emphasizing the importance of that role, it is essential that voluntary associational activity be seen in relation to other and scarcely separable patterns of political behavior. For this reason, this chapter looks first at the development of the local party system in the context of the first four regular municipal elections held in the post-independence period. Second, it identifies the principal primordial groups active in municipal politics and, through examination of the linguistic, caste and religious community affiliations of candidates in these elections, traces the contours of community conflict and collaboration presently influencing local political alignments. Lastly, it presents evidence from a random sampling of candidates in the municipal election of 1969 indicating the enormous involvement of the city's politicians in voluntary associational groups. Our concern, at this point, is to characterize the structure of local politics in general and largely descriptive terms, while at the same time calling attention to the particular structure of voluntary associations upon which later chapters will focus.

THE POLITICAL PARTY SYSTEM

Virtually all analysts agree with Rosenthal that most Indian political parties "are organized on a loose federal basis," more coalitions of factions than parties in the Western sense.[4] Nagpur is no exception. Symptoms of frail party allegiance and pervasive factionalism are readily apparent. Though the first four municipal elections of the post-independence period (1952, 1957, 1962, 1969) have witnessed a variety of attempts at party consolidation, the number of parties, fronts or other political formations *successfully* contesting the elections has grown with each succeeding election. In only one case—the Congress victory in 1957— has any party or coalition of parties managed to win a majority of corporation seats. With the exception of 1957, electoral victories were generally split amongst no less than three important parties or election fronts; and in the two other cases (1952 and 1969) where Congress

---

are readily analogous with the major types of interest aggregation in the West. Perhaps the best recent general analysis of the role of voluntary associations at the district level is Donald B. Rosenthal's essay, " 'Making It' in Maharashtra," *Journal of Politics*, 36 (May 1974), 409–437.

[4]Donald B. Rosenthal, "Factions and Alliances in Indian City Politics," *op. cit.*, 321.

was able to win control of city government, it had to rely on defectors from the ranks both of independents and opposition parties or fronts. Although the first three elections witnessed the steady rise of the Republican Party of India (RPI)[5] and the Bharatiya Jana Sangh (BJS), they managed to defeat Congress and assume governing authority in 1962 principally because of the massive split in the Congress organization itself brought on by the Vidarbhan separatist agitation.[6] Table 1 summarizes information about the four elections.

The political backgrounds of the candidates in the 1969 election testify further to the transient party loyalties of local politicians. Results of a random sampling of the contestants, stratified according to their higher or lower vote-getting capacity, reveal that continuity of political affiliation is relatively uncommon and, further, that it is a generally unreliable index of electoral attractiveness. Table 2, detailing changes in political affiliations among candidates in the 1969 contest, makes clear the slippery nature of organizational identities at the local level. Of the 136 sampled candidates, 76 (55.8 per cent) had a political affiliation, at some time in the past two decades, different from that with which they contested the 1969 election. Twenty-two (16.1 per cent) of these had moved from party to party; 46 (33.8 per cent) from party to independent; and 8 (5.8 per cent) from independent to party.[7] Overall, those with changed affiliations appear somewhat less attractive to the voters, 29 (21.3 per cent) scoring above the median vote as opposed to 47 (34.5 per cent) below. But if the sample's 72 independents, whose

[5]Prior to 1958, the RPI was known as the Scheduled Castes Federation.

[6]Vidarbha is one of four administrative divisions of Maharashtra, and consists of the eight easternmost districts of the state. The Vidarbhan demand for autonomous political status, aired by certain elements of the population ever since the early years of the 20th century, came to the fore during the nationwide controversy over the reorganization of Indian states undertaken in the late 1950s. It reached its greatest pitch with the decision by the government of India (in 1960) to create a single, homogeneous Marathi-speaking state, a decision which threatened to subordinate Vidarbha to the far more populous and industrialized western districts. For a discussion of the various contending claims involved in the development of the Maharashtrian state, consult G. S. Singh, *Maratha Geopolitics and the Indian Nation* (Bombay: Manaktalas, 1966). See also Ram Joshi, "Maharashtra," in *State Politics in India*, Myron Weiner, editor (Princeton: Princeton University Press, 1968), pp. 177-212.

[7]Interestingly, 52 (38.9 per cent of the sample population) of these changes were made in the period immediately preceding the municipal election, suggesting considerable opportunism operating at the time of ticket distribution. Forty-two (30.8 per cent) were dropouts from Congress.

TABLE 1

NAGPUR MUNICIPAL CORPORATION ELECTION RESULTS, 1952-1969[a]

Party	1952		1957		1962		1969	
	Seats won	%-age	Seats won	%-age	Seats won	%-age	Seats won	%-age
Congress	16	38.0	23	54.7	10	23.8	21	28.0
Republican[b]	7	16.6	(9)	21.4	11	26.1	10	13.3
Jana Sangh	1	2.3	(2)	4.7	3	7.1	12	16.0
Samyukta Nagrik Morcha	14	33.3	11	26.1	—		9	12.0
Nag-Vidarbha Andolan Samiti[c]	—		—		11	26.1	(5)	6.6
Janta Aghadi	—		—		—		2	2.6
Lokshahi Aghadi Sthanik	—		—		—		3	4.0
Swatantra Gat Maharashtra	—.		—		—		4	5.3
Nagrik Samiti[d]	—		1	2.3	—		—	
Praja Socialist	—		0	0.0	0	0.0	(0)	0.0
Bolshevik Samyukta	—		0	0.0	—		—	
Socialist	—		0	0.0	1	2.3	(1)	1.3
CPI-Right	—		—		—		(2)	2.6
CPI-Marxist	—		—		—		(1)	1.3
Republican-Ambedkarite	—		—		—		(1)	1.3
Forward Bloc	—		—		—		(0)	0.0
Independents[e]	4	9.5	7	16.6	6	14.2	14	18.6
Total	42	100.0	42	100.0	42	100.0	75	100.0

[a]*Source:* Data on last three elections drawn from corporation election reports. Since 1952 election figures were not available from the corporation, tables provided by the Nagpur city district Congress committee were employed in conjunction with the election report in the *Nagpur Times. Unparenthesized* figures report returns strictly on the basis of election symbols officially assigned to the candidates, which in a few cases may not conform to reality. *Parenthesized* figures indicate that the party contested under the symbol of an electoral front or coalition rather than under its own. Allocation of tickets in such cases was obtained, wherever possible, from responsible party leaders and press reports. *Hyphenated blanks* indicate that the party did not contest the election; *ciphers,* that it contes-

(*Source continued*)

ted but failed to win any seats. The various electoral coalitions (or fronts) reflect little continuity in composition. Party membership of the 1952 Morcha (united civic front) was not obtained. In 1957 the Jana Sangh and the Scheduled Castes Federation contested in a similarly-named Morcha along with several independents. There were no such coalitions in the 1962 municipal election. The 1969 Morcha joined the Nag-Vidarbha Andolan Samiti (NVAS), CPI-Right, CPI-Marxist, RPI-Ambedkarite, Forward Bloc and several independents. The Janta Aghadi (popular front), appearing first in 1969, was a grab-bag of dissident Congressmen, Republicans and NVAS, mixed in with candidates of the Praja Socialists, Samyukta Socialists, Bharatiya Kranti Dal (Indian revolutionary group), Hindu Mahasabha (Hindu assembly), student organizations and a few independents. The Sthanik Swatantra Gat (local independent group), also of recent vintage, was a coalition of dissident Congressmen led by the prominent Colonelbagh faction of the Congress party. Since constituent parties of electoral coalitions are tabulated separately as well as collectively in the table, only the unparenthesized collective figures are cumulative.

[b]Includes the Scheduled Castes Federation which was renamed the Republican Party of India shortly following the 1957 election.

[c]The Nag-Vidarbha Andolan Samiti (Nag-Vidarbha action committee), consisting overwhelmingly of dissident factions of the Congress, spearheaded the Vidarbhan regionalist agitation of the early 1960s.

[d]The Maharashtra Nagrik Samiti (civic committee) was the local branch of the Samyukta (united) Maharashtra Samiti formed to press for the creation of a united Maharashtra state. Locally, it was primarily a coalition of disgruntled Congressmen, Communists and independents. The achievement of its goal in 1960 eliminated the reason for its existence.

[e]The precise definition of an independent, aside from his electoral symbol, would be very troublesome to state. Where party identification hangs so loosely and where party organization is so weak, the distinction between a party candidate and an independent candidate may be slight.

ranks are positively saturated with the has-beens of other parties, are removed from consideration, the reverse becomes true. Whereas independence seems associated generally with lower voter appeal, among the major and minor parties and electoral fronts consistent party loyalty endows very little advantage, if any, in the conduct of an election campaign.[8]

The weakness of party loyalties is perhaps most dramatically visible in the sheer number and political appeal of the (at least nominally unaffiliated) independents. Not since 1952 has the number of unaffiliated candidates fallen below half of the total number of candidates con-

[8]Like party loyalty, political experience is not a major criterion for contestants in local elections. Only 12 candidates (8.8 per cent) of the total sample of 136 had any legislative experience, and all of it was at the municipal level. Only 41 (30.1 per cent) had previously waged an election campaign.

TABLE 2

CHANGES IN POLITICAL AFFILIATIONS OF CANDIDATES, NAGPUR MUNICIPAL
CORPORATION ELECTION, 1969[a]

Record of affiliation	Higher vote-getters		Lower vote-getters		Total	
	No.	%-age	No.	%-age	No.	%-age
One party[b]	29	21.3	5	3.6	34	25.0
Changed status[e]	29	21.3	47	34.5	76	55.8
Party-to-party	15	11.0	7	5.1	22	16.1
Party-to-independent	11	8.0	35	25.7	46	33.8
Independent-to-party[d]	3	2.2	5	3.6	8	5.8
Independent	10	7.3	16	11.7	26	19.1

[a]*Source:* Personal interviews.

[b]Includes six who simultaneously joined a party and entered politics just prior to this election.

[e]Though the table does not reflect the fact, candidates in many instances had changed their status on more than one occasion. The *last* change is recorded here. Changes preceding the election by more than twenty years are not included.

[d]Includes only those who had contested an earlier election as independents.

testing municipal elections.[9] And as was made apparent in Table 1, *successful* independent candidates have grown in number until in 1969 they formed 18.6 per cent of the municipal legislature, an amount sufficient to assure them a prominent voice in any governing coalition.

The reapportionment of wards carried out preliminary to the 1969 contest (in which the number of wards was increased from forty-two to seventy-five) may have given additional encouragement not only to the independents but to the numerous minority and splinter parties operating in the city. Small pockets of opposition strength, previously submerged in the much larger wards, suddenly found themselves outnumbering Congressmen; even the fringe CPI-Marxist group managed this time a quite legitimate entry into city government.

[9]In 1952 the number of candidates was 180; independents numbered 73, or 40.5 per cent of the total. In 1957 the relevant figures were 257 candidates and 132 independents (51.3 per cent); in 1962, 373 candidates and 234 independents (62.7 per cent); and in 1969, 543 candidates and 278 independents (51.1 per cent). Data for 1952 drawn from Philip K. Oldenburg, "Indian Urban Politics, With Particular Reference to the Nagpur Corporation," cited earlier, p. 96; for the three succeeding elections, final result sheets, Nagpur municipal corporation elections, Central Records Department, Nagpur municipal corporation.

Of course, Nagpur's political parties are not entirely without importance. At a minimum, they provide one form of vertical linkage extending from local to regional and national levels of the polity. Through the
media of party organizations, state leaders are able to intervene in urban
politics by influencing, for example, the selection of local party leaders
or the deliberations of local parliamentary boards. Conversely, ambitious local politicians may find the vehicle of party organization vital in
seeking to extend their own reach into wider political arenas. In addition, local political parties perform a number of routine functions—
such as the conduct of intra-organizational elections—which make
them important local agents of political socialization. Parties arbitrate
status claims, distribute material benefits, and provide a platform for
the expression of ideas.[10] And finally, parties help to "discipline" local
politics. Even in the relatively unprogramatic ambience of city politics,
the behavioral effects of organizational ideologies cannot be entirely
ignored.

The fact remains, however, that party organizations are typically
very weak at the local level. Of the major political groups in Nagpur,
only the Jana Sangh can lay claim to substantial organizational unity.[11]
The local Congress organization is saddled with as many as seven factional rivals, a fact which has consistently undermined its natural
strength in the city.[12] The Republican party, in spite of its local reputation for organizational solidarity, has often been ruptured by sub-

[10]According to Donald Rosenthal, parties "are bound to be of particular
importance in a society in which mobility along other dimensions tends to be
restricted, as in the case of the economy, or where the status system is in considerable flux. In the latter instance, where a status structure based on ritual
behavior is being subverted by an emerging conflict between class-based and
egalitarian ethics, the importance of political organizations in recognizing and
advancing demands for the registration of status claims on a society-wide basis
becomes almost as important as the immediate distribution of specific benefits
by government." *The Limited Elite* (Chicago: The University of Chicago Press,
1970), p. 26.

[11]For background on the organizational development of the Jana Sangh,
consult Craig Baxter, *The Jana Sangh: A Biography of an Indian Political Party*,
cited above.

[12]Local factions vary greatly in membership, cohesion and influence. They
are probably as vulnerable to internal rifts as are local party organizations, the
loyalties of followers linked to a certain extent to the success of their leaders.
Cf., Paul Brass' remark that "a faction in the Uttar Pradesh Congress might be
described as a clique with a larger, fluctuating membership." *Factional Politics
in an Indian State, op. cit.*, p. 56.

group feuding.[13] And of the numerous minor political parties and groups, some are clearly factional splinters of the larger parent organizations and some have a life expectancy no greater than the length of an election campaign.

THE SOCIAL CONTEXT

The pattern of politics in Nagpur is heavily influenced by its ethnic history and demographic composition. The city encompasses within its eighty-four square miles of incorporated territory a generous sampling of the caste, tribal, regional, linguistic and religious groups found in South Asia. For many years the hub of political and economic activity in central India, Nagpur naturally attracted migrants from all regions and from all strata of Indian society. Quite as naturally, ethnic identification acted as an important determinant of the pattern of urban settlement. The ex-untouchable Mahars are concentrated in the northern sector of the city; Brahmans, Muslims, merchant and service castes in the high density central sectors; Koshti (weavers) in the northeast; and the Westernized and affluent professionals and civil servants of all communities in the formerly British-settled areas in the western and suburban parts of the city. Apart from mere spatial proximity, the constant social, occupational and associational contacts maintained within these communities tended to reinforce ascriptive identities and to provide ample opportunity for the development of communal political activity.[14]

The Politics of Language. Nagpur's political and economic orientation,

[13]The RPI ranks second to no other party in the number of defections it experiences during local elections. In five heavily RPI precincts in north Nagpur, twenty-six of thirty-five contestants for the five seats in the 1969 municipal election were identified as having been at one time or another members of the RPI. The RPI-Ambedkarite group, led in the 1960s by the (now deceased) lawyer Haridas Awode, has entirely split off from the parent body and contests elections under its own symbol.

[14]In this study, the term communal is not meant to refer solely to religious groups, nor is it intended necessarily to connote aggressive and divisive behavior. It is used in a broad and neutral sense in reference to all types of primordial or sectarian groups—linguistic, caste, tribal, religious, or other racial or ethnic subcultures. For an excellent discussion of *religious* communalism, see Donald E. Smith, *India as a Secular State* (Princeton: Princeton University Press, 1963), pp. 454–489.

at least since the downfall of Maratha power in the mid-19th century, has been to a large extent northward. Its century-long reign as administrative center, first of the British Central Provinces and then briefly of the Indian Madhya Pradesh, forged strong links between it and the overwhelmingly Hindi-speaking heartland with which it was politically associated. This accounts for the presence in the city of a substantial Hindi-speaking community; but Nagpur remains, nonetheless, largely Marathi-speaking. According to the 1961 census (reported in Table 3), Marathi was the mother tongue of 65.8 per cent of the city's population, and Hindi, though second-ranking, of only 15.7 per cent.[15] Viewed

TABLE 3

LINGUISTIC COMMUNITY DISTRIBUTION, NAGPUR CITY POPULATION, 1961[a]

Language	Number of speakers	Per cent of total
Marathi	423,557	65.8
Hindi	101,551	15.7
Urdu[b]	51,094	7.9
Sindhi	14,580	2.2
Gujarati	11,754	1.8
Telugu	11,466	1.7
Punjabi	6,634	1.0
Gondi	6,394	.9
Tamil	6,151	.9
Bengali	4,639	.7
English	1,370	.2
Malayalam	1,186	.1
Others[c]	3,283	.5
Total	643,659	100.0

[a] *Source:* Table C-V: "Mother-tongue," *Census of India*, 1961, Vol. X, Pt. X: "Cities of Maharashtra Census Tables," p. 614.
[b] The language almost exclusively of Nagpur's Muslim population.
[c] Less than 1,000 speakers each.

[15] Though place of birth is not a sure guide to language, it appears that Madhya Pradesh (previously the Central Provinces) has been the chief supplier of the city's Hindi-speaking population. According to the 1961 census, 38,448 migrants to the city claimed Madhya Pradesh as their birth place, which was 46.7 per cent—the largest single group—of the total migrant population (82,303) drawn from outside Maharashtra. Government of India, *Census of India*, 1961, Vol. X, Pt. X (New Delhi: Manager of Publications, 1968), Table D-II, p. 615.

against district figures, Nagpur's Hindi-speakers emerge even more distinctly as a minority enclave. As Table 4 indicates, whereas Marathi is the mother tongue of only 65.8 per cent of Nagpur city's population, it is the mother tongue of 85.9 per cent of the district's rural population.[16]

TABLE 4

DOMINANT LINGUISTIC COMMUNITY DISTRIBUTION, NAGPUR DISTRICT
POPULATION, 1961[a]

Area	Percentage speaking Marathi	Percentage speaking Hindi
Nagpur district	75.9	11.4
Urban[b]	66.7	15.3
Rural	85.9	7.1
Nagpur city	65.8	15.7

[a]*Source*: Table C-V: "Mother-tongue," *Nagpur District Census Handbook*, p.169.

[b]Twelve towns in Nagpur district are classified as urban areas.

Though a statistical minority in city, district and state,[17] Hindi-speakers, in the city of Nagpur at least, have long exercised disproportionate political and economic influence. As early as 1929, at a time when Hindi held undisputed sway as the official language of the area,

[16]Nagpur city's population, third in the state behind Greater Bombay and Poona, tends to swamp Nagpur district, giving the district a considerably greater percentage of urban-to-total population than is true for most of the state. Whereas the percentage of urban-to-total population for the state in 1961 was 28.2 per cent, the corresponding figure for Nagpur district with eleven towns in addition to Nagpur, was 52 per cent. Government of Maharashtra, Census Office, *Nagpur District Census Handbook* (Bombay: Government Printing and Stationery, 1965), p. 11.

[17]Owing to the reorganization of Maharashtra in 1960, the 1961 census does not report the language breakdown for the combined area. However, with the exception of Greater Bombay, the rest of the state can safely be presumed to be overwhelmingly Marathi-speaking. Bombay itself is something of a linguistic enclave in the state. The 1961 census reported a total population for Greater Bombay of 4,152,056, of which the largest *single* language group, but nonetheless a distinct minority, was Marathi with 1,775,114 speakers. Unlike Nagpur, Hindi ranks fourth behind Gujarati and Urdu in Bombay. Reported by Ram Joshi, "Maharashtra," in *State Politics of India*, Table 4.1, p. 183.

Marathi-speakers in the city's municipal council protested against the injustice of conducting all the council's sessions in Hindi when three-fourths of the citizens claimed Marathi as their mother tongue.[18] Leadership of the Nagpur city district Congress committee (NCDCC) even in recent years does not reflect the statistical fact of Marathi predominance.[19] The president and two of the three general secretaries elected to the working committee in 1966 were Hindi-speaking. Only one of the city's four members of the state legislative assembly serving in the state cabinet in 1969 was Hindi-speaking—Madan Gopal Agarwal.[20]

The position of the Hindi-speakers is increasingly untenable. Nagpur's incorporation into reorganized Bombay state in 1956 and then into Maharashtra state in 1960 has all but obliterated the natural support base of the Hindi-speaking community. The reorganizational "outcasting" of the city in effect cut the economic and political head from its linguistic body, transforming the ruling class into a vulnerable minority occupying an enclave that is gradually being engulfed in a Marathi sea. Local Marathi "irredentism" in no sense resembles the volatile force it has become in Bombay, where the militant Shiva Sena (Shivaji's soldiers) poses an imminent threat to the political status of that city's huge non-Maharashtrian population.[21] For Nagpur's so-called "Hindi-siders" are manifestly a statistical minority from whom the trappings of power can be, and have been, won by more conventional means.

In general, the tide has definitely swung in favor of Marathi. Not only is it increasingly the medium in local schools, but in local politics as well. Table 5 indicates a gradual decline in the percentages of Hindi-speaking candidates winning in municipal elections since 1952, offering

[18]Padmakar L. Joshi *et al.*, *Nagpur City Centennial Volume* (Nagpur: Nagpur Municipal Corporation, 1964), p. 158.

[19]The *city* district Congress committee is a separate body from the *district* Congress committee, both having equal status but the latter bearing responsibility only outside of Nagpur city. Not surprisingly, the district Congress committee is dominated by Marathi-speaking persons of cultivating castes.

[20]The only one of the city's four leading newspapers which is generally considered in the Congress camp—the *Navbharat*—is also the only one of the four in the Hindi language. The Jana Sangh-leaning *Tarun Bharat* is in Marathi, and the two English dailies, the *Hitawada* and the *Nagpur Times*, express a neo-Gandhian point of view archly critical of politics in general.

[21]Mary Katzenstein, "Origins of Nativism: The Emergence of the Shiv Sena in Bombay," *Asian Survey*, 13 (April 1973), 386-399.

substantial evidence that the political influence of Hindi-speakers is on the wane.[22] Having dropped from 23.8 to 13.3 per cent of victories in municipal contests, Hindi-speakers, with 15.7 per cent of the city's 1961 population, now are slightly under-represented while Marathi-speakers, with 77.3 per cent of winning candidates in 1969, and 65.8 per cent of the 1961 population, are considerably over-represented. Speakers of languages other than Hindi and Marathi, always woefully

TABLE 5

LINGUISTIC COMMUNITY AFFILIATION, ELECTED MEMBERS OF NAGPUR CITY MUNICIPAL CORPORATION, 1952-1969[a]

Language	1952 Corporators		1957 Corporators		1962 Corporators		1969[b] Corporators	
	No.	%-age	No.	%-age	No.	%-age	No.	%-age
Marathi	29	69.0	31	73.8	35	83.3	58	77.3
Hindi	10	23.8	9	21.4	7	16.6	10	13.3
Other	3	7.1	2	4.7	0	0.0	7	9.3
Total	42	100.0	42	100.0	42	100.0	75	100.0

[a]*Source:* 1952, 1957, and 1962 election data drawn from tables prepared by the NCDCC; 1969 data drawn from personal interviews.

[b]Wards were reapportioned in 1968, raising their number from forty-two to seventy-five.

under-represented, have recently attained some political respectability, winning 9.3 per cent of the seats in 1969, compared with a 1961 population which was 18.4 per cent of the total.

Several interesting points emerge from a comparison of the linguistic and party affiliations of candidates in the 1969 municipal election.

[22]Their relative percentage in the population appears to have remained fairly constant. Between 1951 and 1961, the percentage of Marathi-speakers in the district wavered less than one per cent. G. S. Singh, *Maratha Geopolitics and the Indian Nation,* p. 137. More recent migration would presumably have tilted the population in favor of Marathi. Municipal politics is but one of several competitive arenas in the city, and Hindi-speakers may well retain far more influence in commercial quarters, for example, than is easily discovered. Competition for municipal office is extremely keen, however, and is probably not a bad index of the relative influence of various groups in the population.

Congress, in spite of its Hindi-speaking leadership, appears somewhat niggardly in the distribution of tickets either to Hindi or other minority language groups, and seems least able to assure them victory when they are given tickets. Marathi-speaking candidates, on the other hand, receive a disproportionate number of Congress tickets and reward Congress by giving it almost all of its victories. Table 6 shows the disproportions in the distribution of tickets, and Table 7 indicates the

TABLE 6

LINGUISTIC COMMUNITY AFFILIATION, CONGRESS AND NON-CONGRESS CANDIDATES, NAGPUR MUNICIPAL CORPORATION ELECTION, 1969[a]

Language	%-age of 1961 population	Total candidacies		Congress candidacies		Non-Congress candidacies	
		No.	%-age	No.	%-age	No.	%-age
Marathi	65.8	368	67.7	42	76.3	326	66.8
Hindi	15.7	84	15.4	7	12.7	77	15.7
Other	18.4	61	11.2	6	10.9	55	11.2
Unknown	—	30	5.5	—	—	30	6.1
Total	100.0	543	100.0	55	100.0	488	100.0

[a]*Source:* Personal interviews.

TABLE 7

LINGUISTIC COMMUNITY AFFILIATION, CONGRESS AND NON-CONGRESS WINNING CANDIDATES, NAGPUR MUNICIPAL CORPORATION ELECTION, 1969[a]

Language	%-age of 1961 population	Total seats won		Congress seats won		Non-Congress seats won	
		No.	%-age	No.	%-age	No.	%-age
Marathi	65.8	58	77.3	19	90.4	39	72.2
Hindi	15.7	10	13.3	1	4.7	9	16.6
Other	18.4	7	9.3	1	4.7	6	11.1
Total	100.0	75	100.0	21	100.0	54	100.0

[a]*Source:* Personal interviews.

extreme disparities in winning candidacies. Whereas Congress distributed 76.3 per cent of its tickets to the Marathi community, the corresponding figure for Hindi-speakers was 12.7 per cent, and for other minority language groups only 10.9 per cent. And while Marathi-speakers account for 90.4 per cent of Congress wins, they account for only 72.2 per cent of non-Congress wins. If Congress' alliance with the almost exclusively Marathi-based RPI is taken into account, the disproportions are even more exaggerated.[23] As Table 8 indicates, the Congress-RPI coalition gives Marathi rather complete hegemony in the ruling camp. Whereas only 9.6 per cent of the seats won by the Congress-RPI coalition were filled by non-Marathi-speakers, 31.7 per

TABLE 8

LINGUISTIC COMMUNITY AFFILIATION, CONGRESS-RPI AND OPPOSITION
WINNING CANDIDATES, NAGPUR MUNICIPAL CORPORATION ELECTION, 1969[a]

Language	%-age of 1961 population	Total seats won		Congress-RPI seats won		Opposition seats won	
		No.	%-age	No.	%-age	No.	%-age
Marathi	65.8	58	77.3	28	90.3	30	68.1
Hindi	15.7	10	13.3	2	6.4	8	18.1
Other	18.4	7	9.3	1	3.2	6	13.6
Total	100.0	75	100.0	31	100.0	44	100.0

[a]*Source:* Personal interviews. The total number of RPI candidates was twenty, giving them the best polling results—50 per cent wins—of any group in the city.

[23]The Congress-RPI electoral agreement was forged a few months prior to the 1969 election. *Nagpur Times,* 23 and 28 January 1969.

cent of the seats won by all other parties and independents were filled by this language group. The collective importance of Hindi-speaking and other minority language candidates amongst the opposition is evident.[24]

The Politics of Caste. It would be an overstatement to charge the local Congress with having entirely deserted the non-Marathi-speaking groups in the city, for some of its most powerful leaders, including the general secretary, Rikhabchand Sharma, backed highly cosmopolitan slates of candidates in the 1969 election. It is indisputable, however, that some sort of fissionary process has been occurring, gradually weaning the non-Marathi-speaking communities from the Congress. Whether Congress is actually less hospitable to these groups, or whether they, for reasons of their own, feel more comfortable in the opposition, is not entirely clear in every case. The explanation appears to lie somewhere in the pattern of political coalitions developing between the city's *linguistic* and *caste* communities. The local Congress is gradually adapting to the changed overall linguistic situation, absorbing a greater percentage of the numerically dominant Marathi-speaking community, while at the same time displaying preference for the indigenous traditionally landowning castes of that linguistic group.[25] Simultaneously, the non-Marathi elements are forging coalitions with traditionally town-dwelling, socially low status, or numerically weak Marathi-speaking castes, balancing the scales against the dominant party while at the

[24]The non-Marathi-speaking winners in the 1969 election were politically a very mixed assortment. Excluding the three of this group who contested and won with either the Congress or RPI, the remaining fourteen represented six independent and eight party or election front candidacies. Nine of the fourteen had at one time or another been affiliated with Congress. But other than a common animosity for the Congress, there were few distinctly *political* bonds linking them together. NMC election returns and personal interviews.

[25]Specifically, the local Congress is accommodating more persons of the Kunbi (cultivator) and Maratha (warrior) castes, the former the most numerous in the district, the latter the traditional ruling elite. According to the 1931 census, the Kunbis constituted about nineteen, the Marathas about one per cent of the district population. Next to the Brahmans the Kunbis (in 1931) were the largest proprietary landholders in the district. The Marathas, who appear to have risen from the Kunbis through military service under the great Maratha warrior Shivaji, are also an important landholding class, certainly the most prestigious in view of their imperial past. Government of Maharashtra, *Maharashtra State Gazetteers, Nagpur District,* revised edition (Bombay: Government Printing and Stationery, 1966), pp. 139-142.

same time giving access to power to formerly excluded groups.[26]

Before reviewing the evidence which the city's first four municipal elections provide for this hypothesis, a few observations on the city's two major opposition political parties—the Republican Party of India and the Bharatiya Jana Sangh—are necessary. In the aggregate, the Marathi-speaking castes on the opposition side are an extremely diverse group.[27] But these two (normally) opposition parties present a uniquely homogeneous community front, a fact of great importance in considering the role of caste in local politics.

[26]Of this category, politically of most consequence in the city have been the ex-untouchable Mahars, Brahmans, Telis (oilpressers), Koshtis (weavers) and Kalars (distillers). According to the 1931 census, they constituted, respectively, 17, 4, 8.5, 5, and 1 per cent of the *district* population. The numerically powerful Mahars fall clearly among the "socially low status" elements of the city's population. The bulk of their number in the district is landless agricultural labor; but in migrating into the city in large numbers they have assumed a great variety of occupations. Thousands of them, for example, are employed in the large textile mills of Nagpur. The Telis are also a traditionally low status and fairly numerous group. Few continue to practice their traditional occupation; most, in rural areas, having turned to agricultural labor or, in the city, to a wide variety of occupations, including carpentry, shopkeeping, millworker and so forth. The Koshtis, most of whom speak a distinct dialect mixing Hindi and Marathi, are an almost exclusively towndwelling artisan caste, having migrated to Nagpur in earlier centuries to serve the needs of a royal capital. Economically a precariously positioned group, their large numbers within the city, where they constitute perhaps fifteen per cent of the population, provide them with considerable political leverage. The Kalars, who have long served the city's liquor needs, are numerically small and socially of unquestionably low status. The Brahmans, a traditional elite, would appear to be an exception among these castes. In 1931, they were the district's largest landholders and bore considerable social prestige. Events have thrust them, traditional status notwithstanding, into a socially subordinate role. Within Nagpur city the majority of the Brahmans hold low salaried clerical and governmental positions, adding an economic to the social depression. Angela S. Burger has suggested that India's opposition parties, the Jana Sangh among them, tended to attract primarily the "newly-mobilized," the "defensive," and the "unrealized beneficiaries" of reforms. The "defensives"—those "threatened with loss of status, role, and function by reforms or policies instituted by the dominant party"—appears an apt description of Nagpur's Brahman population. *Opposition in a Dominant-Party System*, p. 11. Background on Nagpur's caste groups is contained in *Nagpur District Gazetteer*, cited earlier, pp. 139-145.

[27]The non-Marathi-speaking elements with whom they are often allied are themselves highly diverse in caste and religious community affiliation. Considering only those of this group who won their election contests on non-Congress

The Marathi-speaking Brahmans are conspicuously identified with the Jana Sangh. They have for long been *communis non grata* so far as the Congress is concerned, a fact mirrored in the powerful anti-Brahman sentiments which arose in this region in the wake of the assassination of Mahatma Gandhi by a Maharashtrian Brahman and former member of the militant Hindu group, Rashtriya Swayamsevak Sangh (RSS). The bitter animosities which surfaced then imposed a barrier between the aggrieved Congress and the tainted community which has not been lifted to this day. While the RSS-influenced BJS put out an over-sized welcome mat for them, the Brahmans found little opportunity thereafter within the Congress.

The local BJS has taken steps to erase its Brahman image by broadening its leadership and distributing election tickets to many other groups. However, it continues to be predominantly the "party of Brahmans" in Nagpur city. Whereas only one Marathi-speaking Brahman served on the twenty-three member working committee of the NCDCC in 1969, there were at least six of this community on the nineteen-member Nagpur district committee of the BJS chosen in the same year.[28] More strikingly, of the forty-five known Brahmans contesting in the 1969 corporation election, at least seventeen were candidates of the BJS, a figure by far the largest of any party in the city.[29]

The formerly untouchable and Marathi-speaking Mahars, like the Brahmans, are closely identified with a single party of the opposition— Republican Party of India.[30] With a census enumeration of over

tickets in the municipal contest of 1969—a group of fifteen—they include persons of eleven separate communities.

[28]Politically, the distinction between Marathi-speaking and other Brahmans is important. The general secretary of the NCDCC is also a Brahman, but a Hindi-speaking Marwadi Brahman, untainted either by the Gandhian episode or by any powerful historical animosities.

[29]Five Brahmans contested with Congress. Information on the caste affiliations of candidates was obtained for 522 of the 543 contesting the election.

[30]The RPI has been technically removed from the ranks of the political opposition due to the 1969 electoral alliance with the Congress. In the 1967 general elections to the state legislative assembly, the RSI ranked second in number of votes polled locally, standing behind Congress but ahead of Jana Sangh. Of the total number of valid votes cast in the city's four legislative constituencies (247,660), the Congress, contesting all four seats, polled 109,928 votes (44.3 per cent), the RPI, contesting two seats, 40,909 (16.5 per cent), and the BJS, also contesting two seats, 31,256 (12.6 per cent). Small parties and independents divided the balance. Government of India, *Report on the Fourth General Elections in India, 1967*, II (New Delhi: Government of India Press, 1968), pp. 365-366.

100,000, the Mahars are one of the largest caste groups in the city.[31] Their domination of the RPI, to say the least, is extensive. Eighteen of the twenty RPI candidates in 1969 were Mahar, giving the party the most monolithic caste composition in the city.

The forging of an electoral alliance between the Congress and the RPI, implemented for the first time in the 1969 election, has given the RPI a powerful "establishment" ally while at the same time giving its coalition partner a potential inroad into the newly mobilized Marathi-speaking lower castes.[32] The alliance is highly fragile, however, and the likelihood of permanence seems small. The pact was drawn up by the state-level party organizations for whom the particular balance of forces in Nagpur—including the problem of an entrenched Hindi-speaking minority—are of little or no relevance. Virtually without exception Congress and RPI leaders, workers, and candidates reported in interview that the alliance's first local tryout in the 1969 election was an almost complete failure. Though top-level decision had successfully divided up the city's wards between the two allies, grassroots decision had the opposite effect. Frustrated aspirants of both parties simply swapped party symbols for independent or splinter party symbols and ran against each other in defiance of their state organization's decision.

Aside from the socially somewhat exclusive BJS and RPI organiza-tions, the rest of the political opposition appears to be generally plura-

---

Judging from the party's record statewide in the same election, Nagpur must be regarded as an RPI stronghold. Contesting 83 seats of 270, the RPI won only 4, securing 6.5 per cent of the total votes polled. Nationwide, the party is even less imposing. Contesting 381 assembly seats in 1967, the RPI won 21 and secured a total of 1.5 per cent of the votes polled. Government of India, Ministry of Information and Broadcasting, *Fourth General Elections: An Analysis* (New Delhi: Publications Division, 1967), pp. 90, 199.

[31]The census figure was obtained by adding together the Buddhist (96,761) and Mahar (7,331) populations, which yielded a total of 104,092. Government of India, *Census of India*, 1961, Vol. X, Pt. X. Table C-VII, p. 614, and Table SCT-III, p. 650. It is true that there are some non-Mahar Buddhists in Nagpur, but there is every indication that their number is slight. With few exceptions the rule holds that most Mahars in Nagpur are Buddhists, and vir-tually all Buddhists are Mahars.

[32]The rags-to-riches saga of the RPI is one of the more pronounced instances of political mobilization in the city. In pre-independence municipal councils the Mahar community had achieved modest representation. Between 1925, when the first popular municipal elections were held in Nagpur, and 1952, when the first post-independence elections were held, Mahars were elected to 20 out of 178 seats (11.2 per cent) in six regular elections. In the four regular elections since

listic in terms of caste composition. But their pluralism is not without pattern. Analysis of the caste or religious community affiliations of corporators elected in the first four regular municipal elections since independence reveals that Congress and non-Congress winning candidates tend to be drawn from markedly different communal groups. Table 9 sets forth the caste or religious community affiliations of all Congress and non-Congress corporators whose caste or religious community has won two or more seats in at least one of the four elections. A glance will indicate that Brahmans and Mahars, as expected, are counted overwhelmingly on the non-Congress side of the ledger. No less interesting is the evident fact that the Congress, though accommodating many communities with respect to ticketing, tends to afford opportunity for municipal office to a rather selective group. Such socially low status Marathi-speaking groups as the Telis and Kalars, and the Urdu-speaking Muslims, have indeed been feted to Congress victories in the past; but their collective record of seats won in the last two elections represents precisely one-third of their tally in the earlier two contests. The almost exclusively towndwelling and originally migrant Koshtis (speaking a Hindi-influenced dialect of Marathi) have rarely won with Congress, in spite of the fact that they are the most numerous community in the city. In contrast, Maratha and Kunbi corporators, representatives respectively of the traditionally most powerful and populous Marathi-speaking castes in the state, are found overwhelmingly on the Congress side of the ledger. Together they account for 34.2 per cent of all Congress victories since independence. More significantly, their share of

---

independence, Mahars won a total of 36 corporation seats (17.9 per cent), in each of the first three elections winning more than any other community group, and equalled in 1969 only by Brahmans. In the elections of 1952, 1957 and 1962, with 42 seats being contested, Mahars scored, respectively, seven, nine and eight victories. In 1969, with the seats expanded to 75, the Mahars won twelve contests. That their aspirations are set much higher is clear from the fact that no less than 110 Mahars contested the 1969 election, a figure which is twenty per cent of the total number of candidacies. Pre-independence election data drawn from charts presented in Padmakar L. Joshi *et al.*, *Nagpur City Centennial Volume*, pp. 143-145. Caste affiliations of corporators in the first three post-independence elections based on tables compiled by the NCDCC; those of the 1969 elected members based on material gathered in interviews with the candidates. The pre-independence electorate was, of course, much smaller than today's, since the grant of full adult suffrage was made after independence was secured. The size of the electorate in 1925, for instance, was only about 38,000, compared with a 1969 figure of 396,451 eligible voters.

TABLE 9

CASTE OR RELIGIOUS COMMUNITY AFFILIATION, CONGRESS AND NON-
CONGRESS WINNING CANDIDATES, NAGPUR MUNICIPAL CORPORATION
ELECTIONS, 1952-1969[a]

Community	Congress seats won					Non-Congress seats won				
	1952	1957	1962	1969	Total	1952	1957	1962	1969	Total
Mahar	0	0	0	0	0	7	9	8	12	36
Brahman	0	0	0	1	1	3	3	4	11	21
Teli	3	3	1	1	8	3	0	2	9	14
Kunbi	3	4	5	5	17	0	0	1	3	4
Koshti	0	2	0	0	2	4	3	4	4	15
Muslim	1	2	1	0	4	2	1	1	3	7
Kalar	1	2	1	0	4	0	0	3	2	5
Maratha	2	1	0	5	8	0	0	1	0	1
Sindhi	1	0	0	1	2	0	0	0	1	1
Nai	0	1	0	2	3	0	0	0	0	0
Others	5	10	3	6	24	7	1	7	9	24
Party total	16	25	11	21	73	26	17	31	54	128

[a]*Source:* 1952, 1957 and 1962 election data from tables prepared by the
NCDCC; 1969 data from personal interviews with candidates.

Congress victories has been *increasing* since independence, ranging from
a low of 20 per cent in 1957 to a high of 47.6 per cent—or almost half
—in 1969. Their pre-eminence in Congress, like the pre-eminence of
Marathi-speakers in general, is a suitable corollary to the merger of
Nagpur in Maharashtra and a tribute to the adaptive capacity of the
local Congress organization.

The Kunbi-Maratha success in Congress no doubt provokes a hostile
reaction by the also Marathi-speaking but socially less well favored
Koshti, Teli and Kalar communities, as well as by such non-Marathi-
speaking groups as the Muslims. Finding poor accommodation in the
Congress, these and similar groups drift into the "free-floating" opposition (that part of it not already overidentified with such groups as the
Mahars or Brahmans). A closer look at the 1969 municipal election will
underscore the point.

Table 10 reveals the community disproportions in the distribution
both of candidacies and of winning candidacies between Congress and

non-Congress contestants. Kunbi and Maratha candidates received
Congress tickets far out of proportion to the number of candidates of
those communities contesting the election. With only 8.8 per cent of

TABLE 10

CASTE OR RELIGIOUS COMMUNITY AFFILIATION, CONGRESS AND NON-CONGRESS
CANDIDATES AND WINNING CANDIDATES, NAGPUR MUNICIPAL CORPORATION
ELECTION, 1969[a]

Community	Total candidacies		Congress		Congress winning		Non-Congress		Non-Congress winning	
	No.	%-age	No.	%-age	No.	%-age	No.	%-age	No.	%-age
Mahar[b]	110	20.2	0	0.0	0	0.0	110	22.5	12	22.2
Teli	55	10.1	4	7.2	1	4.7	51	10.4	9	16.6
Koshti	53	9.7	8	14.5	0	0.0	45	9.2	4	7.4
Kunbi	48	8.8	11	20.0	5	23.8	37	7.5	3	5.5
Brahman	45	8.2	5	9.0	1	4.7	40	8.1	11	20.3
Muslim	33	6.0	3	5.4	0	0.0	30	6.1	3	5.5
Kalar	18	3.3	2	3.6	0	0.0	16	3.2	2	3.7
Maratha	18	3.3	5	9.0	5	23.8	13	2.6	0	0.0
Mehtar	11	2.0	1	1.8	0	0.0	10	2.0	1	1.8
Marwadi	9	1.6	1	1.8	0	0.0	8	1.6	1	1.8
Telenga	9	1.6	1	1.8	1	4.7	8	1.6	0	0.0
Sonar	8	1.4	2	3.6	1	4.7	6	1.2	0	0.0
Christian	7	1.2	1	1.8	0	0.0	6	1.2	0	0.0
Others[c]	97	17.8	11	19.9	7	33.1	86	17.5	8	14.7
Unknown	22	4.0	0	0.0	0	0.0	22	4.5	0	0.0
Total	543	100.0	55	100.0	21	100.0	488	100.0	54	100.0

[a] *Source:* Personal interviews.

[b] Eighteen of the Mahar candidates contested with the RPI, which was in
alliance with the Congress.

[c] Communities with less than seven candidates in the field.

the total number of contestants, ·Kunbis were granted 20 per cent of
Congress tickets and earned 23.8 per cent of its victories. They comprised only 7.5 per cent of opposition tickets, and picked up only 5.5
per cent of opposition victories. Similarly, the Maratha community,
with only 3.3 per cent of candidates in the field, received 9 per cent of
Congress tickets and, significantly, 23.8 per cent of Congress wins. Only

2.6 per cent of opposition candidates were Maratha, and none of them won their contests.

The politically active Teli community, on the other hand, fared considerably better amongst the opposition. Fielding 10.1 per cent of the candidates, it comprised 10.4 per cent of opposition tickets and 7.2 per cent of Congress tickets. However, Telis recorded only 4.7 per cent of Congress wins, while gathering in a revealing 16.6 per cent of opposition victories. Koshti, Muslim and Kalar communities, especially the Koshti, seemingly were dealt an adequate number of Congress tickets; but none of them shared in Congress victories. Though needing no further comment, the importance of the Mahar and Brahman communities among the non-Congress candidacies is especially noteworthy.[33]

There is little doubt that community factors weigh in the selection of candidates in Nagpur politics. Party leaders and workers generally acknowledge it and statistics confirm their observations. It is apparent, too, that coalitions are pieced together in part from the animosities and affections engendered among and between various communities by such acts as the redrawing of state boundaries. Having had their community rug pulled out from under them, Hindi-speakers have quite obviously sought to cushion, if not prevent, their fall by aligning their forces with those Marathi-speaking castes—Koshtis, Telis, Kalars, and even Mahars and Brahmans—who, for want of numbers, social status, or rural roots, have prospects beyond the city just as bleak as the "Hindi-siders." The recession of the Hindi regime is a fact of Nagpur's political life. But so is the vigorous struggle for leadership among Marathi-speaking castes, a fact which gives the Hindi-speakers (in or out of Congress) a considerable lease on life.

[33]The disproportions in ticketing among non-Congress candidates held true even when the numerous independent candidates—who in effect ticket themselves—as well as the caste cohesive BJS and RPI candidates were excluded from consideration. The remaining *organized* opposition, excepting a few tiny and inconsequential parties, consisted of four electoral coalitions—the Samyukta Nagrik Morcha (united civic front), the Lokshahi Aghadi (democratic front), the Janta Aghadi (popular front), and the Sthanik Swatantra Gat (local independent group). Together they fielded 129 candidates, electing 16 of them. The distribution of tickets by these electoral fronts reflects the same community alliance between the Hindi-speaking minority and particular Marathi-speaking castes which we have seen operating within the opposition as a whole. For example, while Congress gave 20 per cent and 9 per cent of its tickets respectively to Kunbis and Marathas, the fronts collectively gave the Kunbis only 9.6 per cent and the Marathas only 1.6 per cent of theirs.

Voluntary Associations

Were we to terminate here our discussion of the structural components of Nagpur politics, our portrait would fall sadly short of reality. Notice must be taken of the profusion of voluntary associations existing apart from the city's party organizations, factions, and traditional ascriptive groups. By "voluntary association" reference is made primarily to the relatively recent and government-promoted institutions of educational management and cooperativism (of which the most prolific forms in Nagpur tend to be credit, housing, labor, consumer and production), but also to communal organizations, wrestling and gymnastic societies, neighborhood committees, and such conventional groups as trade unions, business and professional societies.[34] In practice, we include in our purview only those associations clearly pertinent to municipal politics, specifically those in which recent candidates for municipal office were frequently in occupancy of executive positions.[35] This is much less a constraint than might seem, for the involvement of Nagpur's politicians in local associations is enormous.[36]

[34]It may be objected that some of these associations are, strictly speaking, public or semi-public rather than voluntary. And it is indeed true that government has often played a central role in creating and then subsidizing certain types of association. With the exception of some supervisory responsibilities, government does not *control* them, however, not even in a formal sense. Local autonomy is shielded, in part, by explicit guarantees of participatory democratic procedures and, in further part, by the apparent unwillingness or inability of the Indian government to exert such control. In any event, the imprecise boundary between the public and private domains is a decisive factor, as will be seen in later chapters, accounting for intervention in local voluntary associations by politicians.

[35]This decision, which resulted in the exclusion from the study of student and youth organizations, for example, undoubtedly distorts the actual influence of associational interests in city politics. Candidates in municipal elections are not the only actors, and municipal government is not the only arena, in local politics. In this writer's judgment, however, events pertaining to a municipal election supply a good (albeit imperfect) index to the larger universe of local politics.

[36]Similar behavior has been reported in other Indian cities. Rosenthal, for example, writes that "contrary to expectations which might be held about the development of secondary associations in an underdeveloped nation, Poona and Agra are alive with informal and quasi-formal social groups. The organization of annual festivals, for example, provides an important opportunity for the expression of ward and group rivalries in Poona; the athletic clubs, particularly wrestling associations, are an important base for political action in Poona. In terms of formal organizations, there seems to be an important relationship bet-

A systematic survey of candidates for the office of municipal corporator (councilor) in the 16 March 1969 election exposed pedigrees of associational affiliation impressive both for their quantity and their quality. Eighty-nine (65.4 per cent) of 136 randomly sampled candidates held *executive* positions in at least one voluntary association, and altogether they had 253 such *executive* affiliations to their credit.[37] Table 11 indicates the number and percentages of candidates, by lower

TABLE 11

CURRENT EXECUTIVE LEADERSHIP IN VOLUNTARY ASSOCIATIONS, CANDIDATES
IN NAGPUR MUNICIPAL CORPORATION ELECTION, 1969[a]

Type of association	Higher vote-getters (68)		Lower vote-getters (68)		Total (136)	
	No.	%-age	No.	%-age	No.	%-age
Cooperative	28	20.5	16	11.7	44	32.3
Educational	25	18.3	11	8.0	36	26.4
Trade union	10	7.3	10	7.3	20	14.7
Religious and festival	13	9.5	6	4.4	19	13.9
Civic and social service	12	8.8	7	5.1	19	13.9
Caste	9	6.6	9	6.6	18	13.2
Athletic	11	8.0	5	3.6	16	11.7
Business and professional	9	6.6	3	2.2	12	8.8
Literary and cultural	3	2.2	3	2.2	6	4.4
Other	1	.7	1	.7	2	1.4

[a]*Source:* Personal interviews. Voluntary associational activity was obtained for all candidates in the sample. Since many of the candidates were involved in associational activity falling under more than one category, the percentages are non-cumulative. The table is not a complete measure of associational activity, which would have to take into account the fact that many of the candidates held executive positions in more than one association of the same general classification, and further that these associations vary considerably in such things as size of membership, capital resources, and scope of activities. Past executive leadership or mere membership is excluded from tabulation.

---

ween the commercial activities of the municipal fruit and vegetable market in that city and the Congress party. All of these aspects of economic and social activity remain to be explored for their political content." Donald B. Rosenthal, "Functions of Urban Political Systems," in *Community Structure and Decision-Making: Comparative Analyses*, p. 296.

[37]These figures conceal the fact that a far greater number of the candidates than appears in the tables has an active interest in voluntary associations. Many

and higher vote-getting capacity, affiliated as executives to each type of voluntary association. The larger percentages of candidates are affiliated with the cooperatives (32.3 per cent) and the education socie-ties (26.4 per cent), while such older or more conventional forms of association as trade unions (14.7 per cent), religious and festival socie-ties (13.9 per cent), caste associations (13.2 per cent), and athletic (generally wrestling) societies (11.7 per cent) are relatively less well represented among them.

In interviews, local politicians of every rank and persuasion often reported that their voluntary associational activities played the most significant part in cultivating productive relationships with their consti-tuents. Their claims are given substance by the evident fact that exec-utive leadership in most types of association is generally related to higher vote-getting capacity. This is especially true of the cooperative and education societies. Their managers were found roughly twice as commonly among the higher vote-getters, who occupied 20.5 and 18.3 per cent of the respective executive affiliations, as among the lower vote-getters, for whom the corresponding figures are 11.7 and 8 per cent.

These figures do not, of course, necessarily establish a causal con-nection; they may reflect no more than that whatever qualities enhance a candidate's electoral appeal may also make him a more attractive associational executive.[38] Some affiliations are doubtless more honorific than active. But the impression gained from scores of interviews with associational leaders is that they were *active* executives, highly conver-sant with the technical details of their managerial roles. In many cases they were drawn into public political contests after a lengthy period of associational stewardship, and hence owe their political careers to the reputations built in associational arenas.[39]

Local politicians appear, in fact, to exercise considerable discrimi-nation in the choice of associational career-building opportunities.

---

of those interviewed had served on *past* managing committees or had been active but *untitled* members.

[38]Higher vote-getters do affiliate with markedly greater frequency than lower vote-getters. Of the 253 total unclassified executive affiliations of the sampled candidates, 168 (66.4 per cent) were found among higher vote-getters, and only 85 (33.5 per cent) among the lower vote-getting group.

[39]The same point is made by Donald B. Rosenthal, " 'Making It' in Maha-rashtra: Ambition and Opportunity Structures in Indian District Politics," *op. cit.*, 24.

Table 12, analyzing executive cross-affiliations in all types of association, points up the fact that executive leadership *inclusive* of cooperatives and/or educational societies is far more common among higher vote-getters than is leadership *exclusive* of either or both of these. Whereas 36 (52.9 per cent) of the 68 higher vote-getters are executively affiliated with associations inclusive of education or cooperative societies, 45 (66.1 per cent) of the 68 lower vote-getters are executively affiliated with neither of these. The conclusion is inescapable not only that associational leadership carries political value, but that particular associations are more attractive than others.

CONCLUSION

Having drawn attention to the prominent role of voluntary associations in local politics, it must be re-emphasized that these associations are not the sole determinant of local political behavior (although they are, I believe, an important one). Party, factional and ascriptive ties, among other influences, are also important. But their relative importance in deciding both the style and the fortunes of local political entrepreneurs cannot fairly be judged without full examination of the enormous growth of voluntary associational activity.

TABLE 12

EXECUTIVE CROSS-AFFILIATIONS IN VOLUNTARY ASSOCIATIONS, CANDIDATES IN NAGPUR MUNICIPAL CORPORATION ELECTION, 1969[a]

Type of executive affiliation	Higher vote-getters		Lower vote-getters		Total	
	No.	%-age	No.	%-age	No.	%-age
One or more educational or cooperative societies	36	52.9	23	33.8	59	43.3
Neither educational nor cooperative societies	32	46.1	45	66.1	77	56.6
Number of candidates	68	100.0	68	100.0	136	100.0

[a]*Source:* Personal interviews.

Caste is a central factor in local political calculations. But as this study will make abundantly clear, caste cohesion in electoral arenas is more the exception than the rule in Nagpur politics. Voters are attracted by more than community identification. Such other factors cut across, transmute, and interact with caste, altering its political meaning. In this regard, we might recall André Béteille's wise comment on the political salience of caste in a Tanjore village. Castes, he observed, certainly "do continue to have a virile existence. The question is not whether, as status groups, they provide a basis for political mobilization—for this they evidently do—but what other factors in addition to caste are of importance to the distribution of power, and how such factors interact with one another and with caste."[40]   Similarly, while granting the pervasiveness of factionalism, we shall consider unwarranted the assumption that the character and behavior of factions remain unaltered over time. On the contrary, we will be attempting to discover the directions of factional development under the unmistakable influence of the voluntary associational activity of Nagpur's politicians.

The chapter following examines the development of the associations in Nagpur and, in particular, considers the reasons for their political attractiveness.

[40]*Caste, Class, and Power* (Berkeley: University of California Press, 1965), pp. 224-225. In this connection see also Rajni Kothari's perceptive remarks on the relationship between caste and politics in *Politics in India* (Boston: Little, Brown and Company, 1970), pp. 240-241.

3

The Development of Voluntary Associations

The preceding chapter outlined several prominent characteristics of Nagpur's political environment—the fragmented and factionalized party system, the community cleavages, and the intense associational activity of candidates for municipal office. Factionalism was acknowledged to be the dominant mode of local political organization; community affiliation to loom large in the electoral calculations of local political leaders. It was pointed out, however, that the extensive involvement of local politicians in various types of voluntary association was potentially an important variable in the explanation of local political behavior and, further, that the associational variable might easily be obscured were analysis conceived solely or largely in terms of conventional organizational or social structural models.

This chapter responds to the question: What is the attraction of voluntary associations for local politicians? We know from the discussion thus far that candidates for municipal office are found in considerable numbers on the managing committees of local associations. We know, also, that some types of association seem to possess greater appeal for these politicians than others. We have at least an indication, in the superior polling power of associational activists, that associational management may be a deliberate component of electoral strategy, that is, that whatever other rewards may be gained from associational leadership, a payoff in terms of voter preferences may be among them. Accordingly, discussion now turns to the voluntary aasociations themselves—their growth, structure, membership, financial resources and, in particular, the conditions prompting the solicitous attention of local politicians.

For illustrative purposes, discussion will focus on two major types of associational activity: cooperative and educational. Other types of association—such as wrestling societies—are of considerable importance locally and will be dealt with in later chapters. The task here is to set forth the general functional attributes of cooperative and educational associations which have made them major arenas of local political competition.

COOPERATIVE ASSOCIATIONS

The development of the cooperative movement since independence has been phenomenal, whether judged in terms of number or variety of associations.[1] In the state of Maharashtra alone, there were a total of 38,312 cooperative societies of all kinds, with a total membership of 7,500,000, registered as of 30 June 1967.[2] Of these, Nagpur district claimed (as of 30 June 1969) a total of 1,887 cooperative societies, with a total membership of 319,448.[3] The range of activities contained in the movement is evident in a recent classification of cooperatives registered in Nagpur district, listed on the next page, with their total number in the district[4]:

[1] The cooperative movement has its effective origins in India in the passage by the central government on 25 March 1904, of the Cooperative Credit Societies Act. The first cooperative society in Nagpur district, an urban credit society, was the Nagpur Government Press Cooperative Society, registered on 20 September 1907. According to the district *Gazetteer*, the movement made an auspicious beginning in Nagpur, but a general economic downturn in the 1930s seriously decimated the ranks of the cooperatives. "The war and the post-war period," it reports, "witnessed a considerable progress in the number of societies, their resources and their coverage. In particular, there was a vigorous growth of consumers' movement when the government decided to appoint cooperative societies as agents for distribution of foodgrains that had run in short supply." Government of Maharashtra, *Nagpur District Gazetteer*, p. 377. For a general survey of the Indian cooperative movement, consult C. B. Mamoria and R.D. Saksena, *Co-operation in India* (Allahabad: Kitab Mahal, 1967).

[2] Government of Maharashtra, cooperative department, *Cooperative Societies in Maharashtra State: Government Annual Report (1966-67)* (Bombay: Government Central Press, 1968), p. 2.

[3] Figures supplied by the district deputy registrar cooperative societies, Gandhi Sagar, Nagpur.

[4] "A Note on the Cooperative Movement in Nagpur District," typed report, dated November 1969, prepared for P. P. Dharmadhikari, district deputy

Agricultural credit societies	652
Central cooperative bank	1
Land development bank	1
Processing societies	11
Marketing societies	15
Non-agricultural credit societies	124
Fisheries societies	13
Consumers societies	218
Farming societies	15
Weavers societies	173
Yarn spinning society	1
Industrial producers societies	89
Housing societies	326
Dairying societies	48
Lift irrigation societies	3

The cooperative movement's share of the government's annual budget has generally been substantial. In fiscal 1966-67, for example, state government grants to all the cooperatives in Maharashtra state totalled Rs 27,300,000. In the same period, loans totalled Rs 49,600,999.[5]

Many, perhaps most, of the cooperative associations active in Nagpur district cater largely to rural interests. This is most obviously the case with agricultural credit societies, the single most prolific form of co-operativism in the district. But among the more successful branches of the movement in the Nagpur area (quantitatively speaking) are those based largely in the urban population. These would include the housing, consumer, industrial producer (especially weaver), and non-agricultural credit societies. We will examine two of these—housing and weaver production cooperatives. We turn first to the weaver societies.

Weaver Production Societies. Having reached a peak in Nagpur district earlier than most other types of cooperatives, the number of weaver production societies has tended to level off in recent years. The weaver cooperatives remain, nonetheless, one of the largest associational groups in the Nagpur area. A tabulation made on 30 June 1969 listed 173

---

register cooperative societies, Gandhi Sagar, Nagpur. That a society is registered does not necessarily imply that it is active. For example, the same memo reported that of the eighty-nine industrial producers' societies officially registered, sixty-two were dormant.

[5] Government of Maharashtra, cooperative department, *Cooperative Societies in Maharashtra State: Government Annual Report (1966-67)*, p. 11.

primary cooperative weaver societies in the district, 159 of them employing handloom and 14 of them powerloom production techniques.[6] Nagpur tehsil, an administrative subdivision composed substantially of Nagpur city, holds 134—the great majority of them.[7] Table 13 indicates their progress since 1952.

TABLE 13

PROGRESS OF WEAVERS HANDLOOM AND POWERLOOM PRIMARY COOPERATIVE SOCIETIES, NAGPUR DISTRICT, 1952-1969[a]

Year	Number of societies	Membership
1952	94	?
1957	150	9,110
1961	172	18,441
1965	186	19,212
1969	173	18,823

[a]*Source:* Compiled from *Nagpur District Gazetteer*, p. 385, K. R. Nanekar, *Handloom Industry in Madhya Pradesh* (Nagpur: Nagpur University Press, 1968), p. 67; tables provided by the deputy district registrar cooperative societies; and government of Maharashtra, bureau of economics and statistics, *Socio Economic Review and District Statistical Abstract of Nagpur District (1965-66)* (Bombay: Government Printing and Stationery, 1967?), p. 68. Although official reports do not always distinguish the fact, it is a safe persumption, given the rather recent growth of the local powerloom industry, that powerloom societies are included only in the figures for 1969.

The city and district have a particularly impressive share of the handloom weaver cooperatives operating in the state. In mid-1968, there were 758 handloom weaver societies in Maharashtra, giving Nagpur district—with 159 of them—20 per cent of the total.[8] Large numbers of

[6]"A note on the Cooperative Movement in Nagpur District," *op. cit.*

[7]Figures based on a 30 June 1968 tabulation supplied by the district deputy registrar cooperative societies, Gandhi Sagar, Nagpur.

[8]Government of Maharashtra, commissioner for cooperation and registrar of cooperative societies, Poona, leaflet "Industrial Cooperatives" (Bombay: Government Central Press, 1968?). The number of powerloom cooperatives in Maharashtra is relatively small—only seventy-one in 1967. Nagpur district's share—fourteen—seems oversized in this category, too. Government of Maharashtra, cooperative department, *Cooperative Societies in Maharashtra State: Government Annual Report (1966-67)*, p. 40.

the societies are defunct, but even when their number is subtracted the balance is still large enough to make Nagpur the capital of cooperativism in the state's handloom weaving industry.[9]

The explanation for its prominence is not difficult to discover. Though only a minor textile milling center in comparison with Bombay,[10] Nagpur maintains the state's largest center of handloom weaving. In 1965, of 161,180 handlooms registered in the entire state, the eight eastern districts of Vidarbha altogether held 63,952 of them (39.6 per cent), Nagpur district alone 39,724 (24.6 per cent), and Nagpur city about 30,000 (18.6 per cent) of these.[11]

[9]Of 172 primary weavers' cooperatives registered in Nagpur in 1960-61, for example, 47 were reported not functioning. Government of Maharashtra, *Nagpur District Gazetteer*, p. 384.

[10]Two composite mills (Empress Mills and Model Mills), both predating the 20th century, are located in the city. Together they have over three thousand looms and more than twelve thousand workers. Government of Maharashtra, census office, *Nagpur District Census Handbook*, p. 45. Household powerlooms were not introduced into the city until during World War II; by April 1948 there were approximately seventeen of them installed. Their numbers dwindled, however, in the face of stiff opposition from the handloom interests. Beginning around 1966, household powerlooms have been reintroduced in the city, mainly by Muslim weavers (Momins). Powerlooms numbered over five hundred in 1970, and were located almost entirely in the Muslim section of Mominpura. Figures supplied by an official of the Nagpur Weavers Powerloom Association, interviewed in January 1970.

[11]State, regional and district statistics are from government of Maharashtra, bureau of economics and statistics, *Statistical Abstract of Maharashtra State: 1963-64, 1964-65 and 1965-66*, p. 210. The estimate of the handlooms in Nagpur city itself is drawn from those made by several prominent weaver leaders, whose estimates ranged rather consistently between 25,000 and 35,000 *working* handlooms. In assessing these statistics, two considerations should be borne in mind. The first is that the reliability of officially published statistics is suspect when the industry in question is heavily dependent on government subsidy paid to a considerable extent on the basis of the number of looms claimed in operation. The second and related consideration is that a surprising number of handlooms, though officially registered, are either seasonally or permanently idled. One survey carried out in Nagpur in 1953 revealed that 113 (42 per cent) of 270 looms surveyed were not in operation. And another, conducted in 1955, revealed that 93 (31 per cent) of 296 looms were standing idle. Both were reported in K. R. Nanekar, *Handloom Industry in Madhya Pradesh* (Nagpur: Nagpur University Press, 1968), p. 23. The situation is paralleled statewide, among both household powerlooms and handlooms. Of a total number of 85,339 registered handlooms organized in cooperative societies in the state in 1967, only 28,866 were reported in operation. And of a

The spread of the cooperative movement among Nagpur's handloom weavers is due, in large measure, to the extreme economic vulnerability of a traditional handicraft industry. Prominent among the reasons for its vulnerability is its declining competitive strength against the enormous mechanized wing of the textile industry in the state.

The various branches of India's cotton textile industry have for long been in conflict with one another.[12] The mills, which have risen in the 20th century to a dominant position nationwide in the industry, are clearly on top in the struggle.[13] Their stature in Maharashtra is particularly awesome. The state's eighty-five mills (fifty-five of them in Bombay), while constituting 15.6 per cent of the total mills in India, produced (1967) 24.7 and 33.1 per cent respectively of the nation's yarn and cloth, and employed 31 per cent of the nation's cotton textile workers.[14] The handloom sector, in contrast, is rapidly losing ground both to the household powerloom and, especially, to the textile mills.[15] To the

---

total number of 10,142 registered cooperative powerlooms at that time, only 4,000 were actually in production. Government of Maharashtra, cooperative department, *Cooperative Societies in Maharashtra State: Government Annual Report (1966-67)*, pp. 39-40.

[12]Generally speaking, the cotton textile industry is divided between mill and household looms, the former having obvious advantages in organized efficiency and large-scale mechanization. Household looms themselves are subdivided between powerdriven and handoperated looms, the powerlooms having the disadvantage of small-scale production in comparison with the composite mills and factory powerloom centers, but at the same time bearing lower production costs than the handlooms. The household handloom industry is itself subdivided, in terms of production, between those looms using handspun yarn and those using millmade yarn; those using handspun and handwoven khadi comprise a well known but quite negligible sector of the textile industry, producing generally less than one per cent of the total output of cloth by the entire cotton textile industry of India. K. R. Nanekar, *Handloom Industry in Madhya Pradesh, op. cit.*, pp. 95-96.

[13]The number of composite cotton textile mills throughout India has risen dramatically in the 20th century—from 101 in 1906 to 544 in 1967. K. R. Nanekar, *Handloom Industry in Madhya Pradesh, op. cit.*, p. 98, and government of Maharashtra, bureau of economics and statistics, *Handbook of Basic Statistics of Maharashtra State 1968* (Bombay: Government Central Press, 1969), p. 6.

[14]*Ibid.*, pp. 6, 47. Figures are calculated according to monthly averages. The value of industrial output of *all* branches of the textile industry in Maharashtra is almost twice as great as any other industry in the state.

[15]The household powerloom industry, which is even more concentrated in Maharashtra, though large, is less imposing than the mill sector. According to

suggestion by handloom operators that powerlooms be prohibited from producing women's color saris, which constitute the bulk of the cotton sari market (and almost the entire production of the handloom industry), household powerloom weavers reply that a ban be placed, in compensation, on mill production of various roughcloth goods such as men's dhotis. Mill dominance of the market, and the importance of milled textiles to the Maharashtrian economy, make such an eventuality quite unlikely. Thus, the economic enfeeblement of the handloom sector of the textile industry proceeds on its ineluctable course, slowed by little more than the sheer number of weavers clinging to handloom production techniques. For handloom weaving remains, indeed, the state's largest cottage industry, employing tens of thousands of workers.[16]

Seen from a different angle, the vulnerability of the handloom industry may be traced just as logically to the uneconomic production techniques and conservative marketing practices of the local handloom weavers themselves. According to an administrative official of the Vidarbha Winkar Kendriya Sahakari Saunstha (Vidarbha weavers central cooperative society) (VWCCS)—the apex institution of the local primary handloom societies—the weavers have made hardly any adjustment to their declining market potential.[17] Though superior model looms, such as the frameloom, are available, few of the weavers in Nagpur use them, preferring the reliable but less productive fly-shuttle pitlooms.[18] Ninety

---

1968 figures, Maharashtra, with 96,000 powerlooms, had almost twice as many as any other state. In contrast, the state's handloom textile industry is quite small in comparison with the rest of India, evidence of the state's relatively advanced industrial status. The total number of registered handlooms in India in 1964 was 3,010,000. Only 163,000 (5.4 per cent) were in Maharashtra. Statistics on the powerloom industry supplied by an official of the Nagpur Weavers Powerloom Association; and on the handloom industry, government of Maharashtra, bureau of economics and statistics, *Statistical Abstract of Maharashtra State: 1963-64, 1964-65 and 1965-66*, p. 3.

[16]According to Nanekar, while the mills of India vastly outstrip both household powerlooms and handlooms in amount of production, the handlooms alone employ roughly twice as many workers. *Handloom Industry in Madhya Pradesh, op. cit.*, Table 8.3, p. 103.

[17]Interviewed in January 1970.

[18]Installation of framelooms would require the local weavers, whose homes generally have low ceilings, to partially reconstruct their homes. Though installing newer style looms would probably reduce the work load and improve working conditions, the costs of purchase and installation would not necessarily be offset over the long run by increased productivity. The weavers argue, reports Nanekar, that they "can manipulate the parts of the existing looms

per cent of the local weavers, by this official's estimate, are producing only women's saris on their looms. Though their product is of uncommonly high quality, their market is overwhelmingly rural. And even there the handloom product is waning in popularity. In the cities, according to this informant, women typically purchase only a few handloom products, preferring the more expensive but better looking and more easily maintained synthetic cloths. Since handloom weavers are partially shielded by government restrictions placed on mill production of cotton color saris—restrictions which do not apply to mill production of color saris made of synthetic yarns—they are discouraged from entering the lucrative but unprotected synthetic cloth industry.[19] And finally, while the traditional nine-metre sari continues to decline in popularity, not only in the cities but in the villages (where the five- or

---

with remarkable ease, and that because of this, they can easily adjust the cost of raw material to the ruling market prices." The older devices permit them to get maximum returns in a fluctuating market. "The new devices... limit the capacity of the weaver to manoeuvre and force him to standardize the product. It is agreed that standardization is not likely to improve their economic condition. Of course, the new devices do raise the productivity. But the increase in productivity... is not so substantial as to compensate for the loss suffered on account of standardization....The upshot of the whole argument," he concludes, "is that the weavers would take to improved devices without any opposition, if these devices increased the productivity of looms substantially." *Handloom Industry in Madhya Pradesh, op. cit.,* pp. 51-52. Persons familiar with the weavers' trade report that by slightly reducing the number of "picks" (crosswise weaves) and "ends" (lengthwise weaves) in a sari, the weaver can increase his profits undetected. The standard for 80-count saris, for example, is sixty-two picks and fifty-six ends. By threading one or two picks and ends less per inch, small sums can be surreptitiously earned per sari and the difference will be indistinguishable to the average consumer. The older type looms are apparently more congenial to such economizing practices.

[19]Without protection the weavers would have an even more difficult task in competing with the mills than they have today; and yet the practice of "reserving" certain sectors of the cotton textile industry for the handlooms has tended to bunch weavers together in the production of a very few types of fabrics. The overwhelming majority of handlooms today are producing "reserved" color saris, while the production of other types of cotton textiles has steadily declined. *Ibid.,* pp. 16-17. Also see Nanekar's discussion of the reservation policy, pp. 105-107. Even if there were an economic advantage in entering the synthetic cloth market, the handloom product would inevitably be inferior in appearance to the factory powerloom product, just as are handloom cotton products.

six-metre lengths are increasingly preferred), Nagpur weavers continue their almost total commitment to the longer style.

The Koshtis (weavers) of Nagpur are thus an economic anachronism. Their craft is organized almost exclusively as a household industry, posing economic problems long absent from advanced industrial countries. Whether their predicament is traced to the inability of a household industry to hold its own in an economy increasingly dominated by streamlined mass industrial production, to obsolescent techniques and marketing practices within their own sector, or simply to psychological conservatism, the fact remains that their condition will not easily be relieved. While there is not the slightest chance that they can bring about a legislated return to handloom textile production, domestic handloom weavers are far too numerous in Nagpur to be denied considerable political patronage of their obsolescence.[20] The palliative medium is cooperative association.

Government assistance to the ailing handloom weavers, channeled through their production cooperatives, has taken various forms. Aid direct to the apex society (VWCCS) has been intended to improve its services to the affiliated primaries, such as in the sale of yarn, provision of marketing facilities, and granting of loans.[21] Backed by government,

---

[20]Of a total urban population (1961) of 643,659, weavers (including both Hindus and Muslims) are generally estimated to number between 110,000 and 150,000 (roughly 17 to 23 per cent). Most of these, possibly 80 or 90 per cent, are Hindu weavers, clustered largely in the east-central wards of the city. Koshti is the popular Hindu occupational designation for this group, which includes, in fact, a number of hierarchically arranged subcastes. The smaller Muslim group of weavers, occupationally designated as Momins, resides almost entirely in the single communal ghetto of Mominpura. Unless otherwise stated, Koshti refers here to the entire group, Muslim and Hindu. K. R. Nanekar, *Handloom Industry in Madhya Pradesh*, is the best source on Nagpur weavers. See also N. G. S. Kini, "Caste as a Factor in State Politics," in *State Politics in India*, Iqbal Narain, editor (Meerut: Meenakshi Prakashan, 1967), pp. 562-574.

[21]The official functions of the VWCCS are: (i) supply of raw material to primary societies; (ii) supervision of goods produced by member societies and aid in arranging sales; (iii) provision of financial aid and other help to member societies, and directing and coordinating their activities; (iv) maintenance of demonstration centers and provision of services in preparatory and finishing processes of weaving; (v) advertizing of handloom goods; and (vi) performance of other activities necessary for the rehabilitation and development of the handloom industry. K. R. Nanekar, *Handloom Industry in Madhya Pradesh*, p. 78.

the VWCCS has, in turn, initiated a number of schemes: it operates, or commissions, twelve retail sales centers and thirty-nine wholesale centers in various parts of central India; it manages its own dye house; it has a design-making division to encourage innovation in product design; it operates a seasonal purchase scheme, underwriting weaver losses incurred during the slack (monsoon) season; and it has begun a sales guarantee (or pledge) scheme in which the apex society offers minimum price protection plus low-interest loans affording the weavers flexibility in choosing whether to sell their products through the cooperative organization or on the open market.[22]

Government financial subsidies have been crucial to launching all of these projects. For example, in addition to loans extended through the Nagpur district Central Cooperative Bank totalling over Rs 3,500,000 in fiscal year 1968-69, the apex society received over Rs 1,000,000 in the form of government purchase of shares.[23]

Government aid available direct to the primary societies is also substantial. Loans are provided to members of primary cooperatives for the purchase of shares in the local societies up to 75 per cent of the value of shares.[24] Subsidies or loans are also available for the opening of sales depots, for the setting up of dye houses and dyeing units, for the purchase of tools and equipment. The most common direct form of assistance to the weaver primaries is a government-guaranteed rebate on the wholesale and retail sales of handloom cloth.

Glaring dependence on governmental initiative and financial support has been endemic to the weaver cooperatives virtually from the start.[25] The protracted struggle of the VWCCS is a good illustration.

[22]*Annual Report* (1968-69) of the VWCCS, and "Progress Report" provided by the VWCCS.

[23]*Annual Report* (1968-69). An indication of the central society's dependence on the government lies in the fact that only a small percentage of its share capital has been purchased by its constituent societies. As of 30 June 1969, according to the *Annual Report*, the government had invested a cumulative total of Rs 2,900,000 in shares, the constituent societies only Rs 262,000.

[24]The pattern of current governmental assistance is briefly outlined in the pamphlet *Industrial Cooperatives*, cited earlier.

[25]Though weaver cooperative societies appeared in India in the 1920s, their history is a dismal one up to the close of World War II. In Nagpur, they were virtually non-existent until the late 1930s. Government assistance was meager in those years, and in combination with other factors (lack of indigenous capital, unrestricted competition from the mills, misunderstanding of the cooperative concept, and a generally depressed cotton textile market) the

The VWCCS assumed the status of a central society in 1945 when the provincial government appointed it as the zonal distributor of yarn.[26] Since the handloom industry had long been plagued by the scarcity of yarn, the introduction of a controlled quota system and investiture of the VWCCS as administrative agency gave a boost to cooperativism. "In allotting the yarn," wrote one observer, "the government showed special favour to the central society. This was the most important factor which brought about a mushroom growth of the weavers' cooperatives throughout the province. By 1952, there were 70,000 weavers and about 90,000 handlooms within the cooperative fold."[27]

The end of the controlled yarn scheme in 1951 sharply reversed the situation. By 1953 not more than two weaver cooperatives were active in all of Nagpur district.[28] Once again, however, in a gesture that would be repeated many times in the future, the government intervened in 1954 by making large sums available in the form of interest-free loans and grants for the development of the handloom industry. Since the cooperatives were again made the local distributive medium, older societies were revived and new ones formed.[29] By 1956 local weaver cooperativism was again showing rapid growth. However, the reorganization of states in November of that year reversed its fortunes once more; the VWCCS was bifurcated, its assets apportioned, and the Maharashtrian side (then Bombay state) given territorial responsibility for Vidarbha alone.[30] From 1956 to 1962 the position of the apex institution steadily deteriorated, revived for a few years after 1962 by an

---

movement made little progress. By 1940, not more than 130 weavers were enrolled in the cooperatives in all of the Central Provinces. K. R. Nanekar, *Handloom Industry in Madhya Pradesh, op. cit.*, p. 66.

[26]The VWCCS itself had extraordinarily humble beginnings. It was formally registered as a primary society (the Central Provinces and Berar Weavers Cooperative Society) in December 1934, with seventy-nine members and share capital of thirty-eight rupees. *Ibid.*, p. 77.

[27]*Ibid.*, p. 66.

[28]*Ibid.*, p. 68.

[29]Between 1953 and 1956 weaver cooperatives in eighteen districts of old Madhya Pradesh received government loans totalling over Rs 2,800,000. *Ibid.*, pp. 75-76.

[30]According to an administrative official of the VWCCS, the reorganization seriously undermined the central society. Madhya Pradesh received most of the liquid cash and saleable stock in the settlement; Vidarbha was awarded such frozen assets as the headquarters building itself and older, unsaleable stock.

injection of government loans and grants, but thereafter resumed its downward trend until large governmental inputs, after 1966, set it once again on a forward pace.

Among the weavers, government support and cooperative achievement have always tended to ebb and flow in close communion. Self-sufficiency is a largely unattained goal, at least in so far as the cooperative institutions are concerned. Though large transfusions of government aid have revived weaver cooperatives periodically, their official record locally is one of almost unmitigated economic failure. The apex society has shown a cumulative net loss every year since 1958, amounting in 1969 to Rs 640,000. It suffered its largest loss, Rs 184,652, in fiscal year 1968-69 despite hitherto unmatched government assistance the previous year.[31] The infusion of government aid in 1967 was predicated, in fact, upon the apex society's willingness to give up its autonomy by placing the administration of its accounts in the hands of government officials for a period of several years. The elected managing body thus stepped aside in January 1967, superceded by government administrators.

The uncertain career of the VWCCS has been paralleled by the highly uneven growth of the numerous affiliated primary societies. Only a minority of the weavers has ever affiliated with the cooperative movement, and even then, the connection has often been quite nominal. Of the 41,130 handlooms registered in the district on 30 June 1968, 20,531 were officially listed within the cooperative fold. But of these, according to an official report, only 4,605 were actually in production.[32] Furthermore, many of the active cooperative societies operate independently of one another, maintaining only a nominal connection with the central society. In 1968-69 the VWCCS handled the products of only 1,286 looms, doing business with only 111 of 292 affiliated societies.[33]

[31]Figures supplied by the VWCCS. It is noteworthy that government loans to the VWCCS and finished product retail sales by the society reach their lowest point in almost fifteen years simultaneously in 1961-62, the same period in which the Vidarbhan regionalist movement reached its greatest intensity. Since the Koshtis provided the bulk of the separatist movement's supporters, there may have been some relation between weaver backing of the regionalist movement and government backing of the weaver cooperative movement.

[32]"A Note on the Cooperative Movement in Nagpur District," *op. cit.*

[33]Compiled from the *Annual Report* of the VWCCS for 1968-69, and from a typed "Progress Report" supplied by the society. Though the apex society is technically charged with serving all eight districts of Vidarbha, in practice most of its limited active membership is based in Nagpur city.

The above facts highlight a number of points. First, despite the objective of self-sufficiency the cooperatives remain highly dependent on government support. Dependence is so great that a threat to withdraw government support forced the central society's executive body to relinquish control of its affairs. Second, the affiliated primaries have clearly shown only partial and intermittent interest in the cooperative enterprise: weaver enthusiasm has risen with each fresh injection of government aid, and fallen when aid declined. And third, while members of the primary cooperatives have not been hesitant to apply for the various forms of governmental assistance, they have used the assistance not to strengthen cooperativism as such, but to strengthen their own bargaining power in the free market. The so-called pledge scheme of the VWCCS, noted earlier, was explicitly framed to facilitate just such behavior.[34]

Other reasons may be given for the failure of cooperativism to flourish in Nagpur.[35] But one ineradicable factor appears to be that the weavers employ the cooperative structure principally to obtain government subsidies. The collective economic functions of cooperative associa-

---

[34]The situation was perceptively described some years ago by Nanekar. "Obviously," he wrote in summing up the failure of cooperativism among the Koshtis, "the movement lacks the internal strength of its own and is based on exogenous factors. At one time yarn was easily available through the cooperatives and, therefore, the number of societies increased. The moment this privilege disappeared, the societies began to stop their work. In view of the fact that the yarn business was quite profitable in the past, there was no reason for any society to collapse as soon as the specific situation which had created the cooperative boom was over. The collapse, however, would be easily understood if it is remembered that the cooperatives were not the result of any basic faith in cooperation on the part of the members. They were formed, because they were the best means of advancing the personal gain under the then prevailing government policy. In fact, the cooperatives were taken to be no more than yarn-distributing agencies. Mismanagement, misappropriation and various other malpractices were, therefore, the rule, and not the exception. The rehabilitation of weavers' societies and the revival of the movement in a later period, particularly after 1954, again seems to be very closely associated with liberal government loans and grants. It may thus seem that the weavers' cooperative movement boils down to the formation of cooperatives under a special stimulus. The dissolution of societies seems to be almost natural as soon as the stimulus is withdrawn. Most of these societies owe their existence to government loans and grants. The rebate on handloom cloth ... has now become an important prop. Many societies stop their work completely, if there is a slight delay in the realization of rebate claims from the government." *Handloom Industry in Madhya Pradesh, op. cit.*, pp. 78-79.

[35]On this, see *ibid.*, pp. 80-81.

tions are permitted to atrophy, and free market trading, by members as well as non-members, goes on unabated.

In other words, the cooperatives function as impromptu occupational interest groups with the principal task that of exacting government concessions for their members. For the lobbying of their interests, weavers must rely heavily on the exertion of influence by intermediaries between government and the associations. This is a need for which local politicians are eminently suited. It is a need which has transformed the cooperative societies, primary and apex, into major arenas of political activity in the city of Nagpur. Political support is something all weavers do have to offer local political patrons in exchange for their brokerage activity; and the cooperative societies—the legal instruments created to receive and distribute government developmental subsidies—are logical settings in which to negotiate the transaction. The competition to control the process is intense; fortifying the cooperatives against rival political brokers becomes a central task, displacing others. Since competitive rather than cooperative enterprise thus becomes the norm, existing cleavages in the weaver community are exacerbated and cooperativism becomes a partisan matter. Those weavers excluded from cooperative benefits by essentially *political* decisions become cooperativism's enemies, making it virtually impossible for it to spread on the grounds merely of its economic promise.[36] Those privileged to have control of the cooperative societies and their assets may judge the maintenance of political ties more critical to their survival than the attainment of cooperative objectives.[37] For both incumbent managers and their oppo-

[36]Cooperativism's political promise, according to its critics, is substantial. The presidents and secretaries managing the primary societies allegedly double as "government commission agents," commissioned, that is, as political canvassers for the ruling party. It is charged that the present system of rebate on retail sales of handloom products is regularly used to subsidize such political agents. False accounts are maintained, showing a greater number of looms and members than are actually involved in cooperative production; local government officials, for a concession, are willing to certify the inflated figures. One outspoken opponent, with perhaps some exaggeration, claimed that "every primary society will get an average rebate of about Rs 5,000 each year, and it will all be based on purely paper figures."

[37]It is a matter of dispute precisely which political groups are in control of cooperative interests. Though Congress loyalists have obvious advantages in a state dominated by Congress, there is reason to believe that the representation of weaver interests is open to intermediaries of whatever party affiliation. Only one of the eleven weaver cooperative executives among the candidates

nents, the economically vulnerable and government subsidized cooperative weaver production societies are an inevitably attractive target of political opportunity.

Housing Societies. Cooperative housing societies share many traits in common with the weaver societies.[38] In contrast to the weaver societies, however, the housing associations represent what could not possibly be described as a passing economic anachronism. Demographic and socio-economic transitions have engendered a colossal housing deficit in India, which will surely continue for the balance of this century.[39] The deficit, in turn, has inspired an enormous demand for new and improved housing. The cooperative housing associations are a major vehicle for the expression of this demand. The appearance of such associations in Nagpur would seem to contain considerable opportunity for political entrepreneurship. The opportunity, as we shall soon see, has been enthusiastically seized.

Up until 1956 directors of Nagpur's chief town planning agency—the Nagpur Improvement Trust (NIT)—considered the city rich in land.[40] The agency possessed a surplus of residential plots and, indeed,

---

for municipal office interviewed as part of this study contested on a ticket of the ruling Congress party. And whereas none of the eight Congress Hindu weaver candidates won their elections, two cooperative leaders contesting with opposition parties were among the four Hindu weavers who managed to win. One of the opposition party winners (interviewed in December 1969), an active and prominent leader of the Nagpur Samyukta Socialist Party since 1955, gave no evidence of partisan discrimination. The cooperative society of which he is vice-president receives an annual "cashcredit" loan of Rs 15,000 to cover operating expenses, repayable within one year, from the Nagpur district Central Cooperative Bank. It had recently obtained an additional Rs 15,000 loan, repayable over twenty years, to purchase shares from the Nagpur Weavers Cooperative Spinning Mill. And it regularly claims five per cent rebate on retail sales from its own outlet averaging Rs 300 to Rs 500 daily.

[38]We deal here with those cooperative housing associations engaged primarily in the task of assisting settlers in land acquisition. Later chapters will consider related types of association, such as tenant and slumdweller groups, and neighborhood action committees, whose functions often overlap with those of the cooperative housing societies.

[39]"At the increased rate of construction set for the fourth five-year plan," according to one grim estimate, "it would require more than 120 years just to erase the current deficit." Richard W. Sterling, *Macropolitics: International Relations in a Global Society* (New York: Alfred A. Knopf, 1974), pp. 386-387.

[40]Information about the Trust's role in connection with cooperative housing is from interviews with NIT officials on 26/28 November 1969.

had to employ real estate brokers to canvas for buyers. Since then the situation has altered radically. Tens of thousands of settlers have poured into the hitherto open agricultural lands surrounding the city, indiscriminately occupying hundreds of acres earlier (and somewhat wistfully) designated on the Trust's master plan as "green belt control schemes," driving up land prices, and providing a lucrative field for land sharks, speculators and developers.

In the early years of this urban explosion, settlers simply squatted on vacant (usually government) land or, if they had the means, purchased directly from landowning agriculturists. The potential of this freelance solution to the housing problem was soon exhausted however. The population of the city was growing steadily, magnifying the housing shortage and compounding slum conditions.[41] Recent migrants to the city naturally pressured for new land and housing; but their demands were considerably augmented by inhabitants who had become discontented with widespread overcrowding and lack of sanitation and other amenities in older sectors of the city. The mounting demand and dwindling supply of vacant land inevitably increased the value of privately owned urban-adjacent property, driving prices beyond the means of the ordinary citizen. To all of this were added government controls, applying directly to its own land and indirectly to private lands through reservation of large areas for specified development purposes, intended to bring about the orderly progress of the city and its environs.[42]

As may be ascertained from Table 14, there were very few cooperative housing societies in existence in Nagpur when the encroachments on the city's surroundings began. The appearance and rapid development in Nagpur of the cooperative housing movement—the government-inspired apparatus designed to provide an equitable resolution of the housing problems—is a phenomenon principally of the 1960s. But whether catering to the needs of particular caste groups, occupation or

[41]From a population in 1921 of 145,193, the size of the city has grown to 482,305 in 1951; 643,659 in 1961; and an estimated 800,000 in 1969. Census figures up to 1964 are reported in Padmakar L. Joshi *et al.*, *Nagpur City Centennial Volume*, pp. 26-28. The figures for 1951 include the populations of thirty-four villages (33,206) newly incorporated in the city in that year.

[42]There are four general categories of land ownership in Nagpur: private, municipal, NIT, and state (called *nazul* land, managed by the ministry of revenue). Owing to the NIT's broad development responsibilities, it has blanketed well over half of the city under various schemes, giving itself ample authority to intervene even in respect to privately owned lands.

income groups, or, as was commonly the case, of mixed clientele with little in common but the need for housing, the cooperative societies quickly became the normal mode of organizing settlement.[43]

Among those who took the lead in organizing and managing the cooperatives were numerous local political leaders, some of them with

TABLE 14

GROWTH OF COOPERATIVE HOUSING SOCIETIES IN NAGPUR DISTRICT, 1957-1969[a]

Year	Number of societies	Membership	Share capital (in rupees)	Working capital (in rupees)
1957	22	5,065	11,500	6,415,000
1962	141	14,260	2,410,000	16,437,000
1966	242	23,281	4,396,000	28,016,000
1969	326	33,140	5,795,229	37,549,597

[a]*Source:* Tables provided by the district deputy registrar cooperative societies, Gandhi Sagar, Nagpur; and government of Maharashtra, bureau of economics and statistics, *Socio Economic Review and District Statistical Abstract of Nagpur District (1965-66)*, p. 68. Statistics are not maintained for the city itself, and were not kept for Nagpur tehsil (subdistrict) until recently. However, in Nagpur district, housing societies have been a phenomenon mainly of Nagpur city. Tehsil figures from 30 June 1968, for instance, reveal that Nagpur tehsil, consisting overwhelmingly of urban Nagpur, had 263 of the 306 housing cooperative societies then established in the five tehsils of Nagpur district.

[43]There are seven categories of cooperative housing societies in existence in Nagpur district, of which the more widespread are scheduled caste, scheduled tribe, flood sufferers, low income group, and tenant ownership. *Source:* district deputy registrar cooperative societies, Gandhi Sagar, Nagpur. Where land is settled under the auspices of an organized housing society, the procedure typically follows this pattern: Land is initially purchased by developers from farmers or landlords under the stipulation that the full purchase price will be paid after an agreed period. Option-shares are sold to prospective buyers at a modest price, and then a layout is designed and submitted to the Trust for its approval. Only upon receipt of the Trust's sanction can the society legally finalize the per-plot purchase price and divide costs up among shareholders, who must then undertake to pay for the land in fixed installments to the society. *Source:* Bhausaheb S. Surve, former mayor of Nagpur and housing society executive, interviewed on 12/15 October 1969.

considerable prior experience in land development and housing schemes. From astride the vehicle of the cooperative housing movement they offered land, money with which to build, and government sanction of property rights. Their role was that of intermediary, asking political support in return for aid in obtaining a plot of land, a loan, or title to property.[44]

The necessity for political intercession quickly became apparent, for the local town planning agency was developing its own strategy to meet the housing crisis—a strategy which inadvertently made even more critical the role of the local politician.

By the early 1960s, city planners had come to the realization that the Trust had used up virtually all of its available developed land and that it was now desirable that additional residential areas be created in the urban-adjacent agricultural lands in order to meet the demand for housing. In the decade of the 'sixties, ten large-scale residential schemes were framed. Public notification of them was given in 1963, but sanction for their development was not obtained from the state government until 1968. In the interim Trust officials were obliged to sit by while squatters moved onto the land in droves, organized their societies, planned their layouts and then, finally, turned to the NIT for legal authorization of their unauthorized actions.

As a result, the Trust was thrown into a peculiar dilemma. Responsible for the planned, orderly development of the city, it was now being called upon to regularize the haphazard settlement of the city's outskirts. Trust authorities concede that the settlers' need for land and housing was immediate, and that they could hardly have been expected to wait for the long-delayed legal sanction to arrive from Bombay. But NIT spokesmen insist at the same time that the Trust could not legally approve squatting; that it must first acquire the land for itself, develop

---

[44]One of the ironies of the cooperative housing movement is that it has failed to move very many people into new homes anywhere in India. The explanation lies partly in the fact that most of the cooperative societies are concerned with developing housing sites, not with building houses. The latter responsibility falls to the individual members who, lacking adequate resources of their own and often unable to obtain government loans, only infrequently succeed. It is not surprising, under these conditions, that the cooperatives expend most of their effort defending the substandard squatters' settlements which their lower-class clientele *can* afford.

it, and then sell to individuals rather than to cooperatives.[45] Furthermore, in the Trust's view, to countenance such settlement would be in
the long run to sanction the erosion of its urban development plans.

The dynamics of the situation were obviously not on the side of the
NIT. The settlers typically procured their plots at rates far less than
Trust prices for developed plots, and this was apparently a more important consideration to them than whether their plots came up to the
Trust's minimum standards in size and shape.[46] Morever, the sheer
volume of illicit settlements made unthinkable the idea of forcedly
removing them. Of the NIT's total of twelve residential schemes in
1969, five were purely control schemes, a designation meant to describe
a pre-development "holding" stage. Babulkheda, a ward lying in the
southern outskirts of the city, is the center of one such scheme. An indication of the inappropriateness of the designation lies in the fact that
within its area there were, by 1969, over 1,000 unauthorized structures,
layed out haphazardly, with no provisions for schools, health clinics,
electricity, sewage or water lines, or anything else.

The cooperative associations are the settlers' instrument for unraveling
the dilemma. Four or five, and often more, of the housing cooperatives
are to be found in very nearly all of the Trust's residential schemes, and
where their numbers are large they present a formidable array of collective interest. They are perhaps most formidable in the Sakkardara
Street Scheme, on whose 1,000 acres there were (in 1970) approximately
1,500 unauthorized structures with at least twenty-four cooperative

[45]The Trust capitulated to the demands of the cooperatives early in 1970,
conceding, among other things, that "ownership of the land would be vested
in the society concerned and not shifted to the NIT...." *Hitawada*, 18 January
1970.

[46]The Trust's plot development standards vary in accordance with the
level of income of the group being settled. Low income persons may be settled
on plots laid out twenty to an acre, but the average is more nearly ten to twelve
per acre. The standards of the squatters, on the other hand, are understandably
lower. They obtained their plots, with or without the instrumentation of a
cooperative society, from developers eager to maximize profits by minimizing
plot size, but willing to sell at relatively low rates due to their minimal investment in civic amenities. Ordinarily, the settlers were not in a position to
quibble over the size of the plot or the lack of paved roads, latrines, or water
lines and, having accommodated themselves to necessity, simply refuse to
budge. Having paid typically only Rs 100 to Rs 150, or at most Rs 500, for
their undeveloped plots, the source of their obstinacy is not hard to find. In the
Trust's developed layouts, plots sell for between Rs 2,000 and Rs 3,000, by
the NIT's own admission an obvious incentive to illegal squatting.

housing societies to defend them. Their members may and do use their combined electoral strength to seek the satisfaction of their housing needs. And just as politicians intervene to satisfy weaver demands, so also can they act to give tangible and immediate resolution to demands for new or improved housing.

Thus, housing associations are attractive to politicians in much the same manner as production cooperatives. They provide an elaborate and widespread voluntary associational network organized on the basis of immediate and essential public need. They represent an interest that is highly vulnerable, whether to changing economic conditions, to legal constraints, or simply to the whimsical decisions of government bureaucrats. They provide a major opportunity for political intervention between the aggrieved members and responsible government agencies—such as the Nagpur Improvement Trust. And finally, though few housing cooperatives are directly subsidized by government, the concessions sought from government are incentives to associational activism no less attractive than rebates to production cooperatives.

We turn now, to conclude our sketch of associational development, from cooperatives to *shiksan saunstha*—the education societies which serve as the managing committees of a considerable portion of Nagpur's schools.

EDUCATION SOCIETIES

Anomalous as it may seem in a nominally socialist society, most of Nagpur's schools, while *publicly* financed, are *privately* managed.[47]

---

[47]The situation is duplicated throughout India and in much of Asia. For an excellent general discussion of Asian, and particularly Indian, educational problems, see Gunnar Myrdal, *Asian Drama: An Inquiry into the Poverty of Nations*, III, pp. 1697-1828 (on private management, in particular, pp. 1703-1712). One of the most illuminating accounts of the political environment of Indian educational institutions is Harold Gould, "Educational Structures and Political Processes in Faizabad District, Uttar Pradesh," in *Education and Politics in India*, Susanne H. Rudolph and Lloyd I. Rudolph, editors (Cambridge: Harvard University Press, 1972), pp. 94-120. Additional useful studies of educational politics and public policy are Glynn Wood, "National Planning and Public Demand in Indian Higher Education," *Minerva*, X (January 1972), 83-106; and Donald B. Rosenthal, "Educational Politics and Public Policymaking in Maharashtra, India," *Comparative Education Review*, 18 (February 1974), 79-95.

Government regulatory and supervisory powers, exercised by state, district and municipal agencies, are substantial. But private enterprise, fueled by public subsidy, is spearheading the remarkable growth of educational facilities in the city. This is the case at virtually all levels of education. As will shortly be made clear, this marriage of public and private interests in the educational sector has produced a particularly inviting situation for local political actors.

Even primary schools (grades one through four), hitherto a responsibility chiefly of Nagpur municipal government, are increasingly being established by privately managed societies. Indeed, if the current trend continues there will soon be more private than public primary schools. The municipally operated primary schools increased from 80 to 225 (280 per cent) between 1949 and 1969, on the surface a considerable record of growth.[48] But while the municipal schools continue to hold a slim majority in the city (Table 15), privately managed schools are rapidly

TABLE 15

TYPE AND NUMBER OF PRIMARY SCHOOLS IN NAGPUR CITY, 1968[a]

Controlling agency	Number of schools
Central government	5
State government	1
Municipal corporation	224
Private	181
Total	411

[a]*Source:* Education office, Nagpur Zilla Parishad.

overtaking them. Numbering only 18 in 1932, the private institutions increased to 181 in 1968, and most of that growth was quite recent. Figures available on Nagpur district (largely reflecting growth in the city), indicate that the number of private primary schools rose from 95 in 1962 to 221 in 1968, an increase for the district of over 230 per cent in a period of only six years.[49] More recent data are even more suggestive of the phenomenal growth rate. In the year from March 1968 to March 1969, the number of private primary schools in Nagpur city

[48]Education officer, Nagpur municipal corporation; and Padmakar L. Joshi, *et al., Nagpur City Centennial Volume,* pp. 145-147.
[49]Education office, Nagpur Zilla Parishad.

rose from 181 to 213, giving the private sector 48 per cent of the new total of 443 primary institutions in the city. And in December 1969 there were no less than 132 applications pending with the Nagpur Zilla Parishad (district council) for the registration of private primary schools in the district, many if not most of them to be located in Nagpur city.[50]

Secondary education (grades five through eleven) is virtually the exclusive preserve of private management in Nagpur. One hundred and sixty of the 170 secondary schools in the city in 1968 were privately managed (Table 16). The private schools at the secondary level have virtually no competition from the public sector.[51] And as is the case with primary schools, the private secondary schools continue to proliferate.

TABLE 16

TYPE AND NUMBER OF SECONDARY SCHOOLS IN NAGPUR CITY, 1968[a]

Controlling agency	Number of schools
Central government	1
State government	5
Municipal corporation	4
Private	160
Total	170

[a]*Source:* Education office, Nagpur Zilla Parishad.

Collegiate education, showing the same rapid growth pattern, is also largely under private management in the city. There are eighty colleges affiliated with Nagpur University in the eight-district region of Vidarbha over whose higher education it presides. Twenty-four are in Nagpur district, twenty in Nagpur city itself. Of this last group, seventeen are privately operated.[52] Table 17 makes apparent the recent upsurge in collegiate growth.

[50]*Ibid.*

[51]According to the education officer, Nagpur municipal corporation, the handful of public secondary schools now in existence was established to serve outlying areas of the city ignored by the private societies.

[52]Nagpur University, *Annual Report* (Nagpur: Nagpur University Press, 1969), pp. 4-10.

TABLE 17

GROWTH OF UNIVERSITY AFFILIATED COLLEGES IN NAGPUR CITY, 1930-68[a]

Year	Number of colleges
1930	2
1940	4
1950	6
1960	11
1965	14
1968	20

[a]*Source:* Nagpur University, *Annual Report* (Nagpur: Nagpur University Press, 1969), pp. 110-123.

Figures on enrollment, number of faculty, and government expenditure give further indication both of the scope of the private sector in education and of its substantial share in public funds. As may be seen in Table 18, even the private share of government grants for normally public sector primary education (based on *district* figures) stands at over eleven per cent.[53] The private share of government grants for secondary education in recent years is not specifically determinable from available data, but indications are that it has been and continues to be very large: in 1962 although eighty-six per cent of secondary education in the district was under private management, seventy-one per cent of total expenditure on secondary education was incurred by the government.[54]

Expenditure on primary and secondary education is incurred by the state primarily through grants-in-aid to the Zilla Parishad. Expenditure takes a variety of forms. According to an official source, wards of parents whose annual income does not exceed Rs 1,200 and all students of the

[53]The figure stood at less than five per cent in 1961-62. District figures are naturally biased in favor of public schools due to the rapid growth of rural primary schools. There were 1,275 public and private primary schools in the district outside of Nagpur city in 1968, and the vast majority were public. The growth of private schools in Nagpur district, though increasing in rural areas, remains predominantly an urban phenomenon. In this connection, see Iqbal Narain "Rural Local Politics and Primary School Management," in *Education and Politics in India*, cited above, pp. 148-164.

[54]Government of Maharashtra census office, *Nagpur District Census Handbook*, p. 25.

TABLE 18

COMPARISON OF ENROLLMENT, NUMBER OF TEACHERS, AND GOVERNMENT
GRANTS TO PRIVATE AND PUBLIC PRIMARY SCHOOLS IN NAGPUR DISTRICT,
1967-1968[a]

Controlling agency	Enrollment	Number of teachers	Government grants (in rupees)
Central government	498	10	27,492
State government	160	4	8,736
Zilla Parishad	94,317	3,369	5,595,511
Municipalities[b]	87,166	2,514	5,027,935
Private	31,052	996	1,365,347
Total	213,193	6,893	12,025,021

[a]Source: Education office, Nagpur Zilla Parishad. Separate figures for the
city are not maintained by the education office. Since the private schools
(primary and secondary) are a phenomenon confined to a large degree to Nagpur
city, district figures naturally obscure their relatively greater importance in the
urban environment. In 1968, 181 of the 221 private primary schools and 160
of the 240 private secondary schools in the district were located in Nagpur
city. Recent comparable data on secondary schools in the district were not made
available. But the great scope of private development at the secondary level
may be judged from the fact that secondary education everywhere in the district
lies almost entirely in the private sector: in 1968, 240 of 266 secondary schools
in the district were privately managed. In an earlier period (1961-62), government grants to district secondary schools (most of them private) amounted to
over seven million rupees. It may be noted that the Zilla Parishad serves both as
the office of record for all schools in the district and as the disbursing agency
for state government grants to all urban and rural, public and private, schools
in the district. It is directly responsible for the administration of rural public
schools only.

[b]Includes Nagpur city.

scheduled castes get free education at the cost of the government.[55] In addition to small scholarships for students of the scheduled castes, the government contributes to the maintenance of hostels providing accommodation for scheduled caste students. Private secondary and collegiate institutions, no less than the primary schools, obtain government subsidy through grant-in-aid schemes for maintenance, salaries, building construction and land purchase, equipment, scholarships, loans, and various additional concessions to economically and socially disadvantaged students.[56] Education concessions to so-called "backward class" students, as is clear from data presented in Table 19, alone constitute an enormous budgetary item in Nagpur district. Recipients of concessions form a majority, in fact, of the district's student population. Backward class beneficiaries in fiscal year 1965-66 numbered 170,718, forming over 55 per cent of the total pre-primary through university student population of 308,694 in Nagpur district.[57]

Educational management societies, the privately operated institutions designated to preside over the system described above, vary considerably in terms of number of schools, enrollment and capital investment. They range in size from miniature outfits operating a single, tiny, but grandiloquently styled Montessori pre-school with minimal assets and a few dozen children enrolled, to mammoth systems including every level and branch of education and spreading over vast regions of the state. Nagpur is amply representative of the full range. Two of the city's newer and relatively well provisioned colleges, for example, are part of the Shri Shivaji Shiksan Saunstha (Shri Shivaji education society), founded in 1931, which is one of the largest privately managed educational systems in the state of Maharashtra. Headquartered in Amravati district, it has founded institutions in six districts in the Vidarbhan region.[58] The society has risen from an original three institutions in 1942, with 38 staff members and 250 students, to 126 institutions (including 27 colleges and over 50 secondary schools) in 1968, with 1,925

---

[55] *Ibid.*, p. 24.

[56] *Ibid.*, pp. 25-27.

[57] Government of Maharashtra, bureau of economics and statistics, *Statistical Abstract of Maharashtra State: 1963-64, 1964-65 and 1965-66*, Table 16.2, pp. 283-288.

[58] Information on the society is derived principally from its *Annual Report* for 1967-68.

staff members and enrollment in excess of 36,000.[59] According to the society's *Annual Report*, it held properties and assets in 1968 totalling Rs 14,431,042.

One of the largest locally based education societies is the Yugantar Education Society.[60] Originating in the early 1920s, the Yugantar Society has grown gradually into a complex network of diversified institutions spread through five districts of eastern Maharashtra and into Madhya Pradesh.[61] The Yugantar Society initially concentrated on providing primary school education to persons of the scheduled castes; but as this responsibility was increasingly assumed by government, it took up the establishment, particularly in the post-independence period, of secondary schools and boarding hostels.[62] In recent years, it has diversified even further, founding a college, several tailoring schools, a string of housing societies, and a hospital. The scope of the enter-

[59]The society actually reached its peak in the period 1963-1967, during which the number of institutions reached 216, staff members 2,190, and enrollment 41,590. The sharp drop by 1968 was occasioned, at least in part, by the society's liquidation of those schools lacking adequate financial support from government. It reported fourteen such closures in its *Annual Report* for 1967-68. The society's objectives, spelt out in its constitution, are ambitious nonetheless, testifying to the enormous opportunities existing for educational entrepreneurship. Among other things, the society proposes "to establish, conduct, manage, supervise, and take over educational institutions of various kinds for boys, girls and adults...to undertake and make available facilities for research in all branches of knowledge and to establish institutions for this purpose; to carry on experiments with a view to improving methods of teaching and to establish institutions for this purpose; to encourage physical culture and to start, conduct or manage institutions for this purpose; to encourage women's education by establishing special institutions like hostels, widows' homes and nursing schools, etc.; to establish hostels for poor boys and girls and to open and conduct orphanages...to establish, start, conduct and manage printing presses for publishing books, periodicals, journals and other educational media; to undertake farming, gardening and to acquire or take on lease, or to purchase land for the same purpose; to start other subsidiary activities and institutions such as the establishment of stores, medical aid societies, etc... to organize exhibitions...tournaments...conferences, seminars...." *Amended Constitution*, Shri Shivaji Education Society, Amravati, 1967.

[60]The largest *local* education society is the Citizens' Education Society, discussed in Chapter 5.

[61]Information on the Yugantar Education Society is drawn chiefly from its *Commemorative Volume*, issued on 20 December 1968.

[62]Only two of the society's pre-independence institutions—a hostel founded in 1930 and a high school founded in 1946—continue in existence today.

prise is visible in a 1969 listing of the society's institutions:

Type of institution	Number
Institute of social work	1
Lower secondary schools	3
Secondary night school	1
Primary school	1
Montessori schools	4
Student hostels	15
Tailoring schools	3
Orphanage	1
Hospital	1
Housing societies	8
Total	38

TABLE 19

CONCESSIONS TO BACKWARD CLASS STUDENTS IN NAGPUR DISTRICT, PRE-PRIMARY THROUGH HIGHER EDUCATION, 1965-66[a]

Beneficiary	Enrollment[b]	Educational concession (in rupees)
Scheduled castes	43,693	2,482,037
Scheduled tribes	17,760	381,374
Other backward classes[c]	109,265	4,249,863
Total	170,718	7,113,274

[a]*Source:* Government of Maharashtra, bureau of economics and statistics, *Socio Economic Review and District Statistical Abstract of Nagpur District* (*1965-66*), p. 89.

[b]Enrollment figures exclude students receiving only free education. In the year reported, the number of beneficiaries of so-called "freeships" (i.e., a concession of free education) in the district totalled 71,457 with a total value of Rs 4,507,912. *Ibid.*, p. 90.

[c]Castewise classification of "other backward classes" was terminated in 1960, replaced by a criterion based on income. Persons whose income does not exceed a certain maximum have thereafter been considered part of this category, entitled to the various concessions made available to that class by the government, irrespective of religion or caste. Government of Maharashtra, census office, *Nagpur District Census Handbook*, p. 22.

Well over 2,000 students were enrolled in the Yugantar Society's educational institutions in that year.

The dependence of education societies on government subsidy is acknowledged by virtually all of them, large and small alike. A leader of the Yugantar Society described its dependence in the following terms:

[The society's president] succeeded in getting 9.36 acres of land at Tiger Gap grounds for the society when he was deputy minister in the then government of Madhya Pradesh. For this donation, the society is grateful to the late Ravishankar Shukla, the then chief minister of the Madhya Pradesh government. On this site, the magnificent and beautiful building of the Yugantar Middle School is taking form. . . . The then Madhya Pradesh government contributed one-half of the total expenditure—Rs 157,451—in the form of a grant. . . . In the period 1962-64, the society received Rs 35,000 from the central government as a grant for aiding the construction of an auditorium cum recreation hall costing Rs 75,000. . . .Finance remained a prominent difficulty during this whole period. Though the society devoted itself to a noble and magnificent work, it was mainly a society of and for the poor. And due to this, the society could not raise adequate funds to finish construction and to purchase necessary equipment. Because of this, progress of the society has not been satisfactory.[63]

The manager of a much smaller society in the Mahar (Buddhist) area of north-central Nagpur reported a similar reliance on government assistance. While part of his society's financing had been accomplished through the sale of shares to local friends and associates, augmented by proceeds from a grain ration shop managed by the society, government

---

[63]*Commemorative Volume.* At the inaugural ceremony of a more recent venture, a medical clinic costing Rs 75,000, the society received a substantial boost from the state government. "The chief minister," reported a local weekly newspaper, "complimenting the organizers of the Yugantar Education Society for their new venture also announced a donation of Rs 50,000 from the chief minister's fund for the development of the hospital." *Nagpur Diary,* 21 December 1968. Since the Yugantar Society reserves approximately 90 per cent of its student admissions for persons of the scheduled castes and scheduled tribes, it naturally benefits from government concessions available to these groups.

support has been crucial, in some instances amounting to one hundred per cent of operating expenses.[64]

Granted extreme dependence on government, the opportunity for political intercession is apparent. By the very fact of public-private operational overlap, the scores of education societies which dot Nagpur are natural instruments to influence the transmission of educational resources. On the one hand, they are well-situated to funnel popular demands to government for educational and related benefits. And on the other, they are equally well-situated to bias the local implementation of government educational policy. This mix of public subsidy and discretionary administration inevitably attracts political involvement, for no more liberal mechanism could be devised to facilitate the translation of educational into political resources. In the loosely-regulated and highly decentralized context of the education societies, education policy may be bent to take cognizance of familial and communal ties and of such other considerations as constitute the ingredients of local political allegiance. The system invites politically-inclined discrimination in the hiring of staff, in the admission and continuation of students, in the purchase of texts, and in the awarding of building and maintenance contracts. In spite of official inspection and audit, considerable discretion is available to school managements in determining policy, controlling teacher appointment and termination, and setting salaries. That many teachers do not receive their contracted salary is notorious; and even with the most honest audit procedures it would be difficult to hold managements accountable for the *quality* of education they impart for each rupee of government investment. At the same time, the system magnifies the value of the resourceful political entrepreneur, without whose talents for influencing the extension of official recognition or the authorization of government grants to a society's schools the enterprise would surely collapse. Is it any wonder, then, that "promoting education" is the business of a great many local politicians or that education societies absorb a major share of political energies in Nagpur city?

[64]The society's manager was interviewed in January 1970. Even for the smaller societies, the sums involved are far from paltry. For the year 1968-69, the society's middle school alone received grants totalling Rs 35,000, including payment of teachers' salaries (Rs 25,000) and payment for expenditures on instructional materials, books, and building maintenance (Rs 10,000).

CONCLUSION

The way in which political and associational interests intersect varies somewhat depending on the type of association being examined. Unlike the weaver cooperatives, for example, the city's numerous education societies are in the midst of unprecedented growth, unhandicapped by any ineradicable obsolescence, and aglow with a confidence born of considerable public esteem for their product. The schools they manage sprout so rapidly and are so quickly filled from the ranks of neatly-uniformed students that the education enterprise, academic considerations aside, must be adjudged one of the best pecuniary investments in the city. Although the educational sector is not immune from political intrigue, it probably has a momentum of its own which the handloom cooperatives appear not to have, fortifying the schools to a considerable extent against the complete adulteration of their functions. To note a further contrast, housing cooperatives are much less often the recipients of direct government subsidies than are either the education societies or weaver production cooperatives. In fact, in their characteristic role as defender of squatters' rights, the housing societies are as often as not pitted *against* the implementation of public policy in their pursuit of such concessions as permanent title to illicitly settled land. And finally, while the partnership of government and education society has probably encouraged the entrepreneurship which has endowed Nagpur with some striking educational growth statistics, neither in housing nor in weaver production has the same progress resulted.

All these associations, however, have at least one thing in common: They all provide a decentralized organizational network, privately managed but dependent on government in one way or another, vulnerable to political intervention, and ideal for the conduct of discreet negotiations in which public resources are exchanged for private assurance of political support. It is this set of conditions which marks the voluntary associations of Nagpur as major targets of political opportunity and with the implications of which the balance of this study is concerned. Let us proceed, first, to examine the effects of associational entrepreneurship on leadership style among the local politicians of Nagpur.

4

Voluntary Associations and
Political Leadership

The criteria of successful political leadership in India cannot be established on the basis of any pre-existing formula. The biographies of past leaders reveal all too clearly the enormous diversity in personal assets and talents which has been employed in building political careers.[1] In some cases personal wealth or social status may be crucial factors; in others wit, energy or ambition may play a more determining role. The same attitudes or skills that promote the success of one may be obstacles to the career of another. The attributes that arouse the political loyalties of some groups may cultivate resentment or indifference among others. Indeed, what may have accounted for political advancement in an earlier part of an individual's career may prove disastrous at a later stage.

It remains probable, nonetheless, that certain traits appear with some regularity in political leaders and that such qualities are emulated, with varying degree of success, by those aspiring to replace them. W. H. Morris-Jones' simplified model of political behavior in India is instructive on this point. He identifies three fundamental "languages" or "idioms" of political behavior—modern, traditional, and saintly. While the modern idiom—characteristic of the courts, of parliament, of the English-language press, and of the higher echelons of the leading political

[1]Some of this diversity in leadership styles is made apparent in the outstanding study of village politics in India by F. G. Bailey, *Politics and Social Change: Orissa in 1959.*

parties—is by far the most widespread, both the traditional and saintly idioms have each an important clientele. For example, while the saintly idiom (closely identified with Gandhi's political style) may have little visible effect on actual behavior (and virtually no appeal to politicians operating within the other two idioms), it does influence "standards habitually used by people at large for judging the performance of politicians."[2] What is implicit in Morris-Jones' remark is that politicians respond more or less consciously to popular expectations of them, and order their behavior accordingly. Though few care to tread directly in Gandhi's footsteps, to be sure, few dare to ignore entirely the postulates of the saintly model.

Since popular expectations alter considerably under the impact of changed conditions, so must political leaders modify their personal conduct to assure some kind of consonance between their own behavior and the values of their constituents. Thus, as environmental changes transform the needs and desires of the people, some adjustment in leadership criteria is to be expected.

Mass democratization and unprecedented programs of socio-economic development are among the changes which have been introduced into the political environment of Nagpur. As we have already seen, democratization has summoned new modalities of managing popular demands; and developmental inputs have provided many of the resources with which to respond. How has this altered popular expectations of leaders? What effect has it had on the recruitment of leadership to political organizations? To what extent have traditional role requirements been devalued in the new environment? What new tasks of leadership exist? Have new tasks resulted in the mounting of new criteria of political recruitment? In what ways are voluntary associations a manifestation of these new criteria?

We may begin our response to these questions by looking at the recruitment policies of party and faction leaders in Nagpur.

RECRUITMENT POLICY

The record of Congress party general secretary Rikhabchand Sharma is a particularly apt point of departure, for he exhibits an almost peerless

[2]*The Government and Politics of India* (London: Hutchinson University Library, 1971), p. 60.

talent for adaptation to environmental requirements—new or old.[3] A Hindi-speaking Brahman Marwadi born in Rajasthan over fifty years ago, Sharma has stood at or near the top of the city Congress organization (NCDCC) for almost twenty years, principally by associating to himself the most promising of the city's upcoming politicians. He has assembled a group loyal to him irrespective of party affiliation and representing virtually every community in the city. He claims hundreds of organization workers in all parts of the city from such communities as Teli, Christian, Parsi, Madrasi, Gujarati, Marwadi, Kunbi, Sindhi, Adivasi (tribal aboriginals), Muslim and Harijan. He claims to have successfully crossed so many communal boundaries by responding to discrete and sometimes sectarian demands with rewards drawn as often as not from the resources of government development programs.[4] He has constructed what may be the largest and most effective factional organization in the city of Nagpur.

One means for obtaining a close look at Sharma's recruitment practices is to examine the allocation of Congress tickets to candidates in the 1969 municipal election. The candidates backed by Sharma of course represent only a fraction of his factional allies. But since Congress party nomination is among the most valued rewards in Nagpur (and elsewhere

[3]Interviewed on 30 January 1970.

[4]Sharma gave several examples of his prudent methodology. Some Christians living in a village in the southwestern environs of the city had fallen afoul of their nighbors a few years ago, and were threatened with the closing of their missionary school. Sharma, at the time chairman of the powerful corporation standing committee, obliged the Christians *and* their antagonists by ordering the construction of a new tar road all the way to the village in exchange for the guarantee that the school could stay. Similarly, he endeared himself to the mainly refugee Sindhi population by aiding them to get free land grants for the establishment of two large colonies at Chamarnala and Jaripatka, and by securing a grant of land for four schools for Sindhi youths. He made inroads even among the aboriginal tribals, a group often ignored by Nagpur politicians. They are an especially vulnerable group, for most of them live on government land within the city and lack the wherewithal to purchase land for settlement. Sharma intervened to sanction their illegal dwellings, kept the police from tearing them down, and thereby obliged, according to his estimate, some 4,000 tribals in five separate localities. Muslim affection he earned, in part, by siding with them on two major issues. One concerned the adoption of Urdu as the medium of instruction in Muslim schools, the prohibition on which Sharma was instrumental in lifting. The other concerned the production of colored cotton saris on powerlooms, the Hindu-sponsored prohibition on which Sharma successfully opposed, to the relief, according to him, of some 10,000 local Muslims engaged in the business.

in India), they are likely to be highly important allies. Their collective qualifications are a good index of the criteria of selection adhered to by Sharma.

Eleven of the candidates receiving Congress tickets in the election were backed by Sharma.[5] Caste, language and religious data are known for most of the eleven, and they are a group as cosmopolitan as Sharma claimed.[6] They represent the Hindu, Muslim, Jain and Christian religious communities; the Kunbi, Teli, Kirad, Dhobi and Momin weaver castes; and the Marathi, Hindi, Urdu, Sindhi, Tamil and Banjara (tribal) language groups. Though most of them have impressive political backgrounds, much of their earlier achievement was gained apart from the Congress, an indication of their general independence of party organization. Most of them had occupied positions of influence in party organization or municipal government prior to the 1969 election. At least seven have held executive office on the NCDCC or on one of the fourteen block Congress committees in the city; three were members of the working committee of the NCDCC at the time of the 1969 election. Six had contested municipal elections prior to 1969, three of them winning at least once. As a group they had previously contested thirteen times in municipal elections, winning on four occasions. Perhaps of greatest interest is that *nine* of their thirteen contests (including two victories) were waged *against* Congress nominees. In the 1969 election, five won their races, and none of the eleven fared worse than second place.

Of equal importance to their community spread and political autonomy, they exhibit ample leadership qualities of their own in connec-

[5]To arrive at a fair judgment of the factional apportionment of Congress tickets, which was naturally not published, various methods were employed. Two informed Congress politicians were independently asked to identify each Congress candidate's sponsor on the party's parliamentary board. They provided almost identical responses. Then one of the city's most experienced and high-ranking Congressmen was asked to doublecheck their responses; he reported that they were correct as given. In addition, many of the candidates were frank to admit that they were members of this or that group, and had thereby secured the nomination. Though there remain a few slippery cases among the fifty-five nominees, the results represent a reasonably accurate breakdown of the factional distribution of tickets.

[6]Information was collected on all of them through personal interviews, either directly or with their associates. Interviews were supplemented by perusal of candidate applications to the NCDCC. In two or three cases, alignment of these persons in the Sharma group does not seem especially strong, but for the others factional identification is clear.

tion with voluntary associations. The five who were interviewed alone hold a total of almost thirty executive associational affiliations, including activity in credit, housing and production cooperatives, libraries, caste associations, endowment trusts, labor unions, temple societies, commercial and service associations.

One of them, twenty-eight year old Vijaysingh M. Rathod, the second youngest of 313 applicants for Congress tickets in the election, filed a detailed *curriculum vitae* along with his application which leaves no doubt that he has both remarkable enthusiasm and an instinctive touch for the new politics.[7] His statement filled several pages in the original; it is partially reproduced here, freely translated from Marathi, because it is an especially transparent advertisement of the type of local associational and institutional apparatus which he (and apparently his patron Sharma) considers important.

Political

1) Worked as secretary of the Youth Congress from 1964-1967;. . .
2) Unanimously elected to the block Congress committee from my area;. . .
3) Founder-member of the Gopalnagar Citizens Committee, a public trust. . .also working as advisor for the last three years to the Citizens Committee of Parsodi.

Social

4) Helped in the resettlement of slum and hutment dwellers by getting Improvement Trust sanction for plots in other localities. Aided in securing loan from state government for construction of houses, and now a fine colony has been founded without causing difficulty for the slum and hutment dwellers.
5) Worked as secretary of an action committee formed to solve problems of persons made homeless by clearing of land for the new engineering college.
6) Worked as secretary of an action committee formed to resolve

[7]Applications were made available by the NCDCC. The applicants' diligence in filling out the party forms was sometimes commendable and sometimes not, requiring supplementation in most cases from other sources. Rathod was interviewed on 17 July 1969, and reiterated substantially the same information. Since the election he has extended his list by founding the New Pattern Education Society in his locality. As his numerous activities would suggest, he is a fulltime political worker, otherwise unemployed.

problems of persons made homeless by the Improvement Trust's acquisition of sixty houses in Gopalnagar in 1964-65.

7) Worked as secretary of a protection committee for Nagpur West district in 1965.

8) Worked as member of an anti-price-inflation committee.

9) Worked as member of a rural public service committee opposing the implementation of corporation taxes on the thirty-four villages absorbed into the corporation in 1951. Worked as member of a public service group for the provision of full water supply for these villages, and worked against an increase in water tax and against an increase in the number of tax collection units on the corporation's borders.

10) Organized a week-long program to remove untouchability, and built a road in Gopalnagar in 1965.

11) Helped in getting corporation facilities in the ward. Helped in initiating city bus service for Subhashnagar locality.

12) Founded one cooperative housing society in Vasantnagar in New Babulkheda, and working for the development of this area.

Educational

13) Operated a free study home for poor students in Abhyunkarnagar for three years.

14) Founded a library in Gopalnagar in 1964.

15) Aided in founding a kindergarten and primary school in Gopalnagar and worked to improve educational facilities.

Cooperatives

16) Chief founder of the New Society Housing Society in Gopalnagar, and worked as honorary secretary for the last five years.

17) Served as advisor to the Vijaynagar Cooperative Housing Society, the Mahatma Gandhi Cooperative Housing Society, and the Vasantnagar Cooperative Housing Society.

18) Member of the Nagpur City Cooperative Societies Federation, and working for the development of the cooperative movement.

19) Delegate to the Maharashtra Housing Finance Society in Bombay.

Other

20) Helped in collecting relief fund for storm-affected people of certain localities.

21) Active in celebration of national and religious festivals such as the Ganesh festival. Have arranged devotional singing programs and spiritual talks.

22) Helped in arranging a three-day family planning camp in Gopalnagar.

23) Helped in starting a mobile corporation dispensary service in Gopalnagar.

24) Helped in getting water pipelines and public taps in Gopalnagar.

Rathod's variegated display of leadership in community action committees, housing societies and school and library committees naturally cannot compare with the blue chip enterprises of other Congressmen, who tend to have a considerable advantage in age at least. Many of his activities would appear to have only limited and transient political value. Nonetheless, his accumulating expertise in the management of developmentally-oriented associations would make many of the graying "freedom fighters" blush. His innumerable efforts at intercession, particularly in matters affecting land and housing, require a technical expertise and energetic commitment quite unlike those talents useful to an organizational butterfly. Like many other Nagpur politicians, Rathod reads blueprints as easily as an earlier generation of politicians led satyagraha. He frankly acknowledges that his own political supporters are drawn from among those whom he has personally and directly obliged by securing such things as land rights, approach roads or other civic amenities, and who are appreciative of his constant availability and effectiveness in getting things done for them.

Rathod's ward is one of the largest in the city, comprised of over a score of separate and recently founded residential colonies. As his description makes clear, he has made a deliberate effort to spread his associational net to many colonies beyond his own residence in Gopalnagar. He is a member of the Banjara tribal community, of which he is virtually the exclusive representative in his ward. More than many others, he must function without any significant support from his own community; his reliance on associational resources is for him a natural alternative.[8]

[8]Rathod lost the election, running second (with 1,025 votes) to the BJS candidate (with 1,459 votes). According to Rathod, his defeat was engineered by dissident Congress factions, a fact of which he admits having been blithely unaware at the time. His naivete was visible also in the admitted fact that he made no effort to bring voters to the polls in his ward when they were regis-

Another well known Congress faction leader and member of the 1969 parliamentary board, Ramkrishna P. Samarth, has taken possibly the most frank and deliberate steps in the city to adapt to the new political conditions.[9] He has formed an organization built more squarely on post-independence development innovations than any other faction in or out of Congress. His legal-size personal stationery devotes almost one-half of its space to a catalogue of his executive positions in a great variety of private voluntary associations and institutions. A partial listing of his recent activities (as of 30 September 1966) makes plain his thorough accommodation to the role requirements of contemporary political leadership. Samarth is secretary of the powerful and prestigious Nagpur district Central Cooperative Bank, the apex financial institution for 945 local cooperative societies of all kinds with a total membership around 50,000. He is also

President   Nagpur district Industrial Cooperative Society
                   Bharat Vyayam Shala (gymnastic society)
                   Vidarbha Federation of Cooperative Housing
                   Societies
                   Nagpur Corporation Primary Teachers' Coopera-
                   tive Housing Society

---

tered there but resident elsewhere in the city; he operated on the assumption (dangerous in Nagpur politics) that candidates were to work strictly within their own wards.

[9] His political qualifications to head the move are rather impeccable. A member of Congress since 1937, arrested and jailed in 1943 for his part in the freedom struggle, Samarth worked his way up through the Sewa Dal organization until, by 1950, he was sufficiently powerful to be elected secretary of the NCDCC and also delegate to the all-India Congress committee. He was elected to the corporation in 1952, served as chairman of the standing committee in 1954, and was elected mayor in 1956. For four years, 1956-60, during the states reorganization controversy, he headed a renegade anti-Congress party demanding the creation of a separate state of Maharashtra, and under its banner he was elected to the state legislative council. When the demand was attained, the rebel group was liquidated and Samarth returned to Congress. He has never since been restored to the party's full favor, having been granted no further party offices nor a ticket to contest an election. His political and associational background is drawn from a publicity folder, "Candidature of Shri R. P. Samarth for the Nagpur Parliamentary Constituency No. 21 Along with Brief Review of His Social and Public Work Since Last 30 Years," prepared in 1967 (in English) and provided to the writer

President	Cooperative Education Society
	Sabbani Sporting Club
	Greater Nagpur Development Cooperative Housing Society
	Adhyapak Krida Mandal (teachers sports committee)
	Nagpur Samachar Cooperative Printing Society
	Vidhya Cooperative Housing Society
Vice President	Vidarbha Premier Cooperative Housing Society
	Nagpur Madhyawarti Krida Mandal
	Chatur Singing Academy
Director	Nagpur Divisional Cooperative Board
	Nagpur District Cooperative Board
	Nagpur District Cooperative Marketing Society
Representative	Nagpur Vishal Grahak (supermarket) Cooperative Society
	Nagpur Cooperative Spinning Mill
	Nagpur City Akhada Federation Committee
	Vidarbha Region Khadi Cottage Industry Board

When Samarth applied to contest the parliamentary race in 1967, he submitted to the all-India Congress committee parliamentary board a heavy, bound volume of over a thousand pages containing the carefully prepared recommendations of 1,061 local private institutions and voluntary associations. In much magnified form, it illustrates the type of associational involvement which is increasingly bearing upon the selection of candidates, and not only at the municipal level. Eloquently testifying to Samarth's diverse associational interests, the recommendations were classified as shown on p. 84.[10]

Early in 1970 Samarth initiated his own study of local politics in Nagpur, the format for which further displays his conception of the bases of political recruitment in Nagpur. He distributed a twenty-one page questionnaire to his workers throughout the city; though it does not abide by every canon of social science research, it is markedly utilitarian in design. The types of data requested attest both to his thoroughness and to his recognition of the contemporary needs of

by Samarth. Samarth was briefly interviewed on 16 January 1970.

[10] *Ibid.* In spite of his efforts, Samarth was not awarded the Congress nomination.

Type of recommendation	Number of recommendations
Service cooperative societies	369
Village panchayat samitis	145
Weaver cooperative societies	92
Housing societies	34
Cooperative credit societies	34
Consumer cooperative societies	22
Labor cooperative societies	36
Federations of cooperative institutions	9
Other cooperative institutions	54
Social institutions	28
Education institutions	31
Gymnastic institutions	51
Trade unions	41
Commercial institutions	9
Social welfare institutions	69
Women's associations	13
Personalities in the Muslim community	24
Total	1,061

political organization.[11] Entitled "Ward Public Institutions and Workers Record," it is essentially a socio-demographic survey of the public and private institutions and associations, their scope and leading personnel, in each of the city's seventy-five wards. It raises no questions about attitudes or issues, local or otherwise, being devoted entirely to a mapping of the social, economic, cultural, political, governmental and other structures in the wards. The largest single body of questions was related to private voluntary associations. This category, in much reduced form, is reproduced on p. 85.[12]

[11]It may also attest to his disappointment over the record of his nominees in the municipal election of 1969. Of the six, one achieved victory, four placed second and one third.

[12]A copy of the questionnaire was provided by Samarth. Additional categories in the questionnaire included information about the ward (area, population, community composition); information about political leaders and workers in the various parties active in the ward; information about government agencies and commercial enterprises in the ward; information about public meeting places, *mohalla* (neighborhood) identities, election centers and historical sites; information about prominent local personalities, and information about newspaper publications.

Information about voluntary organizations and private institutions

Trade unions, leadership and membership

Social organizations and leadership

Educational institutions (primary schools, middle and high schools, colleges, training schools, music schools, typing institutes, sewing institutes, vocational training schools, kindergartens, delinquent, disabled and blind boys schools), names of proprietors, headmasters, managing committees, number of teachers and students

Social welfare societies and leadership

Sports societies and leadership

Women's societies and leadership

Cultural societies and leadership

Student organizations and leadership

Religious societies and leadership

Hostels and managers

Public festival committee leaders

Cooperative societies (credit, consumer, weaver, industrial, labor, housing), leadership and membership

Samarth's extraordinary efforts testify powerfully to the altered role of political leadership in Nagpur. A member of the relatively small Kalar caste, Samarth is bound to take an instrumental view of communal affiliations. He has recruited into his organization workers from every corner of the city and spanning every community division. He has managed this principally by spreading his factional umbrella to include a wide assortment of associational structures. He has greatly enhanced his capacity to hold together this coalition of discrete associational interests by competing more successfully than most for control of the local distributive apparatus of government developmental resources.

THE CASE OF MESHRAM VS. WASNIK

The changing nature of leadership role requirements is nowhere better illustrated than in a contest for municipal office waged in one of Nagpur's north wards in 1969. In this contest two powerful figures in the Republican Party of India were pitted against each other, the one —Dr Dharamdas P. Meshram—representing a traditional style of leadership, the other—Dr Madhukar S. Wasnik—virtually the arch-typical model for the emerging political class. A comparison of their backgrounds and the organizations each brought into action in the ward election will dramatize the nature of the shift in leadership criteria of which we have been speaking.

As our discussion will indicate, many factors undoubtedly entered into the calculations of voters faced with a choice between these two men. It will not be possible in the context of this particular ward election to assign definite priority to any single one. Both Meshram and Wasnik possess powerful personalities and above average political acumen; these factors alone, apart from all the circumstances peculiar to the ward, must have had an impact on the election's outcome. And one must consider the fact that one of these two candidates ran under the symbol of a powerful party organization while the other did not.

What a single case such as this can profitably do is to illustrate a *potentially* important factor, regardless of whether it was decisive in this particular event. In the organizational backgrounds of these two men we can see highly contrasting concepts of leadership and of the likely sources of political support. Though their own concepts may have been wide of the mark in determining the outcome of the immediate electoral contest, what they *thought* to be important may be indicative of more general and long-range trends relating to the shift in leadership criteria in Nagpur.

While disavowing any intent to support a monocausal explanation of our own, we must direct our attention at the outset of this discussion to the frequent, and quite simplistic, allegation that the formal backing of the Republican party is the *sine qua non* of electoral success among Nagpur's Mahar-Buddhist voters. The assumption is fairly widespread in Nagpur that whereas voters of other communities may be very calculating in their choice of candidates, voters of the Mahar-Buddhist community blindly follow the elephant symbol of the RPI, planting their "x" willy-nilly wherever the party hierarchy directs, confident that the transcendant will of the founder, Dr Ambedkar, conjoins with their own and party interests. On the surface, the Meshram-Wasnik contest appears to confirm this assumption. Meshram's career had been bound tightly to the RPI and its predecessor, the Scheduled Castes Federation.[13] He was his party's most successful leader for

[13]Meshram was interviewed on 20 November 1969, and on 23 January 1970. The name-change from the Scheduled Castes Federation to the Republican

almost two decades. Following expulsion from the RPI in 1967—and removal from the elephant symbol—his political career reached its lowest ebb. His successful opponent, on the other hand, rose to political prominence only recently and coincident with his affiliation to the RPI.[14] Wasnik's affiliation with the RPI (his first party attachment) dates from February 1969, just prior to the corporation election (his first entry into electoral politics). Equipped with the party's backing and the elephant symbol, many would argue, his victory was a foregone conclusion irrespective of his personal credentials.

Party of India was an obvious necessity following mass conversions of the scheduled caste Mahars to Buddhism in 1956, an event which first occurred at the hands of Dr Ambedkar in Nagpur itself. The change in nomenclature was accomplished on 14 October 1957, within a year of the conversions. The idea for a change in party name was apparently conceived by Dr Ambedkar prior to his death on 6 December 1956, in part to rid his followers of the stigma of caste membership and in part to make the party more attractive to potential groups of supporters not of the scheduled castes. Reported in Padmakar L. Joshi *et al.*, *Nagpur City Centennial Volume*, pp. 25-26. Despite the directive of the RPI's constitution to organize not only Buddhists, but from among Hindu scheduled castes, scheduled tribes and other deprived classes, the Nagpur unit has had only limited success in appealing beyond the Mahar-Buddhist community. The effort to build solidarity among all the "oppressed classes" through conversion to Buddhism has had equally limited success nationwide. Only a tiny fraction of India's vast ex-untouchable population has followed the lead of the Maharashtrian Mahar Dr Ambedkar. Harold Isaacs reports that "the Mahars...are the only ex-untouchables in India who have attempted to take the course of mass conversion as a way out of their sea of troubles. I was told that as many as two and a half million, or about half the total Mahar population, have embraced Buddhism." *India's Ex-Untouchables* (New York: John Day Company, 1964), pp. 172-173. The 65,000,000 Hindu outcastes comprising the legally vanquished category of untouchables constitute about fifteen per cent, or one out of every seven Indians, of the total population, according to the 1961 census (*Ibid.*, p. 25). For background on the Buddhist movement in Maharashtra, consult Eleanor Zelliot, "Buddhism, and Politics in Maharashtra," *South Asian Politics and Religion*, Donald E. Smith, editor (Princeton: Princeton University Press, 1966), pp. 191-212. According to Zelliot (p. 191), the 1961 census recorded a total Buddhist population of 3,250,227, of which 2,789,501 were in Maharashtra. For a wide-ranging discussion of the ex-untouchables, see J. Michael Mahar, editor, *The Untouchables in Contemporary India* (Tucson: The University of Arizona Press, 1972).

[14] Wasnik was interviewed on 30 October 1969.

There may be some validity in this assumption. But it is certainly an exaggeration. For what passes as "exceptional solidarity" in Nagpur would be considered rampant factionalism anywhere else.[15] Nagpur's Mahar-Buddhists are notoriously divided amongst themselves along sub-caste lines; the Republican party, at best, is only a frail thread tying them together. While Mahar-Buddhist candidates can ordinarily depend on their community to support them against candidates of *other* communities, no such rule operates when Mahar-Buddhist candidates contest against each other.[16] For when they do, they almost inevitably jar the delicate coalitional arrangement among the sub-castes which forms the backbone of the RPI. Locally, five sub-castes of the Mahar community are represented—in order of population, Bawane, Ladwan, Barake, Kosare and Somvansh. The Bawane, of which both Meshram and Wasnik are members, comprise about sixty per cent of the total Mahar population in the city; the Somvansh, Dr Ambedkar's sub-caste, are barely represented.[17] The regular RPI is dominated by the Bawane sub-caste[18]; the RPI-Ambedkarite group consists largely of the Barake sub-caste, which numbers about twenty

[15]In 1969, in the first election for the RPI's city executive committee in nine years, three factions emerged clearly: one aligned with the upstart Dr Wasnik, another with the party's regional general secretary Hansraj Gajbhiye, and the third with the longtime trade unionist Vasudeo Ganar. Ganar, who won the post of city president, had earlier been defeated in his race for a seat on the municipal corporation. Ganar charged, and my own investigation confirmed, that his loss in that contest was almost incontestably engineered by rival factions within the party. Ganar was interviewed on 7 July 1969. The party election was reported in the *Nagpur Times*, 29 October 1969.

[16]Many Congress candidates in the 1969 contest reported that the election pact with the RPI had had little effect in their wards, for the Mahar-Buddhists frequently cast their votes for "rebel" candidates of their own community in complete disregard of the agreement and RPI officials. In general, the large size and concentration of the Mahar-Buddhist community in Nagpur's northern wards reduces the need for Mahar politicians to appeal for support beyond their own community, at least in local elections. Numbering almost 100,000, they are surpassed in size locally only by the Hindu weaver community.

[17]Sub-caste ranking in the city is based on estimates given by several RPI leaders.

[18]Rajabhau Khobragade, all-India general secretary (in 1970), Hansraj Gajbhiye, regional general secretary, and Sakharam Meshram, regional president, for example, are all Bawane.

per cent of the total Mahar population in the city.[19] The Mahar-Buddhist community, and by extension the RPI, is dependent for its political success against other communities and parties on its leaders' capacity to subjoin at least three of the sub-castes—Bawane, Ladwan and Kosare—and, increasingly, portions of the non-Mahar scheduled castes.[20]

Returning to our two candidates, let us examine their backgrounds. Meshram entered politics in 1932 as a young man in a youth organization founded by Dr Ambedkar. In 1937 he became a member of Ambedkar's Independent Labor Party. When it merged into the Scheduled Castes Federation in 1942, he was elected ward president, a post he retained for twenty years. In 1946 he was elected to the pre-independence Nagpur city council, and there he remained almost continuously up to 1965.[21] He was chosen deputy mayor in 1954 following his election to the new corporation in 1952 on the ticket of the Scheduled Castes Federation. Re-elected in 1957, he was elevated to the post of president of the renamed city RPI, and served simultaneously as the party's regional vice president.

In 1962, his most triumphant year, Meshram managed to gather in his hands virtually all the positions of power available to an ambitious RPI leader. In this year he successfully contested for the state legislative assembly. Though he did not actually contest the corporation election of 1962, his party was sufficiently strong to bring about his selection to the municipal body.[22] The alliance of opposition parties then in command of the corporation chose him as leader of the opposition, and

[19]Haridas Awode, all-India president (now deceased), and Panjabrao Shambharkar, city president, for example, are Barake. The common assumption among RPI politicians is that the Barake community is almost solidly enrolled in the RPI-Ambedkarite party, which has only token support from the other sub-castes.

[20]Of the twenty candidates who contested the corporation election under the RPI banner in 1969, eighteen are of the Mahar-Buddhist community, and two are of the Mehtar (sweeper) community. The distribution of the Mahar sub-castes reflects the relative strength of the coalition partners. Of the eighteen eight are Bawane, three are Ladwan, three are Kosare, one is Somvansh, and one is Barake. Of the ten who won their contests, six are Bawane, two are Kosare, one is Somvansh, and one is Mehtar.

[21]Ironically, Meshram began his electoral career—as he was to end it—contesting *against* the Scheduled Castes Federation, at that time as later the result of intraparty factionalism.

[22]Prior to 1969, when an entirely direct representative system was installed,

then, to ice the cake, the parties in the alliance elected him mayor of the city.[23] Thus, all in 1962, he was MLA, president of the city RPI, leader of the opposition in the corporation, and mayor of the city.

Rather abruptly, however, the bottom began dropping out of his political edifice. In 1964 he was indecorously removed from the state legislative assembly by a landmark decision of the Indian supreme court[24]; in 1965 the corporation was superseded by the state for maladministration, ingloriously terminating his long tenure in municipal government; and in February 1967 his bid for re-election to the assembly on an RPI ticket was unsuccessful. Meshram charges that his campaign in this last election was sabotaged by secret negotiations allegedly then in progress between the Congress and rival leaders of the RPI, culminating on 15 April 1967, shortly after the local election, in a state-level electoral alliance between the two parties. Linked publicly to a condemnation of the pact made by one of his associates, Meshram, to conclude his political denouement, was obliged to resign from the RPI.[25]

Meshram's efforts to stage a comeback outside of the RPI in the 1969

---

six corporators were selected to municipal office by the elected corporators, two others were elected from reserved trade union constituencies, and six or seven were nominated by such bodies as the Improvement Trust, Chamber of Commerce, and Nagpur University. Padmakar L. Joshi *et al.*, *Nagpur City Centennial Volume*, pp. 179-188.

[23]According to Meshram, he was the first scheduled caste leader so honored in all India. The RPI had formed a ruling alliance with the BJS, NVAS and several independents.

[24]Reported in the *Maharashtra Law Journal*, 1965, pp. 162-169. After a lengthy court battle extending from 1962 to 1965, Meshram was removed on the basis of having fraudulently declared himself a Hindu in order to contest from a constituency reserved for the scheduled castes. His opponents succeeded in convincing the court that he had converted to Buddhism, thereby removing himself from the category of scheduled caste. The entire case is contained in the *Record of Proceedings, Panjabrao vs. D. P. Meshram and Others*, 2 pts., civil appeal number 19 in the supreme court of India, on appeal from the high court of Maharashtra (Nagpur Bench) (New Delhi, 1964).

[25]Advocate Rajendra N. Patil made the indiscreet condemnation of the pact to a press conference on 18 April. He and several others were forced to resign from the RPI along with Meshram. The dissidents appear to have had a similar cause of bitterness about the pact. Four of the group protesting the pact, including Meshram and Patil, had lost their 1967 races for state assembly seats against Congress candidates. Patil was interviewed about his role in the incident on 12 June 1969.

municipal election are an indication of the extent to which his political resources had dwindled. His pre-campaign attempt to secure ample representation for his followers among the then-forming opposition coalitions presented the city's press with a rather amusing and confusing spectacle of desperate maneuvering culminating in Meshram's nearly complete failure. Meshram initially sought to form an alliance with the other small splinter groups comprising the Samyukta Nagrik Morcha (united civic front), a group formed to fight the Congress-RPI alliance. He demanded that his followers, including several who had resigned from the RPI with him in 1967, be allotted ten or more tickets in the sixty-four wards which the Morcha was preparing to contest. Among the Morcha's more prominent leaders were several old rivals of Meshram, including Haridas Awode, head of the RPI-Ambedkarites; not unexpectedly, friction developed over the distribution of tickets and Meshram stormily withdrew.[26]

Before departing the Morcha, Meshram's group had splintered itself; several of his followers founded their own "dissident RPI" party in defiance of their leader, who was in the process, they alleged, of "selling out" their interests to the Morcha.[27]

From the Morcha, Meshram took his bedraggled troop to the Lokshahi Aghadi (democratic front), another coalition of dissident factions formed to contest the election. The Aghadi granted Meshram's following, at the most, five tickets; none of them turned out to be winners.

Wasnik's political credentials are puny in comparison with Meshram's; yet there is a tremendous contrast between the two in the ease with which Wasnik became a party candidate. Wasnik was virtually free to pick his party and his constituency, having sufficient resources of his own to assure at least a good showing however and wherever he chose to contest. According to Wasnik himself, he was asked to apply for the RPI ticket by party leaders who were eager to stop Meshram dead in

[26]Information about the episode is drawn from interviews with various RPI leaders and from reports in the *Nagpur Times* on 6, 15, and 19 February and 10 March 1969.

[27]At one point there were four "RPI" organizations preparing to contest the election: the regular RPI, the RPI-Ambedkarite group, Meshram's original faction, and the splinter-group split off from Meshram's group. There was a strong threat of a fifth stemming from the irritation of the Ganar-Fulzele faction within the regular RPI, which publicly threatened to bolt the party if its leaders were not granted election tickets. The RPI did reconsider its ticketing decisions, and further splintering was avoided.

his tracks and were in need of an attractive candidate.[28] Although the
RPI had publicly already declared a candidate other than Wasnik to
contest in Gurudwara ward, when Wasnik finally made known his
desire to stand the party unhesitatingly chopped its declared candidate
(the Christian A. M. Borkar) from the ticket and replaced him with the
non-resident but popular medic from Indora.[29]

Securing the RPI nomination did not place the party's entire organizational apparatus at Wasnik's disposal. He could count on the support of some RPI workers in the ward, but so could Meshram and
some of the other candidates. In interviews, neither Wasnik nor
Meshram claimed that his own party's organizational support had any
significant impact on the outcome of the election. Wasnik, in fact,
claimed that the local RPI workers canvassed more against than for
him. Both, in any case, had to rely heavily on their own organizational resources.

The differing nature of their organizational resource bases is a key
factor in comprehending their divergent approaches to political leadership: Wasnik comes to politics possessed of sophisticated managerial
experience in large organizations; Meshram comes tied to an earlier formula in which the driving force of his personality is the major pole
around which his organization pivots. Wasnik brings external organizational assets to the local political arena, and with them bridges the gaps
induced by party factionalism and communal antagonisms; Meshram
rose to political pre-eminence on the crest of factional infighting and
communal rivalry, and has few assets to give him any other kind of

[28]Though Wasnik is a latecomer to party politics, he has not been slow to
exploit his recent popularity. Not long after his successful venture into corporation politics, he decided to seek the presidency of the city RPI; he was fore-
stalled from entering the contest only by the reminder that he had not been a
party member for the period required for holding such an office. Unfazed,
Wasnik backed his close associate, Advocate Haribhau M. Salve, for the post.
Salve lost, but Wasnik could at least take satisfaction from having aided in the
defeat of the organization candidate. Wasnik's ambition may have been foreseen
in some quarters of the RPI leadership even before the corporation election.
Wasnik reports that at least one high-ranking RPI personality attempted to
undermine his campaign, in part due to the fear that Wasnik's organizational
strength would soon rival his own.

[29]Borkar contested independently, and garnered 400 votes, only 77 less
than Meshram. His candidacy was aided by the highly cosmopolitan character of the ward's population, which includes many Christians, Sikhs and
Sindhis in addition to the large Mahar-Buddhist community.

leverage. A look at their dissimilar non-political backgrounds will help make the point.

Meshram has lived in Gautamnagar locality in Gurudwara ward all of his life. He has relied on his wits and great energy to achieve his ambitions, for he had few natural advantages in birth, education or occupation. Born an outcaste Mahar, he has no more than a seventh-grade education. As a young man he worked as a building contractor and carpenter, and for two months was a peon (errand boy) in the employ of the Nagpur municipality, a point he would make at a later date not without a trace of pride.[30] After a two-year mainly home-study course in indigenous medicine, he was certified in 1937 as an ayurvedic practitioner.[31] In the same year he became president of the city branch of the Samta Sainik Dal (soldiers for equality corps), an organization founded by Dr Ambedkar to impart para-military training to scheduled caste volunteers. While his political involvement thereafter grew rapidly, his medical practice also expanded until by 1957 he was operating dispensaries in three localities in Nagpur and one even in Bombay.[32]

Despite his ultimate political achievements, Meshram's record is curiously barren of permanent and controlling influence in the various non-party associational structures that were growing up in the city. He is today president of a small local library and of a tiny Buddhist temple in Gautamnagar. He is also head of a local ayurvedic association with sixty-three members, and of a similar regional group with about 700 members. He was on the governing body of the Ambedkar Memorial Committee from 1956 to 1962, but these were the years before it had anything but an empty field to manage.[33] Meshram, finally, is president of the Dr Babasaheb Ambedkar Multi-Purpose High School, but this

[30]Given in testimony before the election tribunal first hearing the case challenging his right to a seat in the state assembly. "Deposition of Dr Dharamdas Meshram," *Record of Proceedings*, I, p. 108.

[31]Certification was made by an out-of-state ayurvedic college. In 1965 he was registered under the Maharashtra Medical Practitioners Act as Doctor of Ayurvedic and Unani Systems of Medicine by the Maharashtra Board of Ayurvedic and Unani Systems of Medicine.

[32]"Deposition of Dr Dharamdas Meshram," *Record of Proceedings*, I, p. 107.

[33]Today, with an impressive and growing array of educational and religious institutions sprouting under its patronage, the Ambedkar Memorial Committee is controlled locally by the Ganar-Fulzele faction of the RPI, not the least cause of antagonism within the party.

is also a dubious distinction since the school has long since ceased to function.

Meshram is a gifted man, with a forceful personality and abundant entrepreneurial talents. He provided aggressive and clever leadership to the Mahar community at a time when it had few other leaders to call upon, and when its lowly status demanded leaders possessed above all of physical courage. Meshram has not the deft managerial talents of his opponent, nor the personality for working towards corporate organizational objectives. But he took his political apprenticeship in an era when his community's right of access to public resources of any kind was still in question, when the qualities of a battler were more admired than those of a negotiator. These skills are not to be belittled, but they do appear to be declining in political utility.

Wasnik, possessing no less energy and wit, has the additional advantages of a sterling education, a prestigious profession and, most importantly, a sure touch for the contingencies of post-independence politics. He graduated from Nagpur Medical College in 1960, a licensed medical practitioner; he fortified his credentials four years later with a diploma in child health. In contrast to Meshram, he speaks fluent English. He is one of the city's most widely known doctors, and could point at the age of thirty-nine to more professional success than most of his colleagues chalk up in a lifetime.

Wasnik began his medical practice in 1963; by 1969 he was operating four clinics scattered about the city, including one at his home in Indora locality and one in Gaddigudam in Gurudwara ward. Though assisted by his wife, who is also a medical graduate, his daily professional routine would seem enough to absorb the energy of even an exceptionally vigorous man.

It obviously does not. In 1967 Wasnik founded the People's Welfare Society, which he serves as general secretary. The society was formed with the twofold objective of providing educational and medical facilities for low income families. In 1968 it opened the College of Arts and Commerce near Wasnik's home in Indora; it is the second college in Nagpur founded by and for the scheduled caste population.[34] Located in the heart of heavily Buddhist north Nagpur, it had already enrolled over 700 students for the 1969-70 year, and had a staff of 17 lecturers. At the same time the society opened a medical policlinic in Indora,

---

[34]The first was the Ambedkar College at Deeksha Bhoomi, managed by the Ambedkar Memorial Committee.

which Wasnik serves as director.[35] He is also president of the society's Health and Medical Welfare Committee, which presently operates a free maternity home in Indora as well as a family planning center, a child welfare center, and a children's park.

On top of his already extensive involvements, Wasnik accepted appointment in 1968 as chairman of the then defunct Nagpur district Bharat Sewak Samaj (national volunteer society) (BSS). Among the various projects which he has utilized to rebuild the organization were the periodic policing of railway travelers in an effort to snag some of the notoriously large crop of ticketless travelers; the distribution of grain, powdered milk and clothing to persons affected in the communal riots of 1968; and a Health Protection Week which promoted the People's Welfare Society's health facilities while at the same time mounting a public drive against various epidemic diseases. Wasnik claims that he has managed to enroll upwards of a thousand volunteers since reviving the BSS.

In between treating patients, founding colleges, and nabbing railway "freeloaders," Wasnik founded the Madusham Housing Development Cooperative Society in 1969, which has plans to construct fifty-one apartment quarters at several sites in the city. He has recently entered the trade union field, having created the Bharatiya Kamgar Sourakshan Samiti (Indian labor protection committee), an independent trade union embracing general labor in the railways, building and other trades. Though Wasnik has not yet become involved in consumer co-operative stores, credit and other types of cooperatives, he avers an intention to do so when the opportunity arises.

Wasnik and Meshram offer a further contrast in their recruitment of campaign workers. Both men are of the same Bawane sub-caste of the Mahar community; whereas Meshram has the advantage of lifelong residency in the ward, Wasnik sits astride an attractive associational network to which supporters can be grafted on terms cutting across neighborhoods, communities, and even old political loyalties. The backgrounds of Wasnik's workers testify to his instrumental approach to political organization; the backgrounds of Meshram's to his reliance on loyalties rooted in lengthy personal association and communal ties.

---

[35]The policlinic is a permanent facility to which a large number of physicians and specialists donate their services once or twice weekly to patients who would otherwise have no access to them. The policlinic sponsors a health insurance scheme by which families, for a very modest fee, are entitled to the free specialized advice of participating physicians.

Wasnik's key workers provide suggestive evidence of a shift in educational and professional qualifications which the sophisticated nature of his associational network requires.[36] Communally, they are quite cosmopolitan, representing the Bengali, Sikh, Pathan, Sindhi and Mahar groups. Mahars dominate among his key workers, but it is significant of his pragmatic approach that they are drawn from all five sub-castes. Meshram, on the other hand, appears to have had far fewer workers, drawn mainly from the Bawane sub-caste and from the less educated laboring class.[37] Whereas Wasnik could enlist workers from all over the city due to the spread of his associational enterprises, Meshram had little support from outside the ward, reflecting his general isolation from an associational resource base.

One of Wasnik's principal local campaign workers, Prabhakar N—, gave an account sharply illustrating how Wasnik's organizational machinery was installed in Gurudwara ward. Prabhakar has resided in the ward all his life. He is a Buddhist convert from the Bawane sub-caste of the Mahars, has a tenth-grade education, and has been since 1945 a government employee. A friend of Meshram's since youth, he was a leading organizer for Meshram until his recruitment to Wasnik's organization. Active in politics since the age of fourteen, he and Meshram formed a local branch of Ambedkar's Independent Labor Party in the late 1930s. In those days, according to him, supporters of Ambedkar's aggressive organization were few in Nagpur, and tackling the Congress monopoly among the scheduled caste population was no mean feat.

Prabhakar worked with Meshram up to 1962 when, with Meshram at the peak of his career, Prabhakar became alienated by what he termed his patron's "unrestrained lust for position and power." In defiance of Prabhakar's counsel to maintain links with his local supporters, to distribute tickets more fairly among the various sub-castes of the Mahar community, and to recruit more educated persons to his organization, Meshram, according to Prabhakar, increasingly ignored the demands of his local constituents, confined his patronage to his Bawane associates, and insisted on attaching uneducated persons to his organization.

In 1963 Dr Wasnik opened a clinic in Gaddigudam, of which Meshram's locality Gautamnagar forms a part. Prabhakar had not known

[36]Wasnik provided the names of eight key workers, of whom three were interviewed. These latter provided descriptions of several additional workers.

[37]Meshram gave the names of four key workers, all of them living in the vicinity of Gautamnagar locality. Two were interviewed, and they provided the name of a fifth key worker, who was also interviewed.

him previously, but soon began to occupy the role of unofficial local advisor to the young doctor. Recognizing Wasnik's political potential, he made suggestions, for instance, on how Wasnik could ingratiate himself in the locality, in his terms, by "sweet talking the poor." Political headway was best made, he advised, by keeping the professional margin of profit small, by giving free injections and cheap medicine, and by making home visitations at no charge.

In 1967 Prabhakar, in fitting tribute to his services, was made an executive member of the eleven-man managing committee of Wasnik's People's Welfare Society, in company with such eminent persons as a college principal, a college professor, a justice of the state high court, the district collector, prominent businessmen and other professional people.[38]

When Wasnik finally decided to contest the municipal election only shortly before the close of nominations, a committee of ten associates, according to Prabhakar, was formed to back his candidacy. The composition of this committee gives an indication of the qualifications Wasnik seeks in enlisting men to his organization. Six are from outside of Gurudwara ward, nine are government employees, seven are college graduates. Two, including Prabhakar, are on the managing committee of the People's Welfare Society. Nine of them are of the Mahar caste, but less than half of these are of Wasnik's own Bawane sub-caste. Indeed, Wasnik received less support from the Bawane community than did Meshram, according to Prabhakar, and was forced to rely mainly on the other Mahar sub-castes and on the mix of Hindu communities resident in the ward.

Gayanarayan N— is a second key worker of Wasnik's. Though he filled a role in Wasnik's campaign apparatus vastly different from Prabhakar's, his experience is a further illustration of Wasnik's mode of infiltrating the ward. Like Prabhakar, Gayanarayan is a Buddhist convert of Bawane sub-caste, and a lifelong resident of Gautamnagar. Now over fifty years old, he was for two decades a supporter of Meshram. For fifteen years—up to 1965—he was secretary under Meshram of the ward branch of the RPI. He sought municipal office himself in 1962, but was unable to secure a party ticket.

In describing some of the reasons why his old comrade Meshram had fallen from grace in the locality, Gayanarayan noted that Meshram had

---

[38]Listed in an undated bulletin of the People's Welfare Society, "Proposed Residential College," provided by Dr Wasnik.

increasingly begun to neglect organizational tasks locally. Up to the 1960s, he had been a responsive and accessible worker for local residents, but thereafter had failed to keep up local contacts and to respond to the people's demands. If they approached him for help in getting employment, he refused to help them. When he was mayor and MLA, he was never available to students, for example, who were in need of his signature on their caste certificates.[39]

Wasnik, in Gayanarayan's opinion, behaved in a reverse manner. He carefully cultivated local contacts, often giving medical assistance to the poor, such as free injections and free medicine. Gayanarayan admits that Wasnik has the advantage of greater personal wealth. Four times annually, for instance, he gives generous donations of Rs 300 to Rs 400 to local religious anniversary and festival committees constituted at the time of each celebration. During the election year of 1969, Gayanarayan was himself treasurer of two such committees formed to organize the commemorations of the Lord Buddha and Dr Ambedkar birth-anniversary celebrations.

The accounts of Prabhakar and Gayanarayan illustrate the manner in which an outside and upstart organization established itself in the ward. Prabhakar, one of the area's most astute political organizers, with thorough knowledge of local personalities, petty jealousies and rivalries, was literally drafted into the apex institution of Wasnik's organizational network—the People's Welfare Society. Gayanarayan, on the other hand, was gradually weaned from Meshram by making him the recipient and local distributor of certain cash investments of the Wasnik organization. For both of them, Wasnik's candidacy was, if in no other way, materially attractive, rewarding them both with positions from which to manage the distribution of various material benefits, whether in the form of cash, medical care or admission to an educational institution. Meshram, lacking either professional success or lucrative associational contacts, was in no position to make similar rewards. A look at some of his supporters will conclude the narrative.

The three key workers of Meshram who were interviewed are all lifelong neighbors of his in Gautamnagar, possess no more than a primary school education, and have virtually no associational affiliations.

---

[39]In order to qualify for receipt of government educational stipends, students of the scheduled castes, scheduled tribes or backward classes must have the authorized signature of an MLA, or of a district honorary magistrate. Religious conversion to Buddhism does not disqualify a student from such grants.

Namdeorao N— is a herdsman, or milkman, Ghowli by caste, and the owner of six buffaloes. He has been a member of the SCF-RPI since the middle 1940s, but has never held any office in the party. He has a fourth grade education. He has worked for Meshram from the beginning of his neighbor's political career. Other than his having been secretary of a local milkmen's association two decades ago, he has been a leader in no associations and presently belongs to none. Ramrao R—, a second key worker, is a millworker in one of Nagpur's two textile mills. Educated to the fourth grade, he is a Buddhist convert of the Bawane sub-caste. A close neighbor and relative of Meshram, he has worked for him from the start of Meshram's career. At one time employed by Meshram as a peon in the RPI headquarters, Ramrao once served as secretary of the ward branch of the party. Ramrao has never had any associational affiliations whatsoever.

The third worker, Sukhman N—, is a Buddhist convert of the Barake sub-caste of the Mahar community. Educated to the fourth grade, he is today a government employee in a railway workshop. He is the organizer of the local branch of a railway union, with fifteen affiliated members living in the ward. Otherwise, he is presently active in no associations. In earlier years he worked with Meshram in the local library association and in the local Buddhist association but nowadays, he pointed out, persons like himself are being replaced in such organizations by younger and better educated personalities. Having worked for Meshram since 1942, Sukhman considers him to have been an outstanding and aggressive leader, but admits that only a half dozen or so active political workers in the ward are willing to organize on his behalf today.

On election day, Wasnik won 1,207 votes (38.2 per cent of the total) as against Meshram's third place tally of 477 (15.1 per cent).[40] In his defense, Meshram produced several hand-drawn maps showing, rather persuasively, that half or more of his electoral base of support had been shaved from Gurudwara ward by the reapportionment of wards carried out just prior to the election. The removed sector, according to him, was inhabited mainly by persons of the Bawane sub-caste, from whom he could readily anticipate support. His own ward, on the

[40]The balance was split among six other candidates: a Sikh, a Christian, two Hindi-speakers, and two other Mahars. The two latter candidates, one of the Barake and one of the Ladwan sub-caste, collectively polled only 55 votes.

other hand, had absorbed several highly cosmopolitan colonies—Christians, Sikhs, Hindi-speakers—from which he anticipated little or no support.

Meshram's regrets over reapportionment are probably well-founded, but they only go further to indicate the narrow communal base upon which he calculated strategy. For Wasnik, of the same community sub-caste as Meshram but of a strikingly different "caste" of developmental entrepreneurs, the reshaping of the ward's boundaries posed an opportunity for pragmatic negotiations rather than a cause for alarm. Wasnik's plurality victory is an indication that he too, like most other winners in the election, did not succeed in circumventing all the local, communal and partisan cleavages in the ward.[41] But there is no doubt that his energetic investment in voluntary associations and the skillful installation of his associational network into the ward greatly assisted him in bridging over the differences that remained such impenetrable barriers to his opponents.

SUMMARY

The criteria of successful political leadership are changing in Nagpur. As this chapter has attempted to demonstrate, newcomers like Dr Wasnik or Vijaysingh Rathod, and oldtimers like Rikhabchand Sharma or Ramkrishna Samarth have conscientiously adapted themselves to the pragmatic mode of post-independence politics. They are likely no more energetic or ingenious than the more traditional leaders they are displacing; each of them, however, has clearly seen the light of associational politics and is actively seeking command of developmental resources apparently valued by the electorate. Age is not an insurmountable barrier to developmental entrepreneurship, but the younger politicians can undoubtedly make the transition with greater ease: Dr Meshram, an ayurvedic practitioner born in 1913, served his political apprenticeship in the 1930s when development planning was a foreign and exotic idea; Dr Wasnik, a graduate of the Nagpur Medical College, was born in 1930 and has grown up in an era thoroughly impregnated with the developmental ethos.

Primordial affiliations may be as highly valued as formerly, but

[41]Only ten of the seventy-five victors managed to secure a majority of the votes cast in their wards.

they are by their very nature relatively fixed and non-negotiable ingredients of the environment. Wasnik's support, like Meshram's, was drawn largely from the Mahar-Buddhist community. However, he has taken steps to broaden his appeal beyond any particular sub-caste of that community; recruitment to his organization is based on criteria other than mere community membership. As Meshram's experience testifies, communal solidarity, particularly when pushed to the sub-caste level, can be an electoral albatross.

The political exploitation of developmental resources may amount to no more than the concession of a tar road or access to a policlinic; the political value of such concessions does not lie in their magnitude, but rather in the fact that they are fluid and negotiable, readily exchangeable in the discrete process of negotiating political support among heterogeneous populations. Traditional political leaders tended to operate in territorially and communally more exclusive environments. Leaders related to followers on a largely personalistic basis and depended on resources, such as traditional status or kinship solidarity, internal to the local environment for gaining and retaining political support. Newer leaders, such as Wasnik or Samarth, operate in a multitude of dispersed arenas where local and primordial linkages are necessarily reduced in value; they and their followers relate increasingly on a pragmatic and material basis, wherein the exchange of support relies less on the manipulation of symbols of communal solidarity than on the transfer of resources such as have been intruded into the local environment by government development programs.

Successful political leadership increasingly depends on the capacity of individuals to enter into pragmatic negotiations with broad and highly differentiated sectors of the electorate, and to compete for development resources in numerous and diverse arenas. Such skills are valued as can bring discrete local and community groups into common associational frameworks where their interests can be jointly and materially served. Older skills remain in use, but there is a discernible tendency for local political organizations to prefer individuals better adapted to function as developmental entrepreneurs than as primordial chieftains. One can only conclude that the same preference is increasingly guiding the choices of voters.

5

Voluntary Associations and Political Organization (I)

Political organizations in Nagpur are major competitors for control of the voluntary associational apparatus which has been described in preceding chapters. This has consequences not only for the associations, but for the political organizations competing for management of them. As we have seen, associational entrepreneurship is an increasingly valued trait among local political leaders, sharply affecting organizational recruitment criteria. And with the emergence of a new type of leadership, some change in the means and ends of organized political action is to be expected. For the way in which leaders conceive the process of building political support is bound to influence the determination of organizational strategy and the setting of organizational goals. The change will not be total and may be manifest more in some groups than in others; but the same environmental conditions attracting *individual* politicians to associational arenas perforce dictate *organizational* adaptation as well. This chapter is an effort to describe and analyze the changes which have occurred in post-independence local political organization and, specifically, to illuminate those changes generated by voluntary associations. Its focus is the faction, by far the most pervasive and powerful medium of political organization in India.

THE NATURE OF FACTIONS

The concept of faction is itself rather abstract, and as Donald Rosenthal advises in his own effort at more exact specification, distinctions among factions may be as fundamental as the distinctions dividing factional from party organization.[1] Perhaps we can ease the task of visualizing the changes in factional organization in Nagpur by first reviewing some of the conceptual formulations of faction present in the work of leading analysts.

Myron Weiner, for example, has defined *faction* as "a group with an articulated set of goals, operating within a larger organization but not created by or with the approval of the parent body." Rooted in a highly personalistic form of allegiance, "the faction assumes many of the functions of the traditional joint family, caste system, and village organization. Like groups in the traditional order, the faction is virtually 'closed' to outsiders."[2] Factionally-organized politicians, he explained in a later study, take an instrumental view of caste. "The point is," Weiner claimed,

> that party politicians are typically loyal to their faction, not to their caste (and often not to their party), and that factions typically cut across caste. When candidates of antagonistic castes oppose one another in an election, they readily make electoral appeals to caste since caste constitutes a potential voting bank. When one faction is manifestly multi-caste in leadership and the other is predominantly from one caste, the first group will typically denounce the second on the basis of 'casteism' in order to reduce its appeal to other castes. When...candidates are from the same caste, neither is likely to make caste an issue at all; both will bargain intensively for the support of multi-caste village factions.[3]

Thus, while Weiner conceives factions as retaining flexibility in regard to the traditional social structure, they remain, in his view, essentially "closed" and personalistic, thereby lacking the capacity to aggregate broad societal interests. Though Weiner acknowledges material consi-

---

[1]Rosenthal depicts a fourfold typology of factions, based on his study of the municipal politics of Agra and Poona. He distinguishes personal followings, machines, primordial groups and ideational groups. He treats them as ideal types, visible generally as tendencies "frequently found within a single political party or political group." "Factions and Alliances in Indian City Politics," *Midwest Journal of Political Science*, X (August 1966), 324-325.

[2]*Party Politics in India: The Development of a Multi-Party System*, pp. 237-238.

[3]*Party Building in a New Nation: The Indian National Congress*, p. 154.

derations in the expectations of factional followers, his concept comes closest to Rosenthal's definition of a "personal following" as "the result of the attachment which people have to a person or to his house 'and not from regard for political principles, loyalty to the party he represents, or in expectation of material rewards'. Followers attempt to enhance the political influence of the leader and, in turn, benefit from his advancement, but the prestige of the leader is a major interest in their relationship with other groups."[4] If Weiner is correct in his assumption that factions assume traditional functions, such as those of the caste system or the joint family, the conclusion would seem inescapable that the rigidities and divisiveness of traditional society have been transferred relatively untransformed to faction, rendering the pursuit of power as segmented as ever.

Paul Brass, who has probably articulated the role of Indian party factions more fully than any other investigator, considerably reinforces Weiner's position. Factions, in Brass' view, form the intermediate linkage between traditional and modern organizational forms. Factional loyalties, he wrote in his study of the Congress party of Uttar Pradesh,

provide the link between the parochial units of Indian society— family, village, caste—and the political parties. Factional loyalty in the Uttar Pradesh Congress replaces party loyalty. Factional politics is an intermediate, perhaps a transitional, form of politics. It is something 'more' than parochial politics—a politics based upon language, caste, tribe, or religion—and something 'less' than party politics in the European and American sense, involving an impersonal allegiance to a party as an institution or as an ideology.[5]

The faction, according to Brass, is a facet of the traditional order,

[4]"Factions and Alliances in Indian City Politics," *op. cit.*, 324. Rosenthal's quotation is from Edward C. Banfield and James Q. Wilson, *City Politics* (Cambridge: Harvard-MIT University Presses, 1963), p. 129.

[5]*Factional Politics in an Indian State: The Congress Party in Uttar Pradesh*, p. 154. He defines faction specifically (p. 237) as "a vertical structure of power which crosscuts caste and class divisions...an organization based upon the ties between a leader and his followers, an economic patron and his dependents, a lawyer and his clients. There are vertical ties, some of which flow directly out of the traditional hierarchical order; others, like the lawyer-client ties are modern forms of association, based upon mutual service rather than traditional loyalties. Most factions are based upon a combination of traditional loyalties and individual interests."

an indigenous form of loyalty akin to lineage, caste, village or regional loyalties.[6] It is rooted in traditional leader-follower relationships, and the personality of the leader serves as the focal point of all its actions. "Factions and factional conflict," he notes, "are organized completely around personalities and around personal enmities among party leaders."[7] And further, "a faction in the Uttar Pradesh Congress might be described as a clique with a larger, fluctuating membership."[8] Though it belongs to the traditional order, the faction functions as a transmission belt from the modernizing political party to the traditional society. While it "traditionalizes" modern political organization, it also "modernizes" the traditional social structure.[9]

Though Brass thus acknowledges the intermediate, "modernizing" functions of traditional factional organization, and asserts more affirmatively than Weiner that the associational ties binding leader to follower are as often instrumental as affective, he insists that factions are fundamentally antithetical to modern forms of interest aggregation and the effective transmission of group political demands. Factional conflicts, he argues, have little to do with policies or issues, and inhibit voting on the basis of party, ideology, or even economic self-interest. In Deoria district (Uttar Pradesh) he found, for example, that factional politics sometimes corresponded with fundamental economic issues: the language of politics in this major cane sugar producing area generally concerned the price of sugar-cane, factory wages, and demands for greater political participation; dominant Congress factions were identified with the big sugar producers. Nonetheless, voting itself rarely related to such considerations. "Factional conflicts and economic conflicts," he reports, "are independent variables; neither one determines the form of the other."[10] The relative paucity in Uttar Pradesh of organized interests—in the form of peasant organizations, trade unions, or caste associations—leaves the field clear, according to Brass, for the factional organization of discrete interests cutting across caste and class lines. "Factions," Brass concludes,

are alternative forms of political organization to interest groups and are based upon conflicting principles. Factions are vertical structures

[6] *Ibid.*, p. 238.
[7] *Ibid.*, p. 54.
[8] *Ibid.*, p. 56.
[9] *Ibid.*, p. 3.
[10] *Ibid.*, pp. 134-135.

of power oriented towards influence, that is, towards the establishment of links which will provide for the transmission of favors and services. Interest groups are associations oriented towards the promotion of the long-term interests of a generalized category in the population. Factions inhibit the organization of interests because they are based upon ties which unite opposed interests. The members of a faction come from different social and economic groups in the society, united by a desire for personal privileges.[11]

If these commentators have not been misunderstood, the vertical and segmental aggregation of interests represented by factional political organization is conceived as inimical to the growth of institutions capable of hammering countless private interests into a form amenable to broad, long-range and impersonal government action. Though perhaps a departure from earlier forms of organization, factions still lack the "horse-trading" and integrative character normally presumed intrinsic to democratic party organization.[12] Concerned with the establishment of linkages for the transmission of personal favors and services, and governed by the need to obtain concessions for discrete categories of the population, they are essentially indifferent to the interests of socially generalized sectors of the population and to the protection and fostering of such interests in legislative arenas.

How does this formulation stand up under the impact of massive developmental change and mass participation in democratic politics? Let us examine the evidence from the factional politics of Nagpur city.

THE TRANSFORMATION OF FACTIONAL CONFLICT

For illustrative purposes, we focus now on an historically rooted conflict between two powerful factional alignments in the local Congress party

[11]*Ibid.*, p. 244.

[12]For some illustrative discussions of the ideal traits of political party organizations, refer to Joseph LaPalombara and Myron Weiner, editors, *Political Parties and Political Development* (Princeton: Princeton University Press, 1966), especially the editors' essay, "The Origin and Development of Political Parties," pp. 3-42; and Fred W. Riggs, "Comparative Politics and the Study of Political Parties: A Structural Approach," *Approaches to the Study of Party Organization*, William J. Crotty, editor (Boston: Allyn and Bacon, Inc., 1968), pp. 45-104.

organization—the Nawabpura and the Colonelbag groups. Both display today a *modus operandi* markedly different from pre-independence days. In exploring changes in the mode of conflict between them, we will have an opportunity to view the impact of competition for control of voluntary associational management on factional leadership, strategy and employment of political resources and, more importantly, to assess whether these changes represent a substantive transformation in the nature of factions.

In their beginnings, both the Nawabpura and Colonelbag groups were little more than extraordinarily boisterous street gangs, organized in several wards of the city's east side.[13] Their institutional strength at the time consisted almost exclusively of competing networks of small neighborhood wrestling gymnasiums (akhadas), of which the Colonelbag group was reputed to have controlled about forty and the Nawabpura group about seventy.[14] The akhadas naturally attracted the more muscular elements of their localities, men interested in body-building exercises and traditional wrestling. Their ardor for physical exertion appears to have spilled over on occasion into street fights featuring such lethal weapons as swords, spears and clubs.

Both the Nawabpura and the Colonelbag groups took definite shape in the middle of the 1930s when the independence movement was in full swing. The Nawabpura group was the more socially prestigious of the

[13]Nawabpura was originally a Muslim quarter in which was located the palace of a Muslim zamindar, one of a class of landlords frequently referred to as "nawabs." Following disastrous communal riots in the mid-1920s, the local nawab and most of his Muslim followers fled the locality, leaving only the name behind. It is the same area in which the Rashtriya Swayamsewak Sangh (RSS) was founded in 1925, and was once the home of the RSS's founder, Dr Keshao B. Hedgewar. Historical background on the area was related by Pandurang T. Kadu, sixty year old resident of Nawabpura and a prominent leader of the Nawabpura group since its founding, interviewed on 23 December 1969. Colonelbag (also spelled Karnalbag) formerly was an open area belonging to the estate of the last indigenous ruler preceding British takeover in the 1850s. With the establishment in 1877 of Jamshet Tata's Model Mills, Nagpur's first cotton-textile mill, the area rapidly filled up with laborers' colonies. Background on the Colonelbag area was provided by Advocate Haribhau R. Dhoble, resident and a leading political figure, interviewed on four occasions beginning 25 July 1969. Both factional groups have exercised considerable influence beyond their immediate localities almost from the beginning, but the local designations continue in use.

[14]Dadarao Tembhekar, an associate of the Nawabpura group and presently secretary of the Nagpur City Akhada Federation Committee, interviewed on 18 December 1969, and 24 January 1970.

two, having had the patronage of the former royal family of the Bhonsales, whose somewhat dilapidated palace lies buffer-like between the Nawabpura and Colonelbag localities. Colonelbag, lying in the shadow of the tall smokestacks of Model Mills, was ideally situated to permit its muscular lords to serve as patrons (albeit of less noble blood than the Bhonsales) of the thousands of migrant laborers recruited for work in the mills.

The precise basis for the onset of rivalry between the two groups is problematic. The thwarted ambitions of the formerly ruling Marathas, on the Nawabpura side, and the upward mobility of the migrant Kunbis, on the Colonelbag side, may have been an important component. Both castes are Marathi-speaking, the Marathas tracing their warrior status back to the great folk-hero and military chieftain, Shivaji, the largely rural and lower caste farmer Kunbis numerically outstripping every other caste in Nagpur district.[15] Kunbis consider themselves equally descended from the retinue of the great Shivaji, and many of their leaders, among them the Kunbi leaders of the Colonelbag group, take pains to identify their caste as Maratha rather than as Kunbi. Heavy urban migration by the Kunbis in the present century upset the political ecology and perhaps threatened the traditional status claims of the Marathas. In any event, neither faction consists today exclusively of any single caste, and both appear to have been at least somewhat mixed in their clientele from the very beginning.

The more immediate early-day catalyst for the "blood feud" of these two Congress factions may be somewhat apocryphal, but probably is not untypical of their competitive style in the rough-and-tumble 'thirties. Their henchmen practiced various bodily arts in their association with the local akhadas, developing skills ranging from sword-fighting to wrestling. The akhadas, or networks of akhadas, were deemed to have certain territorial prerogatives, such as provision of various services or personnel for local wedding parties. Some akhadas trained exhibition spearmen or swordsmen, for instance, whose unique skill provided entertainment at local functions. These services provided paid employment for the akhada members; and their natural capacity for physical coercion must have been advantageous in monopolizing jobs within a faction's area of influence. The violation by one group of another's

---

[15]The 1908 edition of the district *Gazetteer* stated that the Kunbis were the most numerous in the district, constituting twenty per cent of the population. Government of Maharashtra, *Maharashtra State Gazetteers, Nagpur District*, p. 140.

territorial rights was sometimes *casus belli*. Gang fights would ensue, the lethal weaponry of combatants occasionally resulting in dead and gravely wounded. Several informants alleged that it was just such an instance which first brought the Colonelbag and Nawabpura groups into headlong conflict. According to a Nawabpura leader, a Colonelbag-patronized wedding procession invaded Nawabpura territory in 1938, and the resulting bloody fracas gave rise to a deadly enmity that continues to this day.[16]

The leaders of both groups are quick to point out the honorable roles they and their associates played in the lengthy freedom struggle preceding the grant of independence in 1947. There is no doubt that their "professional" services, if not also their patriotism, would have been highly valued in the nationalist struggle, whose non-violent ethos was observed on occasion only in the breach. Domaji Deshmukh, the aging but still robust founder of the Colonelbag group, and his younger brother, Ishwar, both point to stiff jail terms meted out by the British— Domaji to five of them and Ishwar to one of a year and a half imposed for his participation in the Quit India movement of 1942.[17] The Nawabpura group, its leadership organized more or less formally ever since 1936 as the Rashtriya Shivaji Mandal (national Shivaji council), has a similarly patriotic past. It lists nine of its members who were jailed by the British, and it annually commemorates the hanging by the British of one of its youthful associates at the unveiling of whose statue in Nawabpura Prime Minister Jawaharlal Nehru was himself present.[18]

Nonetheless, not all their independence struggles were motivated merely by patriotism. An informant who was an associate of the Colonelbag group for twelve years from 1944 to 1956 reported that the faction's patriotic and other socially esteemed activities were often a screen for less noble endeavors. His own services included a period as secretary of the Nagrik Unnathi Mandal (citizens development council), a

[16]Sakharam D. Choudhary, the generally acknowledged founder of the Nawabpura faction, interviewed on 18 April 1969. Another source, in the 1930s an RSS organizer, reported having watched several pitched battles between these two groups involving hundreds of men and considerable bloodletting.

[17]Domaji Deshmukh was interviewed on 17 November, Ishwar on 22 November 1969.

[18]Related by M.M. Wade, joint secretary of the Rashtriya Shivaji Mandal, interviewed on 18 November 1969. A public trust not formally registered until 1962, the Shivaji Mandal was for some time roughly synonymous with the Nawabpura group, the faction's subsequent organizational diversification makes such a comparison somewhat less valid today.

Colonelbag affiliate which, among other things, sponsored a Gandhian Charka Sangh (spinning society), mass physical training organizations, and an RSS-like uniformed social service corps called the Bajarang Dal (Hanuman corps).[19] According to him, the Colonelbag faction in those days was a highly effective and well organized group which gained wide recognition for its nationalist activities. But at the same time, in his opinion, it was earning its bad reputation by indulging in a variety of unscrupulous activities. For example, up to the early 1950s, its agents collected five to twenty-five rupees monthly from every household in Colonelbag and vicinity, ostensibly voluntarily solicited to support the group's worthy projects, but in fact coerced to support its leaders and their associates.

A similar tale is told by another informant, an articulate and prominent foe of the Colonelbag faction, who grew up in Colonelbag in the independence era. He described his youthful disillusionment with local political leaders in these words:

> Though my interests as a youth were largely non-political, I was aware even as a teenager of the oppression of the poor people in my locality. For instance, people would often come to my home requesting loans of money from my mother for such things as paying compulsory subscriptions to the sponsors of various religious festivals, such as the Ganpathi festival occurring every September. Compulsory subscriptions were a type of activity which certain bad elements in the Colonelbag area engaged in for their own selfish ends. During the pre-independence period, certain political leaders of the nationalist movement revived ostensibly religious or cultural festivals to bring masses of people together under the noses of the British in order to foster a national consciousness in them. Under the garb of Shivaji's anniversary, or the Ganpathi festival, or similar occasions, leaders all over India propagandized for the nationalist movement without violating British restrictions on such types of political gatherings. Some local politicians took advantage of the opportunity thus provided and coerced donations to so-called festival committees far larger than the expected one or so rupees supposedly voluntarily subscribed from each individual or family. In fact, some unscrupulous leaders imposed collective subscriptions on localities as high as 1,000 or 1,500 rupees, which the inhabitants, be they howsoever

---

[19]Hanuman, locally called Bajarang, is the Hindu god of strength.

poor, had to pay or face beatings from the goondas who served to enforce the will of the festival committees. Only part of the large sums collected from whole localities, or from groups of mill workers, would actually be spent on festival preparation, the bulk being used to enrich the profiteers feeding on this unjust system.[20]

In the early post-independence years, both the Nawabpura and Colonelbag groups began to assume a mantle of legitimacy.[21] They early shed their too-obvious links with "goondas" and street gangs. The Congress Sewa Dal (service corps) tended to side with the Nawabpura group, and provided it with a ready and quite respectable component of organized youths to serve as its militant arm. Not to be outdone, and certain that it could not rely on the Sewa Dal volunteers, the Colonelbag group formed their own service association, the aforementioned Bajarang Dal. Bajarang volunteers came to Congress functions dressed in black pants, white shirts and saffron caps, and for a while

[20]Notes of the interview were taken almost verbatim, but some liberties have been taken to assure that the respondent's remarks are easily comprehended. Another informant, a school headmaster, lifelong resident of Colonelbag, and a political opponent of the Colonelbag faction, described the local atmosphere in his youth in similar terms as one permeated with violent rivalry between akhadas. Many of them were utterly devoid of patriotism, in his opinion, and were no more than muscle-squads organized to enrich their leaders. One tactic employed by the Colonelbag group, he charged, involved extorting up to one-half of millworkers' salaries through the mechanism of a private "employment agency" operated by the faction. Colonelbag leaders established an *adda* (booth) near the main gate of Model Mills to which those laborers indebted to the Colonelbag group's influence for their jobs were obliged to regularly pay a "commission" or face the threat of violent retaliation. The Colonelbag faction had such influence with the mill management, in this informant's judgment, that some of their henchmen were kept on the mill's payroll without actually having to work there.

[21]Virtually all respondents agreed that the violent activities characteristic of the earlier period had largely ceased by the early 1950s. A top leader of the Nawabpura group candidly admitted that his organization indulged in a disreputable brand of activities at one stage of its history; by the middle of the 1950s, he insisted, it had left its gangland behavior entirely behind. Even the most outspoken critics of the Colonelbag group's past behavior acknowledged a softening in its tactics in recent years. Stray incidents of violence are still reported, but neither group commands automatic and total authority in any locality. It is usually conceded, however, that fear of both groups, based on their past reputations, is not uncommon among some of the residents of their original localities.

the surfeit of Congress "dals" was something of an embarrassment.[22]

The Nawabpura group has responded to the post-independence environment through the diversification of its activities into various developmental fields. Pandurang T. Kadu, a prominent Nawabpura figure, has been president of the Rashtriya Shivaji Mandal since its founding in 1936. He and a group of associates founded the Chitnispura Friends Cooperative Credit Society around 1950, and Kadu has served as its vice president from the start. The venture was so successful that by the middle of the 1960s the credit society was turned into a bank; it has quickly risen to prominence among the city's cooperative banking institutions. Kadu entered other fields also, occupying managerial positions in educational, housing and physical training associations. Sakharam D. Choudhary, another Nawabpura leader, founder and lifelong secretary of the Rashtriya Shivaji Mandal, has nurtured the organization into what its leaders claim is the oldest and largest operation of its kind in the entire city. It continues its decades-long function of assisting persons in the immediate locality (essentially Nawabpura and Chitnispura) with their wedding ceremonies, employment and financial problems. It also assumes responsibility, as in former days, for arranging the Shivaji anniversary celebration, Ganpathi festivals, and Republic and Independence Day commemorations. But its major functions surround the multipurpose institutions of which it now serves as an overarching supervisory committee. In 1958 it founded the Sarwa Service Credit Cooperative Society, presently enrolling about a thousand shareholders and serving all of Nagpur and its environs. The Shivaji Mandal, in addition, operates a library, and in the early 1960s opened a consumers' cooperative store. At the same time it expanded into education, opening the Shri Shivaji High School, to which it added a primary school in 1969. It still continues to manage a physical exercise association—the Shivaji Vyayam Shala—which dates back to the Shivaji Mandal's founding in 1936. The Shivaji Mandal and its affiliated institutions, according to its leaders, constitute an association of about five thousand persons in Nagpur and surrounding rural areas.

Nawabpura leaders have all the while been intensely interested in municipal politics. Kadu, for instance, has stood in three municipal

---

[22]One informant related that on the occasion of a formal visit to Nagpur by Prime Minister Nehru in the middle 1950s, the Bajarang Dal managed to intrude its volunteers into the meeting ground along with volunteers of the Sewa Dal. The prime minister, surprised by the act, objected that only the Sewa Dal was to perform the service function of the Congress organization.

elections since independence. He was elected a corporator in 1957, and in 1962 served as deputy mayor of the city. Choudhary, contesting his first election in 1969, secured the highest vote (2,763) in the entire city of Nagpur in a field of 543 candidates, an impressive indication that the organizational diversification of the Nawabpura group has not meant the deterioration of its popular hold.

In matters of diversification and innovation, the Colonelbag group is far from laggard. Always something of a family faction, with the two Kunbi brothers, Domaji and Ishwar Deshmukh, sharing responsibilities of leadership, the Colonelbag group is locally renowned for its extraordinary achievements in many fields. But all of their other activities pale in comparison to the entreprencurial talents the Deshmukh brothers have displayed in the field of education. They and their associates today manage the largest private educational system in the city of Nagpur, a complex of fourteen diverse institutions within and outside the city, commanding an immense budget and growing with amazing rapidity. According to a recent publicity pamphlet, the Nagrik Shiksan Mandal (citizens education society) was founded on 5 May 1955, under the inspiration of Domaji and active headship of Ishwar Deshmukh.[23] It began on a small scale with the opening near Model Mills of the Rashtriya Vidyalay (national high school), which opened with a student body of 150. It followed with the establishment in 1956 of a Citizens Training College for Primary Teachers, also in Colonelbag. It has since spread to virtually every category of education, and has under construction a large complex of institutions on an eight and a half acre site in Hanumannagar on the southern edge of the city. It has also established several schools in rural areas, including several in the Deshmukh's own ancestral village of Kuhi. The fourteen presently existing institutions, with approximately four thousand students enrolled, make a list impressive above all for the scope of educational activities represented[24]:

[23]*Citizens Education Society, Nagpur—Objectives and Operation*, n.d. (1969?).

[24]*Ibid.* The same source lists the facilities under construction in Hanumannagar which will greatly add to the size of the education society's investment. With their estimated costs, they are as follows:

1)	Gymnasium	Rs 350,000
2)	Stadium	Rs 250,000
3)	Swimming pool	Rs 100,000
4)	Students hostel	Rs 400,000
5)	Teachers quarters	Rs 400,000
6)	Sports guesthouse	Rs 100,000
7)	Administrative block	Rs 200,000

 1) Training Institute for Physical Education
 2) National Institute of Social Work
 3) Panchayati Raj Training Center
 4) National Teachers Training College, Junior College of Education
 5) National High School, Branch Number 1
 6) National High School, Branch Number 2
 7) Citizens Teachers Training College, Junior College of Education
 8) National High School, Branch Number 3
 9) Rukhwadashram High School
10) Tailoring School
11) National Primary School and Kindergarten
12) Citizens Primary School
13) National Kindergarten
14) National Gymnastic School

The Colonelbag leaders are as active politically as their Nawabpura counterparts. Domaji, the elder and less educated brother, though never having contested an election, has been active in local politics since 1930 and is widely regarded as one of the most powerful Congressmen in Nagpur. Ishwar, who holds a law degree, has been highly successful in obtaining influential political and governmental posts. In 1955 he was elected president of the NCDCC, in which capacity he served for three years. In 1958, while completing his legal training, he was granted a ticket to contest a bye-election to the state legislative council. He won, and then in 1960 was re-elected to a six-year term. In 1961, in an exceptional case, he was selected to the municipal corporation by the Congress majority, an action made possible through the resignation of a friendly sitting corporator. Ishwar has been a member of the all-India Congress committee, and since 1966 has been a trustee of the Nagpur Improvement Trust. In 1968 he was appointed regional chairman of the influential Maharashtra State Transport Commission.[25]

To sum up, the Nawabpura and Colonelbag factions have moved from the streets into an elaborate array of institutions. They have exchanged a personal and corporal brand of competition for one of administrative coups and counter-coups, wherein they strive to capture government concessions and grants rather than defend the borders of their erstwhile fiefdoms. Political competition between them probably dates back very nearly to their origins; the *mode* of competition has certainly changed

[25]In 1969, Ishwar suffered a stunning upset in the municipal election; the defeat, according to all accounts, was engineered by a coalition of Congress party leaders desirous of trimming the billowing sails of the Deshmukh flotilla.

with the change in the character of the factions themselves. Where once it may have been possible literally to beat one's opposition into submission, it is increasingly required that one be able to best him with managerial finesse. Here, bargaining and not bullying is the critical factor in forging electoral alliances, and institutional rather than protoplasmic muscle backs up the bargainers.

The Akhada Dispute

A particularly good example of the changed mode of competition is to be found in a recent dispute between the Nawabpura and Colonelbag factions over control of a large wrestling federation in the city—the Nagpur City Akhada Federation Committee (NCAFC). The dispute among the members of this committee, a body joining together leaders of the numerous traditional local wrestling akhadas, brings sharply into focus the political vulnerability and utility of *any* association responsible for the implementation of development programs.

Akhadas have long occupied a place in the power structure of their localities, if for no other reason than that they were suitable recruiting grounds for husky political henchmen. But while their older role seems well on its way to extinction, modern developmental programing, which includes the building of the nation's bodies as well as its minds, has infused the old wrestling and body-building organizations with new purposes, new roles, and—most importantly—new resources. In so doing, it has posed a lure to faction leaders, who are increasingly willing and able to use the newfangled paraphernalia of managing committees, constitutions, bye-laws, and periodic elections of officers to achieve their ends.

Let us look first at the background to the dispute.

Sports of all kinds are highly popular and highly organized among the citizens of Nagpur city. Throngs of spectators are attracted to sports events as diverse from one another as gentlemanly cricket and bicep-thumping traditional wrestling. Scores of private clubs sponsor meets for enthusiasts of badminton, table tennis, weight-lifting, and football, as for those sports, like *kabbade*, *kho-kho* and traditional wrestling, which have been self-consciously revived in independent India.

Most local sports groups are organized under one of three general types of voluntary athletic association—akhadas, vyayam shalas, or krida mandals. The distinctions among them are somewhat blurry, but generally they fall somewhere on a continuum stretching from traditional Indian to contemporary Western sports. Akhadas are the most traditional athletic association of the three, found most commonly in the older sectors of the city among the weaver communities. They provide facilities for traditional wrestling and exercise, and sponsor their more outstanding members in a variety of citywide contests.[26] Vyayam shalas, a more recent phenomenon, are gymnastic clubs combining traditional wrestling with contemporary forms of exercise and sport. Many saw their birth in the independence struggle when mass physical training and exercise received the blessing of nationalist leaders. Krida mandals, or sports councils, on the other hand, are largely a post-independence phenomenon devoted to the promotion of a wide variety of mainly contemporary sports and games.

Together the three types comprise an imposing array of local associations. There are 110 akhadas and vyayam shalas in the city of Nagpur, and from 150 to 200 krida mandals.[27] All types are increasing in number year by year.[28]

Part of their growth may be attributable to the support extended to the athletic associations by the government. Thirty-five of the akhadas, for instance, are presently receiving annual state grants of from Rs 300 to Rs 1,000, disbursed through the akhada federation. Considerable sums are made available to promote particular sports, such as wrestling. Since 1960, the state of Maharashtra has budgeted Rs 200,000 per annum to be apportioned among the state's twenty-six districts exclusively in the form of honoraria to student and non-student winning wrestlers in state selection tournaments. Tournament winners may receive from Rs 30 to Rs 75 monthly; state champions may receive a monthly honorarium as high as Rs 150 rupees. Nagpur district's current share is about

[26]The term akhada refers to a small enclosed arena, typically about $18' \times 21'$, housing a small sunken wrestling pit cushioned with soft red dirt (*mutti*).

[27]Technical data concerning the city's sports associations are drawn from interviews with Dadarao Tembhekar, secretary of the Nagpur City Akhada Federation Committee, on 18 December 1969, and 24 January 1970; Vithalrao Darwekar, leading wrestling promoter and would-be president of the NCAFC, on 18 December 1969; and Narayan T. Murkute, executive member and permanent trustee of the NCAFC and president of the Nagpur District Wrestlers Association, on 23 December 1969. Figures are reported as of the end of 1969. According to Murkute, within Nagpur *district* there are currently 500 akhadas and vyayam shalas.

[28]Even the tradition-minded akhadas are growing in number. According to Tembhekar, ten new ones opened in the previous five years.

Rs 10,000, distributed in the 1968-69 period among twenty-three wrestlers, eleven of them in the city itself.[29]

Most of the sports associations in the city are organized into federations, the largest and oldest of which is the Nagpur City Akhada Federation Committee. Sixty-six akhadas and vyayam shalas are presently affiliated with it.[30] It was born, informally, in the late 1940s. According to Dadarao Tembhekar, its secretary, several Congress leaders created the organization in an early effort to bring about a less troublesome relationship among akhadas than then existed. At the time of its founding the Colonelbag group was reputed to control about forty akhadas, the Nawabpura group about seventy.

Tembhekar, who is the delegate to the NCAFC from the Shivaji Vyayam Shala in Nawabpura, the oldest institution founded by the Nawabpura group's Rashtriya Shivaji Mandal, stoutly insists that the federation has been mainly successful in keeping purely political considerations out of its operations.[31] Or at least it was, he regretfully adds, up until 1969.

Politics intruded itself in the wake of a large state government grant authorizing the federation to construct a stadium in Siraspeth in the southeastern sector of the city. According to Tembhekar, the government agreed to pay sixty per cent of the total estimated cost of Rs 700,000. A first installment of Rs 5,000 had already been received in early 1969, and construction was underway.[32] Tembhekar admits that the lucrative grant turned the NCAFC, accustomed to handling more piddling sums, into a battleground. Two men now claimed to be its president—one supported by the Colonelbag group, the other by the Nawabpura group and its allies. Rectification was ultimately sought through the courts, where it had to be determined whose associates were

[29]Though the funds are distributed directly through a local government agency—the social welfare department of the Zilla Parishad—authority for allocation is vested, in the case of wrestling, in the Maharashtra State Wrestling Conference, a semi-private body presided over in 1969 by the State Revenue Minister Balasaheb Desai.

[30]Official NCAFC roster, dated 25 October 1969, provided by Tembhekar.

[31]Ordinarily the NCAFC performs such functions as providing professional coaches to member akhadas, arranging selection tournaments, and operating coaching and training camps several times each year. According to Tembhekar, there are about 450-550 tournament wrestlers in Nagpur, 200-250 of them students.

[32]It is located not far from the Colonelbag group's own new stadium, also under construction, in Hanumannagar.

to preside over the expanded assets of the federation.[33]

The evolution of the dispute over leadership of the federation is interesting as an example of the legal-constitutional brand of competition now commonly indulged in even by those not far removed from the skullcracking, armtwisting problem-resolving methods of yesteryear. The final date for submission of delegate names and fees in the triannual registration of akhadas and vyayam shalas with the federation fell on 15 July 1969. The Colonelbag group, relatively weaker in akhada affiliations, submitted the names of representatives from a large number of krida mandals and contemporary sports associations among which it had greater influence; it hoped to "stack" the representation in its favor, according to Tembhekar, increasing the likelihood of a stronger Colonelbag voice on the executive committee.[34]

The legitimacy of the Colonelbag slate was quickly challenged in federation meetings by the allies of other political factions. At a meeting of the federation's working committee on 27 July 1969, attended among others by Domaji Deshmukh, Tembhekar reported that during scrutiny of the ninety-three registration forms submitted, it was found that some of the sports groups were of doubtful qualification for membership in the federation. The working committee unanimously agreed to constitute an inspection committee of three persons, including Tembhekar, to investigate the matter and submit a report prior to the next general meeting of the federation.[35]

---

[33]Hitherto the NCAFC had total assets amounting only to about Rs 200,000.

[34]The hand of Colonelbag is visible, for instance, in the sport club affiliations of one such representative, B.D. Bhoyar, interviewed on 28 January 1970. A degree-bearing physical education instructor, Bhoyar is an executive in such associations as the Vidarbha Best Physique and Weightlifting Association, founded in 1967; the Vidarbha Athletic Association, founded in 1960; the Vidarbha Cycling Association, founded in 1960; and the Vidarbha Gymnastic Association, founded in 1969. Ishwar Deshmukh, Colonelbag leader, is president of all of these. Names of representatives from two were submitted for inclusion in the federation. It should be understood that the appearance of Deshmukh's name as president of this or that association is not evidence of Colonelbag *domination*. Individual sports groups are often run by elected managing committees, subject to the same constitutional constraints as the federation. A Nawabpura associate and political foe of Ishwar Deshmukh informed the writer that he and his associates had deliberately elected Ishwar president of the Vidarbha Volleyball Association "in order to get government grants." Ishwar, he pointed out, was the only member of the Colonelbag group in the management and was removable—democratically—at the others' discretion.

[35]Minutes of the meeting of the working committee, NCAFC, 27 July 1969.

The subsequent general meeting was held in an affiliated vyayam shala (gymnasium) on the evening of 14 September 1969. It was well-attended by seventy-one representatives of akhadas, vyayam shalas, and krida mandals. It was convened specifically to consider procedures for filling the vacant post of the federation's director. The nationally-known and respected Sant Tukdoji Maharaj, director (sanghatan sanghchalak) of the NCAFC since its formation in 1946, had died in August, adding a successional to the already critical constitutional crisis.

However, the general meeting never got this far in its deliberations. It had hardly begun when Dhondbaji Hedau, erstwhile wrestler, former MLA and prominent political leader among the Koshti weavers, rose to challenge the credentials of the representatives in attendance at the meeting. Hedau pointed out that the federation's constitution sanctioned representation only by duly-registered traditional akhadas. His allies in the assembly rose to point out that among those in attendance were delegates of a number of krida mandals, as well as of such quite untraditional groups as the Vidarbha Cycling Association and the Vidarbha Weightlifting Association. There already existed, these spokesmen insisted, separate federations for their activities—the Nagpur District Kabbadi Association, the Nagpur District Kho-Kho Association, among others—and they should join those rather than a federation designed exclusively for traditional akhadas. One after another, the pro-akhada delegates joined the chorus demanding retention of a pristine construction of the constitution, only to be answered by the pro-krida mandal forces demanding their inclusion. Not unpersuasively, these delegates argued that akhadas which included in their programs sports activities typically associated with krida mandals had all along been registered with the federation. So why, they asked, could not krida mandals be affiliated in their own right?

The meeting reached a climax when Tembhekar, in his capacity as secretary, stood up to declare that he had not received membership fees from the protesting krida mandals, and ordered their representatives to leave the meeting. At this, Colonelbag leader Domaji Deshmukh and other krida mandal proponents, according to the minutes of the meeting, began "abusing" their antagonists; the situation so deteriorated that the members "were coming to blows."[36] The president of the host gymnasium averted a more physical showdown by requesting a temporary

[36]"Report of the General Meeting," NCAFC, 14 September 1969.

adjournment. Feelings had reached such a pitch, however, that the delegates simply went home, and the meeting dissolved entirely.

At this point the federation divided into two groups, both claiming status as *the* legitimate federation. When the Nawabpura-led general body reconvened on 25 October to consider the same problem of succession, it was a much more homogeneous but quite shrunken group of thirty-three delegates. It hammered through a series of resolutions dealing with the constitutional and successional crises. Sant Tukdoji Maharaj, enjoying the trust of all, had been constitutionally empowered to *select* the federation's executive committee. The constitution did not specify, however, what procedure was to be followed in the event of the director's demise. The delegates decided, since there was no great personality available with whom to replace Sant Tukdoji, the next best course was to amend the constitution to provide for the direct democratic election of the sanghchalak and of the executive committee by the federation's general body.[37]

In the meantime the krida mandal forces met separately and agreed to the appointment of Sant Damodar Maharaj as federation director. On 28 November 1969, they convened a general meeting at which the new director, in accord with his constitutional prerogatives, chose a new executive committee. Their names were promptly submitted for approval to the Nagpur district Charitable Trusts Commission, whose sanction of their slate of officers was a necessary precondition for the redirection of government funds to the reconstituted executive committee.[38] The Nawabpura-led federation responded by taking legal action to block such a decision, and there the matter rested in early 1970.

The dispute described here concerns more than constitutional niceties or rival conceptions of the proper development of sports in India. The antagonists are obviously not ideologically committed to either a loose or strict constructionist view of constitutionality. The "strict" constructionists—the Nawabpura forces—were not averse to amending the constitution to fit their own needs. Nor does it seem that either side is exclusively or irrevocably committed to either traditional or modern sports. Ramkrishna P. Samarth, a noted Congress faction leader, though siding in this dispute with pro-akhada forces, is himself president of the

[37]"Report of the General Meeting," NCAFC, 25 October 1969.

[38]The new president of the rebel federation, Vithalrao Darwekar, interviewed on 18 December 1969, claimed a membership of sixty akhadas and thirty-two krida mandals.

Nagpura District Krida Mandal Association.[39]

Both sides candidly acknowledge the role of government development funds in catalyzing their argument. Both sides, the preceding discussion has made clear, are developmentally oriented, having invested heavily in associational enterprises vested with the authority to administer local development programs. Other factors, such as personal antagonisms or caste rivalry, are imbedded in their competition. But the dispute did not flare into the proportions described until a well-financed government project for athletic development injected a new component into local associational activity.

Recognition by the disputants that athletic associations constitute a very large interest group in Nagpur is a second factor accounting for the intensity of the struggle. Both the Nawabpura and Colonelbag factions patronize a diverse assortment of associations, ranging from credit and banking institutions to housing cooperatives and education societies. Their political fortunes rest in part on their capacity to aggregate diverse interests cutting across community and locality boundaries. The popularity of wrestling associations among the politically important Hindu and Muslim weaver communities, neither of which has any significant links with either of the two factions, represents an opportunity for the faction leaders to make political capital from the resources of a government developmental program.

The introduction of democratic and constitutional procedures in most associations on the receiving end of government developmental resources has produced more than mere paper acknowledgment of such practices. They have become a dominant mode of competitive politics, affixing a legitimacy to democratic procedures which rhetoric alone would never have achieved.[40] Factions have to confront the fact that the democratization of local associations has put bargaining authority in many more hands than formerly. Faction leaders are pushed to organize authority in a more corporate form than may have been necessary in the more localized and personalized factional alignments of pre-development years. Competition for control of an agency even as simple as the akhada federation is complicated by the spatial spread of

---

[39]Samarth's background is discussed in Chapter 4, above.

[40]The system affords the government opportunity to further its own developmental objectives by acting as guarantor of associational constitutionality. Having the right to arbitrate such disputes as arise over the legitimacy of rival pretenders to executive authority in these associations, it is favorably situated to exercise at least some influence in the expenditure of its funds.

sixty-six affiliates, not to mention their social differentiation among community groups. The Nawabpura faction in this case was dependent on the support of the Samarth faction, which has considerable influence among the Kalar and Koshti communities, and on the former MLA, Dhondbaji Hedau, one of the most prominent Koshti leaders. The Colonelbag faction endowed the presidency of its rebel federation on Vithalrao Darwekar of the Nai (barber) caste, a man with considerable independent following among the Koshtis.[41] Faction leaders thus gradually learn that it may be advantageous to agree to corporate management of associations, sharing authority with other leaders and factions, rather than to insist on monopoly control.

The scope of factional activities in Nagpur has been so transformed that contemporary factions bear little resemblance to their predecessors of even a few decades ago. Conflict has moved from the streets into managing committees, and disputes are resolved through the adroit manipulation of constitutional rules rather than through the confrontation of brute strength; what were once racketeering gangs indulging often in violent confrontation are today dispersed managerial enterprises engaging in rather more pacific struggles for control of associational networks. As the terms of competition have altered, factions have been led to an increasingly corporate style of leadership, socially aggregative recruitment policy, diversification of arenas of conflict, and to heavy reliance on the resources of voluntary associations.

SUMMARY

This chapter has given us little reason to alter the prevailing concept of Indian political *party* organization; granted certain exceptions, Nagpur's political parties are beset with factionalism untempered by feelings of party allegiance. It has given us some reasons, however, for wishing to modify prevailing concepts of *factional* organization. Some of Nagpur's factional groups are probably not far removed in form and practice from the definitions given by Weiner and Brass; but most are focused not simply on the personality of the leader but on the capacity of the faction to serve the material interests of a relatively broad stratum of the urban population. Factions have certainly not grown less competitive and are

[41]The Nawabpura faction, according to Tembhekar, also sought to enlist Darwekar as president of its federation.

not visibly melting into either an overarching party organizational structure or functionally specific interest associations; but they have definitely
assumed functions modifying their customary role as personality oriented
"cliques" organized entirely around personal enmities.

If the standard formulations of faction are not a precise fit for the
organizational media found operating in Nagpur, what alternative con-
ceptualization can be found which will be more suitable?

One effort has attempted to link the Indian type of organization to
the so-called "machine" model whose prototypes flourished in America
at the close of the 19th and beginning of the 20th century. According to
James C. Scott, conditions in many of the developing countries, including
India, bear remarkable resemblance to those obtaining in America in the
heyday of the big city machines, and the oddity is that not more of them
have developed machine-style political organizations.[42] "The machine,"
in Scott's opinion,

> is not the disciplined, ideological party held together by class ties
> and common programs that arose in continental Europe. Neither
> is it typically a charismatic party, depending on a belief in the almost
> superhuman qualities of its leader to insure internal cohesion. The
> machine is rather a non-ideological organization interested less in
> political principle than in securing and holding office for its leaders
> and distributing income to those who run it and work for it. It relies
> on what it accomplishes in a concrete way for its supporters, not on
> what it stands for. A machine may in fact be likened to a business in
> which all members are stockholders and dividends are paid in accor-
> dance with what has been invested.[43]

The American urban machine's chief distinguishing characteristic,
according to Scott, lay in the "cement" binding leaders and followers.
Though ties based on charisma, coercion or ideology were not entirely
absent, they were "definitely subsidiary to the concrete, particularistic
rewards that represented its staple means of political coordination. It
is the predominance of these reward networks—the special quality of the
ties between leaders and followers—that distinguishes the machine
party from the non-machine party."[44]

[42]"Corruption, Machine Politics, and Political Change," *American Political
Science Review*, LXIII (December 1969), 1142-1158.

[43]*Ibid.*, 1143-1144.

[44]*Ibid.*, 1144.

It distinguishes as well the machine organization from the factional organization described by Paul Brass. Brass' conception of faction is similar to the machine model in that both are oriented towards the establishment of influence-linkages for the transmission of favors and services. Brass' concept diverges from Scott's in the emphasis Brass places on the *indigenous* nature of factions and on the importance of personal loyalties deriving from the *traditional* hierarchical order. Whereas Brass considers the faction *leader* the focal point of factional activity and his personal ambitions the very reason for the faction's existence, Scott's machine *boss* is a creature fashioned out of his own concrete acts, for which he is held popularly accountable. "Given its principal concern for retaining office," wrote Scott,

> the machine was a responsive, informal context within which bargaining based on reciprocity relationships was facilitated. Leaders of the machine were rarely in a position to dictate because those who supported them did so on the basis of value received or anticipated. The machine for the most part accepted its electoral clients as they were and responded to their needs in a manner that would elicit their support. The pragmatic, opportunistic orientation of the machine made it a flexible institution that could accommodate new groups and leaders in highly dynamic situations.[45]

Brass, in arguing that factions often inhibit the effective transmission of group political demands, even those rooted in self-interest, places his concept of Indian political organization squarely outside the pale of the machine model. For the machine, in Scott's construction, is organized precisely to absorb and consolidate a wide spectrum of interests, particularly "self-interests." Where the social context is such that political demands *other* than those rooted in material self-interests are unlikely to arise, broad popular support, in Scott's view, is hardly obtainable otherwise than through responsiveness to the interests of individuals. "Forging a wide coalition of interests," he writes,

> in social contexts that resemble the features of the U.S. at the turn of the century or most new nations today, inevitably means developing a capacity to distribute short-run material incentives among potential clienteles. Few, if any, durable political bonds except that of material

[45] *Ibid.*

self-interest are available to build a large political party among poor, heterogeneous, transitional populations. Self-interest thus provides the necessary political cement when neither a traditional governing elite nor a ruling group based on ideological or class interest is available.... The central fact about a political 'machine' is that it aims at the 'political consolidation of the beneficiaries' of the patronage and graft system. Whereas non-machine corruption often has a random and sporadic character or aims only at the consolidation of narrow elites who control wealth or armed force, the machine must remain popular to survive and must consequently meet the demands of a broad stratum.[46]

Whereas the opportunistic and reciprocal relationship between leaders and followers described by Scott appears to be an apt characterization of the behavior of political groups in Nagpur, and a definite advance over prevailing conceptions of factional organization, the machine model is not perfectly adapted to the Indian environment.[47] For one thing, the fragmentation of local factions requires an intense continuous competition for control of patronage which the very term "machine" does little to conjure up. For another, Nagpur's factions have achieved a higher degree of *long-run* and *institutionalized* patronage than the erstwhile American machines.

Scott's argument that machine politics is directed to the administrative or enforcement stage of legislation, while clearly pertinent to Nagpur

[46]*Ibid.*, 1151, 1154. Scott's quotation is from V.O. Key, Jr., *The Techniques of Political Graft in the United States* (Chicago: University of Chicago Libraries, 1936), p. 394.

[47]A number of commentators have remarked concerning their absence, generally attributing it to the lack of autonomy of local political groups and to the lack of command by any one of them over the distribution of patronage. In a monograph based on his experience in Indore (Madhya Pradesh), Rodney Jones tentatively accounted for the weakness of nascent political machines in that city to "the lack of autonomy of local patronage distribution processes from high level influences, the fragmentation of bureaucratic agencies through which state government patronage is distributed and the high degree of ascriptive pluralism of the population with its concomitants for vigorous factional competition within the dominant party." "Towards Comparative Urban Studies: A Linkage Model of Urban Politics in India," unpublished paper prepared for delivery at the annual meeting of the International Studies Association, Pittsburgh, 3-5 April 1970, 23. Myron Weiner reaches similar conclusions in his discussion of the Congress organization in Madurai city (Tamil Nadu), in *Party Building in a New Nation: The Indian National Congress*, p. 449.

politics, overlooks this last aspect—the enormous, continuous and legitimate patronage available from voluntary associational institutions. He writes that

> a large portion of individual demands, and even group demands, in developing nations reach the political system, not before laws are passed, but rather at the enforcement stage. Influence before legislation is passed often takes the form of 'pressure-group politics'; *influence at the enforcement stage often takes the form of 'corruption' and has seldom been treated as the alternative means of interest articulation which in fact it is*. . . .Couched as it is in universalistic language, legislation is not a suitable vehicle for the expression of particularistic interests. Influence at the enforcement level—whether it meets the legal definition of corruption or not—is, on the other hand, almost exclusively particularistic. It is scarcely surprising, then, that many of the narrow, parochial demands characteristic of new nations should make their weight felt during the implementation of legislation rather than during its passage.[48]

That this orientation typically leads to corruption is an overstatement. Though the Indian organizations are dependent on porkbarreled development financing and the favored allocation of public works, just as were American big city machines they rely much more heavily than their earlier Western counterparts on *public* and *legal* mechanisms of distribution. Political groups in Nagpur have assumed management of a large share of local developmental enterprises—such institutions as schools, cooperatives, and housing societies—through which they quite legally and openly dispense goods and services of every sort. Graft aud corruption are present; there is no evidence to indicate, however, that they have greater importance in the competition for political support than the distribution of such thoroughly legitimate favors as admission to a school or health clinic, acquisition of a cooperative rebate, or sanction of a housing loan.

Scott misses the crux of the matter arising from the very different legal and developmental context confronting contemporary Indian politicians. "Saddled with the 'very latest' in terms of civil service regulations," he argues, "politicians in the new nations must regularly

---

[48]"Corruption, Machine Politics, and Political Change," *op. cit.*, 1142-1143. Italics in the original.

resort to practices that are either highly questionable or transparently illegal to find jobs for some of the party workers."[49] In fact, Nagpur's politicians have "solved" this problem by absorbing a voluntary associational structure enabling them to exploit the already fuzzy boundary between public and private sectors of the system. Institutionalized and openly subsidized, their "machines" bear a remarkable legitimacy restrained by no inherent need for corruption.

How, then, may we characterize the dominant type of political organization in Nagpur? Those local organizations we have discussed in this chapter appear to be an imperfect blend of traditional factional and machine traits. They have at least three distinct properties setting them apart somewhat from either traditional faction or machine models: they are characteristically corporate in management, functionally organized to manage a diverse set of enterprises, and development oriented in terms of the type of enterprises over which they seek to gain and retain command.

Corporate structure is revealed in the declining importance of a single leader or boss and in the rising importance of leadership shared among more or less equal entrepreneurs having autonomous command of saleable political assets of their own. Such leaders are bound together less by devotion to particular personalities than by mutual calculation of material advantages to be gained through cooperation. Their autonomy is guaranteed by the fragmentation of political-bureaucratic arenas (by the multiplication of democratically-elected associational managements which comprise the heart of the patronage system) over which no single leader can gain full control.

The functional diversity of factions derives from recognition by faction leaders that the tenure of the factional relationship rests on corporate capacity to satisfy the highly diverse demands of constituent voters. Factions are vulnerable both to government whimsy in the not always stable realm of development programing, and to the even more arbitrary decisions of voters. Dispersed investment of factional energies and resources into a variety of associational enterprises commanding the distribution of different developmental benefits admired and sought by the voting public provides insulation against momentary setbacks in any particular arena and assures the expansion of factional appeal to wider and varied sectors of the electorate.

The developmental orientation of factions involves little more than

[49] *Ibid.*, 1152.

the understanding that many governmental resources are being deliberately poured into a myriad development projects, while at the same time popular taste for the product of these projects is steadily rising. Political capital is available elsewhere—in caste and kinship affiliations, in ideological commitments, in charismatic personality, and so on—but it is increasingly obvious that developmental inputs are a principal— perhaps *the* principal—resource currently in use in Nagpur.

In such ways as these local factions have been transformed by the development-laden post-independence political process into managerial syndicates responsible for the direct local distribution of palpable benefits and the production of political support. If it is to fairly represent the reality of political organization as found in Nagpur, a concept of faction must be framed upon recognition of this transformation, in particular upon the capacity of factions to institutionalize the transmission of popular demands on government.

Nagpur's factions manage the multiple demands of diverse publics not so much through the short-term extraction of favors from influential contacts as through the establishment and expansion of developmental structures such as schools, cooperatives, and other associations whose fortunes are heavily dependent on quite long-range development planning. Voter demands remain, indeed, highly discrete and intermittent; but by linking their organizations institutionally to the enforcement or implementation stage of legislative enactment, local politicians have devised a formula for giving coherence and continuity to this otherwise anarchic pattern of demand articulation. The organizations they have devised in a sense serve as coalitions of pressure groups, at one time extracting concessions for education societies and the publics they represent, at another time performing the same task for credit, production and housing cooperatives, for sporting clubs, health and welfare associations, until they have spread their representational services, and their political power, to a large and highly differentiated segment of the urban populace. That aggregation occurs thusly under the auspices of factional organizations distinct from organizations (namely, political parties and functional interest groups) commonly performing this function in Western countries should not be understood as a negation of interest representation.[50]

Factions as exist in Nagpur may be described as "alternative forms

---

[50]Brass is keenly aware of the importance of government patronage to factional organizations. We differ mainly in the emphasis he places on the essentially

of political organization to interest groups. . . based upon conflicting principles." But they do not necessarily "inhibit the organization of interests because they are based upon ties which unite opposed interests."[51] For this to be true, one would have to assume that the "opposed interests"—modern ones of class and ideology; traditional ones of kin, caste, religious community and neighborhood—do not share a *common* and *transcendent* interest in exploiting the patronage system so generously provided by the ruling elite's developmental ambitions. How can we assault factions for uniting antagonistic class interests, for example, while denying (as many do) that class ideology has anything much to do with Indian politics?[52] Where class interests are weakly defined, as they appear to be in India, what difference does it make if factions largely ignore them? Perhaps more than any other agency in Nagpur, factions are *fostering* the organization of interests, deliberately creating and giving political direction to literally hundreds of associations concerned with virtually every conceivable and long-term need of the population. The modern faction does not come close to being a "party" in indigenous dress, "held together by a sense of moral dedication to a common purpose"[53]; but it *is* an aggregation of interests cutting across *both* modern and traditional barriers in the common quest for the material benefits of national development.

---

short-term favors and privileges transacted between faction leaders and government authorities. *Factional Politics in an Indian State: The Congress Party in Uttar Pradesh*, p. 231.

[51]*Ibid.*, p. 244.

[52]*Ibid.*, p. 233. The efforts of one author to demonstrate that fundamental economic interests and ideological preferences *do* play a significant role in the political behavior of factions have met with considerable objection. See Mary C. Carras, *The Dynamics of Indian Political Factions: A Study of District Councils in the State of Maharashtra*, cited earlier. For an effective rejoinder, see Donald B.Rosenthal, "Sources of District Congress Factionalism in Maharashtra," *Economic and Political Weekly*, VII (19 August 1972), 1725-1746.

[53]F.G. Bailey, *Politics and Social Change: Orissa in 1959*, p. 141.

6

Voluntary Associations and Political Organization (II)

In spite of the prevalence of factionalism in Nagpur city politics, there are some political parties which appear to have an organizational coherence, disciplined cadre and programatic orientation conforming fairly well to the Western prototype. The Communist party, for example, is generally considered to have greater ideological motivation than other local parties; and the Republican party, as was pointed out inChapter 4, is often claimed to have a dependable resource in the communal solidarity of the former untouchables. The Bharatiya Jana Sangh, as will shortly be shown, is almost unanimously judged to have extraordinary reserves of both ideological and communal solidarity.

In this chapter, in which we examine the Jana Sangh party organization, the point will not be to suggest that the BJS or any other organization does not rely to an important extent on just such resources; such a claim would be difficult, if not impossible, to substantiate. Locally, the Jana Sangh does appear to have a tight-knit organization, remarkably free of overt factionalism, headed by a cadre of ideologically committed leaders. It pays great attention to indoctrination of its workers in party policy, and insists upon a degree of discipline among them rarely paralleled in other political organizations.

It will rather be the intent here to suggest that the BJS is subject to the same forces acting upon other political organizations, and must adapt to these forces if it is to retain viable political credentials of any sort. It competes in the same environment of highly particularistic demands, channeled through a multitude of voluntary associational structures, responded to often from the palpable resources of government development programs. Though the dedication of party cadre to long-range socio-economic and cultural goals may not be diminished at all with the realization, party leaders, in formulating organizational strategy, could hardly be unaware that purely ideological or communal symbols are not enough to manage demands in an "indulgent" mass participant system; they are unlikely to miss the fact that party growth, aside from party maintenance, does not occur in isolation from, but in direct competition with the strategies of opposition groups. Since the opposition groups are often more successful than the Jana Sangh and are clearly inclined towards pragmatism in the calculation of political opportunity, some Jana Sangh "borrowing" of organizational strategy from its opponents would not be surprising.

The discussion in this chapter will deal with the evidence of an alteration in organizational strategy by the local BJS in its effort to enlarge its base of support and to provide a genuine alternative to Congress. The terms of analysis remain essentially the same as in preceding chapters: we will examine organizational recruitment criteria, modes of managing popular demands, and overall strategy for handling inter-party competition.

Prior to examining the evidence for the proposition that BJS organizational strategy has been significantly remodeled, we must first ask what it has been, or at least what it has been thought to be.

THE JANA SANGH AND HINDU REVIVALISM

The Jana Sangh has long been described as the contemporary political bearer of Hindu traditionalism and cultural revitalization.[1] In an

[1] Among the many studies of communalist and cultural revivalist phenomena in India are B.R. Purohit, *Hindu Revivalism and Indian Nationalism* (Sagar, Madhya Pradesh: Sathi Prakashan, 1965); Vincent Watson, "Communal Politics in India and the United States: A Comparative Analysis," Research Paper No. 10 (Atlanta: School of Arts and Sciences, Georgia State College, 1965); Guenter Lewy, *Militant Hindu Nationalism: The Early Phase*, Report prepared for the U.S. Department of Defense, Advanced Research Projects Agency, April 1967; Richard D. Lambert, "Hindu Communal Groups in Indian Politics," in *Leadership and Political Institutions in India*, Richard L. Park and Irene Tinker, editors (Princeton: Princeton University Press, 1959), pp. 211-224; Richard M. Fontera, "Cultural Pluralism and Communalism: The Development of the Government of India Act of 1935" (unpublished Ph.D. dissertation,

early work, Myron Weiner suggested that the BJS was a fundamentally anti-system party representing the post-independence continuation of the communalist phenomenon. Tracing the historical roots of caste and religious communal exclusivism, Weiner pointed to the evolution of the Brahmo Samaj as a sort of pro-West thesis; the Arya Samaj soon appeared as the pro-Hindu antithesis, followed by Ramakrishna, Swami Vivekananda, the Theosophical Society, Tilak, the Hindu Mahasabha, the Rashtriya Swayamsewak Sangh, the Ram Rajya Parishad, and ultimately the Jana Sangh. The "mood" and "general outlook" of the communal parties he described as anti-Western, militarist and violent, lacking interest in the political process, lacking concern for economic questions, and lacking either conscious understanding or defense of the democratic system.[2]

Similar interpretations of the communalist and revitalist bias of the Jana Sangh have been made in more recent years by scholars, both Indian and Western. Ram Joshi, an Indian political scientist, has asserted, for instance, that "although the Jana Sangh has grown steadily in organization and influence, its appeal is largely confined to the militant Hindu communalists. It is a party of Hindu communalism, traditionalism, and social conservatism."[3]

New York University, 1964); Donald E. Smith, *India as a Secular State,* cited earlier, especially pp. 454-489; and Jean A. Curran, Jr., *Militant Hinduism in Indian Politics: A Study of the R.S.S.* (New York: International Secretariat, Institute of Pacific Relations, 1951). For a lucid discussion of cultural revitalization movements in general, see Anthony F.C. Wallace, *Culture and Personality* (New York: Random House, 1961), especially pp. 143-156.

[2]*Party Politics in India: The Development of a Multi-Party System*, pp. 164-167. Weiner speculated that communalism had shifted both its targets and its geographic base in the post-independene period. "Since independence," he observed (p. 170), "the Hindu Mahasabha and other like-minded organizations have been shifting increasingly from their anti-Islam emphasis to opposition to the Westernized Indian community, which they feel now dominates the central government." Whereas communal forces were strongest in Bengal, Punjab and Maharashtra, their strength now lies more in "areas where the Western impact has been the weakest. Anti-Westernization rather than anti-Islam feeling is increasingly providing the new basis for Hindu communalism."

[3]"Maharashtra," in *State Politics in India*, pp. 200-201. Harold Gould, an anthropologist, drew similar conclusions from his study of Faizabad constituency in Uttar Pradesh, one of the few intensive empirical studies of local Jana Sangh political behavior. He found that the BJS exploits the inevitable social stresses following in the wake of rapid social change and industrialization. Gould de-

Some commentators have seen in the steady growth of the Jana Sangh and other conservative parties, especially as manifested in the 1967 general elections, confirmation that an ideological crossroads had been reached and that India's political future was likely to be shaped much more than formerly by its militant cultural revitalists. Lloyd and Susanne Rudolph pointed out, for example, that

> organized efforts to pursue power in the name of tradition were relatively unsuccessful until the fourth general election in 1967, when they made impressive gains. Two political parties that attempted to do so in the immediate post-independence period, the Ram Rajya Parishad and the Hindu Mahasabha, are moribund. Two others, however, the Jana Sangh and Swatantra parties, particularly the former, have succeeded in introducing traditional ideology into public dialogue and political competition.

The Rudolphs went so far as to say that some of the Jana Sangh's appeals "constitute a potential challenge to the present public hegemony

---

clared that "protest has shifted its emphasis to a preoccupation with the threat of a secular assault upon the traditional institutions that have sustained the status and the security of many Indians. This preoccupation," he argued, "has grown and turned support toward communal parties in direct ratio to the occurrence of stress born of the attempt to industrialize Indian society. As managers of protest, the communal parties play up the solidarities, the securities, the privileged access to scarce resources which social structures like caste, religion, and ethnolinguistic community have always afforded Indians and whose survival depends upon the retention of salient features of the traditional culture pattern.... Communal parties manage the protest of those who see the dissolution of various particularistic aspects of the traditional social order as destructive of their personal chances for survival and prosperity." The Jana Sangh in particular, he notes, "is communal in the sense that it appeals strongly to parochial sensibilities: in other words, the party endeavors to make people feel that their best hope for security and prosperity lies in reliance upon a group whose identity is determined in personalistic terms....By stressing the point that it works for a modern India rooted in the old Hindu traditions, it makes Hindus feel that they can have the best that the modern world has to offer while simultaneously forming 'one caste' (*ek jat*) of coreligionists with particularistic claims on one another. They will homogenize themselves against the 'other castes' who pose numerous dangers to the survival of Mother India (*Bharat Mata*)—the Muslims, the Christians, the Chinese, Westernized Indians, etc." "Religion and Politics in a U.P. Constituency," in *South Asian Politics and Religion*, Donald E. Smith, editor (Princeton: Princeton University Press, 1966), pp. 53, 66.

of modernity in India."[4]

In word and deed the Jana Sangh's adherents have certainly provided grounds for such interpretations. And the party's close association with the outspokenly culturally revitalistic Rashtriya Swayamsewak Sangh (RSS) seems to offer even more conclusive evidence that the BJS is little likely to play an accommodative brand of politics.[5] Paul Brass declares that

a major reason for the survival and success of the Jana Sangh, at a time when other Hindu political parties have declined, is the support which the Jana Sangh has always had from the Rashtriya Swayam-sewak Sangh (RSS). . . . The RSS maintains a continuing interest in the Jana Sangh; RSS members are in controlling positions in both the legislatures and the party organization. The RSS does not tolerate factionalism either in its own organization or in the Jana Sangh. Members of the Jana Sangh who break party discipline are quickly.

[4]*The Modernity of Tradition: Political Development in India* (Chicago: The University of Chicago Press, 1967), p. 130. Norman Palmer, writing in May 1967, indicated his feeling that "the outcome of the elections may be interpreted as a reaction against the Western-trained and Western-oriented leaders and groups which have determined the nature of the Indian state and have made the basic national and international decisions since independence, and as an indication of a reversion against the failures, real or fancied, of the efforts at modernization." This trend, he concluded, underlies "one of the most significant aspects of the Indian political scene, namely the acceleration of 'the Indianization of Indian politics'." "India's Fourth General Election," *Asian Survey*, VII (May 1967), 276-277.

[5]Craig Baxter, an historian of the Jana Sangh, has written that since a flurry of defections in 1954-55, "the Jana Sangh organization came almost completely under the control of persons associated with the RSS." Militant RSS leadership has given the party its peculiar cohesion. As a consequence, he noted, factionalism "has been all but non-existent in the Jana Sangh." "The Jana Sangh: A Brief History," in *South Asian Politics and Religion*, p. 89. Baxter expands on this topic in his *The Jana Sangh: A Biography of an Indian Political Party*, cited earlier, especially pp. 314-315. The founding of the Jana Sangh and its embryonic fusion with the RSS is the subject of an illuminating essay by the British historian Bruce D. Graham, "Syama Prasad Mookerjee and the Communalist Alternative," in *Soundings in Modern Asian History*, D. A. Low, editor (Berkeley: University of California Press, 1968), pp. 330-374. The only detailed study of the RSS available to scholars is the dated monograph by J. A. Curran, Jr., *Militant Hinduism in Indian Politics: A Study of the R.S.S.*, cited earlier. Written prior to the founding of the BJS, it offers no insight into the party's relationship with the RSS.

and permanently expelled from the organization.[6]

The urban political arena of Nagpur, the city wherein the RSS was born and continues to maintain a national headquarters, might seem an unlikely spot at which to observe the evidence for the deflation—or at least deflection—of revitalist dogma. But let us turn to the evidence.

THE TRANSFORMATION OF ORGANIZATIONAL STRATEGY

A change in organizational priorities is frankly acknowledged by BJS leaders. Babanrao Deshpande, the party's fulltime organizing secretary for the entire eight-district region of Vidarbha, provided a detailed district by district analysis of BJS strength in the region, an analysis notable chiefly for its emphasis on the need for socially-dispersed recruitment and associational enterprise.[7] He admitted, firstly, that the party was weakest in those districts where its social composition was most exclusive, particularly where it was Brahman-dominated. And secondly, he weighed party strength not merely in terms of the number of public offices to which its candidates have been elected, but in terms of the number of voluntary developmental associations infiltrated and controlled.

For instance, Deshpande asserted that the BJS had its strongest base in the region in the district of Buldhana. It is strongest there, he stated, because "from top to bottom" it is composed of "common men"— in other words, of persons of Maratha, Kunbi and Mali caste— "without a single Brahman" in the organization. Electorally the party has done well in Buldhana, in which it has been contesting elections since 1952. It controls one municipality and a number of small towns and villages; it has elected councillors in other municipalities and has elected a man to the zilla parishad (district panchayat). An equally strong indicator of party success, however, lies in the fact that the

---

[6]"Uttar Pradesh," in *State Politics in India*, p. 90.

[7]Interviewed on 31 January 1970. Deshpande, a Brahman, has been an RSS member since childhood and remains a dedicated activist in the organization. He was arrested in 1948 after the assassination of Gandhi, and was imprisoned for nine months. Upon release he went to work as a district organizer for the RSS in Akola district. With the founding of the BJS, he became a fulltime party worker; since 1955 he has been its regional organizing secretary. In 1968-69, Deshpande served as joint secretary of the state party organization.

BJS controls six high schools and two colleges in the district, four urban cooperative banks (one created by the party, the others successfully infiltrated), many rural cooperative credit societies, and a number of sale-purchase associations whose monopoly purchasing, milling and marketing facilities, according to Deshpande, are vital in the countryside.

In contrast, the party is weakest, according to Deshpande, in Yeotmal district, where it has voting support largely among the educated Brahman class, and controls only one high school and one college.

Deshpande ranked Nagpur district fourth in the region in party strength, but noted that its strength was almost exclusively within the city. It had never managed to elect anyone to the zilla parishad; and though controlling about 100 of the 800 gram panchayats (village councils) in the district, the party had thus far failed to gain command of any sale-purchase societies, and controlled only eight to ten rural cooperative credit societies. Within the city, however, the BJS not only had a creditable electoral record, but controlled, among many other associations and institutions, four colleges and innumerable high schools, primary schools and pre-school kindergartens. Its weakness in Nagpur district as a whole, Deshpande suggested, was due to its socially narrow base among the educated upper castes in combination with an enduring and widespread anti-Brahman sentiment.[8]

SOCIAL COMPOSITION

The social composition of the Nagpur district committee of the Jana Sangh (elected in 1968) confirms Deshpande's claim that party leadership locally tends to be drawn from the educated professional class. Of the nineteen members, ten are occupationally professionals (lawyers, doctors, professors) or at least professionally educated.[9] Community identifications are less uniform, however, indicating that the party has made a deliberate effort to incorporate representatives from many of the city's dominant caste groups. At least six are Brahmans in caste, a

[8]Ram Joshi reports that in Maharashtra as a whole the Jana Sangh's main source of support "lies in the Brahman middle class from urban localities, in contrast to Uttar Pradesh, Rajasthan, or Madhya Pradesh, where the party has some rural support." "Maharashtra," in *State Politics in India*, pp. 200-201.

[9]Information on the BJS district committee was derived from interviews with six of its members.

proportion of the total which is probably modest judged in comparison with the voting support provided to the party by the city's Brahman community. All are Hindu (with the exception of a Parsi); but in addition to the Brahman caste, representation is spread to include the Kunbi, Teli, Maratha, Sindhi, Bari, Koshti, Vaishya and Marwadi communities.

The political limitations of social exclusivism are recognized by members of the Nagpur district committee. Dr Ramprakash S. Ahuja, a Punjabi Hindu refugee from Lahore, in 1969 district general secretary and president of the working committee of the city unit of the party, relates that local leaders became sharply aware of the Jana Sangh's socially narrow appeal at the time of the 1962 elections. Since the middle 1960s, he notes, they have been taking deliberate steps to broaden its social base of support.[10] Among Brahmans, Sindhis and Hindi-speaking Telis, he explains, the party has long had good support; but these were distinctly minority communities in the city. In recent years, therefore, the party has set out to woo the numerically powerful and normally Congress-voting Kunbi and Koshti communities and, Ahuja insists, is presently encouraging informal contacts even with the traditionally hostile Muslims, Christians and scheduled castes.

The criteria adopted in the selection of party candidates for the 1969 corporation election give more concrete evidence of the change in recruitment policy. Dr Ahuja states that the party's parliamentary board, in deciding among the applicants for electoral tickets, gave consideration to four major qualifications: active party membership; personal influence in the constituency; financial ability to support candidacy; and attractiveness to voters, including such factors as community affiliation, level of education, and political experience. He exemplified the pragmatism underlying these criteria. In one ward two applicants were considered for the party's nomination; one was a deserving and active party worker, but unfortunately he was, in Ahuja's words, a "goodie-goodie" with little personal influence or voter attractiveness. In his place the party chose an organizationally less active man of the numerically dominant Teli community who was, moreover, politically shrewd, experienced, and independently wealthy.

In another ward, the parliamentary board chose a non-party candidate, Sonar (goldsmith) in caste and moneylender in occupation, because he appeared to be influential in the business community and was consi-

[10]Ahuja was interviewed on four occasions beginning 25 March 1969.

dered a man of integrity; according to Ahuja it was an opportunity for the party to make an entering wedge into an important business group. In another case the party leadership settled on a scheduled caste Mahar candidate who was also a party worker and RSS activist, an infrequent combination which seemed to offer opportunity for making headway in a community from which the BJS has thus far been almost totally excluded.

Data available on all fifty-five party candidates support the contention that the party spread its tickets far and wide, though it must be admitted that in many cases little more than a token gesture is apparent.[11] Tickets were distributed among twenty different communities.[12] Of the eleven candidates who *won* their contests, eight are Brahmans; and of the twenty-two candidates who received a vote above the city-wide party median of 570 votes, Brahmans ranked high with ten (45.4 per cent).[13] While the Brahmans—with at least seventeen of the total fifty-five candidates[14]—are thus the party's first line of defense, it is just as apparent that backup is being sought on a large scale from the numerically significant Koshti, Kunbi and Teli communities, not normally included in the Jana Sangh's phalanx, who together received sixteen tickets.

Brahman fealty to the Jana Sangh is a mixed blessing: on the one hand it seems to assure the reliable support of an important and influential minority; four of the eight winning candidates who were interviewed specifically attributed their victory in large part to the 'overwhelming

[11]Twenty-two of the fifty-five Jana Sangh candidates were interviewed; community background on the others was obtained indirectly from knowledgeable sources.

[12]Community identification is known for all but three of the BJS candidates.

[13]Ten of the eleven winners contested from wards in which Brahmans constitute a significant proportion of the voting population, seven from wards in which Brahmans are the largest single caste group. Nagpur's Brahman population lives clustered in three quite distinct areas of the city—Mahal, Dhantoli, and the southwestern Civil Station sector. Mahal, from where the Bhonsale kings ruled in pre-British days, is the old and densely populated core of the city; Dhantoli, in pre-independence days a fashionable suburb settled by the growing professional class patronized by the British, consists mainly of large old bungalows, grown seedy with time but sumptuous in comparison with most of the city; the Civil Station area, grown up almost entirely since independence, consists of a score of new housing colonies (e.g., Ambazari, Shankarnagar, Ramdaspeth) settled principally by the city's prosperous middle classes—doctors, lawyers, businessmen and upper-ranking government servants.

[14]By way of comparison, only five of the fifty-five Congress candidates are Brahmans.

support of Brahmans.[15] But at the same time the general unpopularity of Brahmans makes their close identity with the party a considerable inconvenience.[16] For the Nagpur unit of the BJS, the social extension of its support base is contingent to a large degree on its capacity to make a *convincing* display of its non-Brahmanical plans; this helps explain the party's extraordinarily ambitious and locally unprecedented effort to blanket fifty-five wards (most of them with few Brahman residents) with its candidates, a number precisely equal to the number contesting under the banner of the undeniably socially aggressive Congress party.[17]

Another indication of the party's intention to present a more heterogeneous electoral front is visible in the relatively large number of tickets distributed to non-party persons. Information available on all but three of the fifty-five candidates reveals that twenty-three (forty-two per cent) had little or no Jana Sangh background prior to the election in

[15]Two of the other four candidates were not asked the question about Brahman support; a third claimed not to have calculated caste support; and the fourth was clearly elected with the support of other communities. The four reporting large-scale Brahman support estimated anywhere from one-third to ninety per cent of their vote from that source. One of the four, himself not a Brahman, reported that Brahman loyalty to the BJS was so solid and so large in his ward that the party (in his words) "could run a light pole and win."

[16]Dr Ahuja admitted that the party was disappointed in the results of the 1969 election even though it made significant gains over previous years; his disappointment derived from the fact that its victories occurred almost entirely in wards where it anticipated victory based on previous electoral experience, not in wards where victory was dependent on the successful introduction of its new strategy. The only party victory in 1969 untinged with Brahman support was in a ward on the outskirts of the city where a landlord Kunbi won under the party banner largely owing to his influence among Kunbi farmers. He had joined the party just prior to the election, having had no previous contact with it in any form. The candidate in question was Wasudeo Shingane, interviewed on 29 July 1969.

[17]In 1962, for instance, the BJS ran only thirteen candidates (for forty-two seats). Philip Oldenburg, "Indian Urban Politics, with Particular Reference to the Nagpur Corporation," p. 96. The party's efforts in this regard cannot be explained as a simple case of balancing the ticket in accord with numerical community strength in each ward. Many candidates appear to have been nominated purely for "display" purposes—to provide the party with material evidence of its will to extend itself into a large number of hitherto ignored groups. Tickets granted to a Muslim and a Christian, for example, were surely "wasted" in this manner. Together the two received but a few score votes.

1969.[18] Their performance at the polls, generally, was much less creditable than that of the party stalwarts: only four of them tallied a vote above the party median. Their collective failure underscores the difficulties involved in sallying forth from the Jana Sangh citadels.

Dispersion socially among non-Brahmans and organizationally among non-party workers is undoubtedly made more complicated by the local party's heavy reliance on the RSS. Though the precise nature of the linkage between it and the party is difficult to establish, the *importance* of the linkage was frankly acknowledged by most of the Jana Sangh candidates who were interviewed. Since the RSS provides the party with the core of its workers—superbly organized, dedicated and presumably costless—among what social groups and where in the city *the*y are organized is surely a major factor influencing party decisions, among other things about recruitment policy and the allocation of tickets.

Of the forty-four candidates on whom relevant information is available, twenty-one have an RSS background.[19] Of these, fourteen received a total of votes above the party median; nine won their contests, a rather striking figure in view of the fact that the party had a total of only eleven winners.[20]

The social composition of the RSS organization is not easily discovered, but evidence is sufficient to indicate that the largest component in Nagpur is provided by the Brahman community. It was repeatedly affirmed by Jana Sangh candidates and workers in the Brahman-populated wards that virtually every household in their localities contained at least one RSS member. This accounts for the fact that seven of the nine winning RSS-affiliated candidates are also Brahmans.[21]

---

[18]This figure includes a few who joined the BJS at the time of the 1967 elections. At least seven of the twenty-three had earlier been active workers in other parties—Congress, NVAS, and the RPI.

[19]The number of RSS "sympathizers" would undoubtedly enlarge the figure. Since many Brahmans are in government employment, they may be expected to guard against any *overt* affiliation with an organization that has been under government attack for decades.

[20]Six of the eight winners who were interviewed reported lifelong RSS affiliation, most of them having been leaders in the organization at one time or another. The seventh respondent is a retired Brahman military officer, whose career effectively barred participation. And the eighth is a landlord Kunbi, the party's only "exceptional" winner.

[21]On the other hand, an indication that the RSS is itself socially somewhat aggregative lies in the fact that of the twenty-one BJS candidates of known RSS background, only nine are Brahmans.

The strategy of social dispersion is clearly in evidence; but it is just as obvious that the backbone of the BJS locally continues to be Brahman and RSS. The seventeen Brahman candidates (thirty per cent of the number of candidates) earned forty-four per cent of the total party vote; the twenty-one known RSS candidates (thirty-eight per cent of the number of candidates), of whom nine are Brahmans, earned fifty-nine per cent of the party vote. Candidates who were either Brahman or RSS, or both (twenty-nine candidates, or fifty-three per cent of the number of candidates) earned sixty-nine per cent of the party total.[22]

The Nagpur Jana Sangh has a long distance to go before it can describe itself as socially inclusive. This should not be used to conceal the equally important fact, however, that the party is aware of the narrowness of its social base of support and is taking steps to overcome it. It should not be forgotten that the party's opponents have nothing to gain from the Jana Sangh's success in this maneuver and much to gain from keeping alive in public consciousness the Brahman/RSS identification with the party.

ASSOCIATIONAL MANAGEMENT

In line with the observations of the party's regional organizer, Deshpande, local BJS leaders are frank to acknowledge not only their socially expansionist program, but a drive to be *materially* more appealing as well. Moreover, by virtue of their close association with the party, at least some elements of the RSS appear in agreement that a development orientation, one servicing the palpable instead of merely the psychological or spiritual needs of the people, will be more attractive to potential recruits to *either* of the two organizations than simply hanging out a welcome mat. That the BJS, in league with numerous individual RSS members, is thus remodeling itself to manage the material demands of its constituents is supported both by the statements of organizational leaders as by the heavy investment of energy by organizational workers in voluntary associations of all kinds. In certain spheres of developmental entrepreneurship, the BJS is considerably outclassed by the Congress; but there is no gainsaying that it has made impressive progress

[22]Calculations are based on NMC election returns.

in this direction.[23]

Most of the Jana Sangh candidates interviewed as part of this study revealed activities in voluntary associations. They hold executive posts in a great range of such associations, including cooperative banking and credit; housing and area development; health, welfare and education.

The Jana Sangh has been working in some of these fields longer than in others. Its establishment of networks of schools—from kindergartens through colleges—is a phenomenon which has been commented upon by many observers elsewhere in India, and presumably has a relatively lengthy history.[24] In the field of cooperative banking, the Jana Sangh locally appears to have a foothold going back at least to the early 1960s. Manohar Kholkute, a lifelong RSS member and formerly secretary of the Nagpur district Jana Sangh committee, aided in the founding and has been a director since 1963 of the Nagpur Citizens Cooperative Bank. The present district treasurer of the Jana Sangh, Vasantrao

[23]To what extent the RSS has been inspirational in these matters is questionable. Informed observers of the local RSS, in conversations with the author, tended to give it less credit than is implied in these pages. One particularly astute observer (a Congress Brahman), although admitting that the RSS does have a "progressive" wing, insisted that the Nagpur branch was mainly a stagnant collection of Brahmans, typically low-middle class economically, inspired by the Nazi vision, lacking program, support from intellectuals, or any mass appeal. Since the RSS organization did not form part of this study, I am not prepared to make a judgment on the correctness of his assessment. I did encounter enough specific instances where RSS workers displayed impressive energy and practical wisdom to suggest caution in characterizing the organization as a whole.

[24]Paul Brass remarks, for instance, that "Jana Sangh and RSS members are active in educational activities of all sorts. Many RSS members teach in schools and some have founded educational institutions. The Jana Sangh is attempting to establish in U.P. a network of private schools, controlled by party members and sympathizers, where the values which the party supports may be taught." "Uttar Pradesh," in *State Politics in India*, pp. 92-93. Angela Burger reports in her study of U.P. MLAs that a surprising number of them had set up schools. Though the Jana Sangh MLAs lagged behind their Socialist and Praja Socialist colleagues in this regard, twenty-five per cent of them had established one or two schools, and over fourteen per cent had established three or more. *Opposition in a Dominant-Party System*, pp. 224-225. In Nagpur schools often bear the reputation of belonging to one or another party, not entirely without justification. The principal of the Mohota Science College, for example, is B. N. Varadpande, chief (deputy *sanghchalak*) of the Nagpur RSS. V. B. Phatak, a senior lecturer in chemistry on his staff, is general secretary of the Nagpur RSS; and another senior lecturer in chemistry, Manoharrao Shende, is a lifelong RSS activist, in 1970 joint secretary of both the district committee and the city work-

Salpekar, and Dr Ahuja are also on the bank's board of directors.[25]

According to the party's district joint secretary, Manoharrao Shende, the BJS has also been active for some time in housing cooperatives, but its strategy has thus far emphasized infiltrating old established societies and only secondarily founding new ones. For instance, the party has had at least one or two representatives among the directors of the large and well-capitalized Vidarbha Premier Cooperative Housing Society for more than a decade, while the Dharampeth Housing Development Cooperative Society, founded in 1959, is headed entirely by persons sympathetic with the Jana Sangh.[26]

Exemplary of more recent involvement, local party workers founded, according to Shende, at least five credit cooperatives in the last few months of 1969.

ADAPTATION IN CHITNIS PARK

Examples of the versatile and energetic adaptation of the new strategy to local conditions abound in the testimony of Jana Sangh party workers. An examination of a few such cases will illustrate the scope of these activities; it may also indicate that the qualities of leadership, found of increasing value in other political organizations in Nagpur, are achieving an analogous position in the Jana Sangh party organization. As we have seen, post-independence politics increasingly places a premium on instrumental attitudes towards community relationships, on skill in aggregating discrete groups into a wide variety of associational structures, and on capacity for competing against other groups in dispersed associational arenas. There is some evidence that these are gradually supplanting the attitudes and skills suitable for fostering communal and ideological solidarity in the Jana Sangh organization.

---

ing committee of the BJS. Shende was interviewed in this connection on 10 January 1970.

[25]Kholkute was interviewed on 23 October 1969; Salpekar on 23 January 1970. Kholkute is also a state director, Maharashtra Cooperative Banks Association, and was formerly director, Maharashtra State Cooperative Bank, and vice-chairman, Nagpur District Central Cooperative Bank.

[26]The current (1970) president of the Dharampeth society, Lawyer G. K. Athawale, an RSS worker for twenty years, is also regional general secretary of the BJS-affiliated trade union combine—the Bharatiya Mazdur Sangh (Indian workers' union). Athawale was interviewed on 20 December 1969.

In Chitnis Park ward, located in the heavily Brahman Mahal area of the city, the party's evolving strategy is readily apparent. Diwakar Dhakras, the BJS winning candidate in that ward in the 1969 election, came to the party with ordinarily perfectly acceptable credentials—he is a Brahman, well educated, and an active worker in the RSS.[27] His credentials were marred by the fact, however, that he had few activities outside of the RSS, few contacts outside of the Brahman community, and little experience in competitive politics. The manner in which he waged a successful election campaign is illustrative of the new party priorities.

Dhakras, who is in his late thirties, has been a member of the RSS since the age of fourteen As a young man in his native Bhandara district, he was in charge of a local RSS shaka (unit); after coming to Nagpur he eventually became chief of an RSS branch, having eight or ten affiliated shakas. Though he presently holds no offices in the organization, he is an active daily participant in RSS functions in Chitnis Park.[28]

Dhakras joined the BJS at the time of its founding in 1951; up to 1967, however, he was politically inactive. In that year he was made secretary of the Nagpur central constituency, one of four such posts in the city bearing responsibility for organizing party activities.

Thus, apart from his business (he operates a printing press establishment in Chitnis Park) Dhakras' time in recent years has been absorbed largely in RSS and party activities; he admitted having otherwise a very thin record of associational work to his credit, particularly among the people of Chitnis Park. When the party asked him to contest the municipal election only a few months prior to the event, he was obliged to rely heavily on the cultivation of the ward which his associates in the RSS and party had already performed.

The background and energetic pursuits of one such associate—the youthful Baban Nandanpawar—are particularly indicative of the new currents in the party.[29] A high school teacher since 1961, Nandanpawar comes from the same basic mold as Dhakras: he is a Brahman, college educated, and a lifelong member of the RSS.[30] But in contrast to

---

[27]Interviewed on 12 January 1970.

[28]According to Dhakras, Chitnis Park ward holds six shakas with a total active membership of about two hundred, ranging upwards from the age of eight.

[29]Nandanpawar, then twenty-nine years old, was interviewed on 18 January 1970.

[30]Active in the RSS from the age of six, Nandanpawar is a flute-player in the marching band shaka which meets at the nearby headquarters building of the RSS.

Dhakras, he had for some years been highly active among the people of Chitnis Park, and was therefore a valuable campaign worker.

Nandanpawar joined the BJS in 1965 and was immediately appointed organizing secretary of the Nagpur central constituency, assigned to work chiefly among persons of the scheduled castes and scheduled tribes. He has since then devoted about two hours daily to the investigation and resolution of such problems as street drainage and water supply, quality of food supply, and admission to schools and hospitals. He is active in the cooperative movement: secretary and founder of a credit cooperative established at his high school in 1967, and an executive in another credit cooperative created in 1966 among local teachers.

Though Nandanpawar freely acknowledges the importance of Brahman and RSS support to Dhakras' victory, he is emphatic that the role of intermediation on behalf of heterogeneous community groups has by far the greater impact on electoral outcomes in general. Dhakras did not receive the full support of either Brahmans or RSS members, he points out, and was heavily dependent on the goodwill generated among other communities by party workers like himself. Three of the four candidates in the ward were Brahman, a fact which considerably reduced communal solidarity. According to Nandanpawar, Dhakras (whose total vote was 1,685) received barely 500 of the 1,000 Brahman votes in the ward. Even the RSS apparently failed to maintain a solid front. Nandanpawar estimates that of the 500 active and inactive members of the RSS in the ward, about twenty per cent threw their votes to other candidates. The split in RSS ranks he attributes to personal friendships, family and caste ties, divisions which easily take on importance in such a small-scale election.

It is not surprising why Dhakras' credentials—Brahman community, RSS affiliation, and advanced education—were not adequate insurance of electoral victory. And we can understand why *since* the election he has picked up the voluntary associational gauntlet himself. Late in 1969, Dhakras and his associates founded the Vivekananda Credit Cooperative Society, part of a party plan, according to Dhakras, which aims at the creation of at least one such society to service the credit needs of every three wards. Additionally, Dhakras has even more recently been instrumental (and again, he points out, in accord with party policy) in securing loans for small businessmen in his locality, a policy made feasible by the nationalization of private banking firms carried out in 1969. Thus far, states Dhakras, loans ranging from Rs 200 to Rs 4,000 have been obtained, principally for about forty or fifty

Mochis (shoemakers), in addition to several cycle-renters, tailors and other small shopkeepers. He and his workers prepare "creditworthiness" studies of individuals in their area, he explains, on the basis of which banks are persuaded to grant loans.

In the Chitnis Park case we have seen evidence of the Jana Sangh's increasing concern for instrumental community relationships and for greater investment in developmental entrepreneurship. In the next case, we will view the manner in which the BJS has infiltrated a particularly important associational arena—the weaver cooperatives—from which it has ordinarily been excluded. The party's efforts in this direction must be judged mere pinpricks, but the political importance of the Koshtis in Nagpur endows Jana Sangh strategy in their regard with more than passing interest.[31]

PENETRATION OF THE WEAVER COMMUNITY

The Koshtis have long been considered a Congress preserve, though an extremely unruly one, and no other party organization has yet managed to permanently unite them in opposition. In the early 1960s, the Vidarbhan separatists succeeded in organizing many of the weavers behind the banner of the NVAS, and in the general and municipal elections of 1962 the Congress took a considerable beating.[32] But the Vidarbhan banner ceased soon to wave so bravely, and many of its more prominent leaders eventually returned to the Congress fold. The granting of the Congress parliamentary ticket for the Nagpur constituency to a leading Koshti politician in 1967 sealed the fate of the NVAS, at least for the time being.

The Koshtis are a quarrelsome lot, however, divided amongst themselves, a fact which encourages opposition groups to seek their favor despite the unfavorable odds. In 1967, the Jana Sangh granted its own parliamentary ticket to N.M. Belekar, a Koshti, an elderly lawyer prominent in the cooperative movement in the 1940s and 1950s.[33] Since victory was quite beyond the party's potential in Nagpur, the ploy was obviously designed with an eye on future strategy.

Belekar, who placed fourth in the election with 35,332 votes (9.95

[31]Background of the Koshtis is related in Chapter 3, above.
[32]The Vidarbhan movement is noted in Chapter 2, above.
[33]Interviewed on 14 December 1969.

per cent of the total), behind the Congress, Communist and NVAS candidates, admits that the tactic did not carry the Jana Sangh very far into the Koshti wards. He estimates that he received hardly five to seven per cent of the weaver vote, and only a negligible number actively campaigned for him. None of the numerous cooperative organizations among them backed his candidacy. His support amongst the weavers, according to him, came solely from those whom he had personally obliged at some time in the past.

Belekar, who only became affiliated with the BJS shortly prior to the 1967 election, nonetheless is confident that gains can be made by the party. Congress' dismal showing among the weavers in the municipal election of 1969, he notes, is patent evidence that the weavers continue to be dissatisfied with that party.[34] According to him, part of their dissatisfaction lies in the fact that the provision of credit, a commodity much needed in the economically fluctuating handloom industry, has all along been the exclusive prerogative of the Congress-dominated cooperative organizations, whose judgment of credit-worthiness has always been guided more by political than economic considerations. The Jana Sangh's recent promotion of direct bank loans to individual weavers, in his opinion, has therefore great appeal.

In addition to giving support to such demands as for direct bank loans, production subsidies in the slack season, and a ban on powerloom production of colored saris, the BJS has also sought to make headway among the weavers by infiltrating the cooperative organizations themselves. In this tactic, the party has already had a minor but nonetheless significant success. The particular object of its attention was the Winkar Dukandar Samyukta Saunstha (united society of weavers and merchants), into whose managing committee the party succeeded in installing a party worker after a prolonged and bitter struggle.

The United Society is a marketing cooperative created in May 1949, charged with such tasks (according to its constitution) as standardizing the quality and improving the sales of handloom saris, contributing to the welfare of weavers, and encouraging cooperation among weavers and between weavers and the cloth merchants and wholesalers. It serves primarily the Hindu weavers of Nagpur city selling their handloom products through the open handloom market in Gandhibagh.[35]

---

[34]Not one of the eight Congress Koshti candidates contesting the 1969 election won his race.

[35]This excludes Momin Muslim handloom products, household powerloom

According to the president of the United Society, Krushnarao Zunke[36], the Jana Sangh's successful intruder, the association has always functioned in a renegade capacity; it is in essence an effort to introduce the cooperative principle on a limited scale in the free market arena where it stands in competitive relationship to the immense Congress-patronized handloom cooperative system.

The United Society's income is obtained from a modest fee charged for the stamp which must be affixed to every handloom product sold in the Gandhibagh market. Zunke states that the association processes an average of 165,000 saris per month, earning a net profit annually of about Rs 30,000. The society's income is not large enough to spark a civil war among the weavers, but certainly is substantial enough to be an attractive asset. Though it is not presently a recipient of government development funds, the society does have the advantage of being positioned very strategically astride the biggest commercial center in the city.[37]

Zunke was elected president of the United Society in February 1969; from 1952 to 1969, according to him, no election to its managing committee had been held. For most of the period, the association had been dominated by the lanky ex-wrestler Dhondbaji Hedau, former MLA and Koshti political leader since 1952.[38] During these years, Zunke relates, the association achieved little but the construction of a high school for weaver students, most of its funds having been swallowed by its managing committee.

---

and factory products, and cooperative handloom products, for all of which separate marketing facilities exist.

[36]Interviewed on 17 December 1969. He is a college graduate, Koshti by caste, and at one time or another has been an independent weaver, master weaver, commission agent and cloth merchant.

[37]The Gandhibagh market is reputedly one of the world's largest remaining handloom markets; though something of an economic museumpiece, it is one of the most exciting spots in the city, reminiscent simultaneously of the Wall Street stock exchange and a crowded Sears-Roebuck salesroom. Some of Gandhibagh market's two hundred or more private cloth merchants and wholesalers have a gross annual business individually, according to Zunke, as high as two million rupees.

[38]Interviewed on 19 December 1969. A fifty year old illiterate, Hedau rode the Vidarbhan movement to victory in 1962 in both corporation and state legislative elections. He was president of the United Society for fifteen years. For his role in the akhada dispute involving the NCAFC, see Chapter 5, above.

Zunke's affiliation with the Jana Sangh came in the middle of a court battle to legally force the managers of the United Society to hold an election for the choosing of new officers.[39] Spending Rs 2,000 of his own resources, Zunke finally won his case, heard before the Charitable Trusts Commission, which ultimately sanctioned an election.[40]

The election was vigorously contested: thirty-one weavers stood for the eleven weaver seats on the managing committee, and 12,447 weaver members cast their ballots, a rather impressive turnout for an election of such apparently limited scope.[41] The results gave Zunke and his associates only a narrow margin of authority on the new managing committee; only eight of the seventeen members clearly support him.[42] He is dependent for his position on the committee to a number of political independents, and for this reason admits to having softpedalled his affiliation with the BJS.

It would be unwarranted to assume that the Jana Sangh had herewith clinched its bid for political support among the Koshtis: the United Society is a minor enterprise, dependent almost entirely on private rather than governmental resources, and liable to be removed from the Jana Sangh orbit in the same way it was gained. Nonetheless, the episode testifies to the party's awareness that political headway must be won bit by bit through earnest and prolonged competition in the diverse and scattered arenas of voluntary association. In such arenas, it must also be aware, ideological and communal solidarity count for much less than pragmatic bargaining; organizational partisanship for much less than the qualities of developmental entrepreneurship.

[39]Up until the 1967 general elections, Zunke had belonged to no political party; at that time, along with Belekar, he joined the BJS. However, his elder brother had been a prominent politician among the weavers, twice contesting against Hedau.

[40]The old leaders attempted to thwart his plans, according to Zunke, by conducting an impromptu "show of hands" election on 19 March 1968; but their effort was held to be invalid by the commission.

[41]The association's constitution is somewhat ambiguous, but a member is considered to be anyone engaged in the handloom production or handloom products sales business. According to a map prepared for the election, the eleven electoral zones of the weaver community embrace parts or all of nineteen pre-reapportionment wards, or approximately fifty-eight mohallas.

[42]The weavers are entitled to eleven, the merchants to six of the United Society's managing positions.

SUMMARY

Followers of the Jana Sangh are not likely to quickly forget the party's natal mission, for its task of reinvigorating and purifying India's allegedly emasculated and adulterated culture is regularly reaffirmed for it by RSS leaders. Certainly it would be a great mistake for scholars to fly to the extreme of denigrating every instance of ideological expression as mere rhetoric; the endless hours of indoctrination which youthful RSS recruits receive at daily meetings of the shaka, at summer encampments, and at great public gatherings cannot but have an effect on the political attitudes and behavior of those of them who pass as adults into the Jana Sangh political organization.

Nonetheless, the Nagpur branch of the Bharatiya Jana Sangh is today clearly altering its organizational strategy. The change is visible in at least two major ways: for one, the party is striving to enlarge its social base of support, de-homogenizing its community composition and making itself attractive and accessible to groups hitherto excluded; and for another, it is giving its program a concretely developmental orientation by actively competing for influence or control in associations where management can directly influence the distribution of government developmental resources.

The probable effect of the first has been to introduce greater social incongruity into the organization, in terms of the socio-economic status of its members, and with it heightened discontinuity in agreement on organizational objectives. The restoration of the traditional hierarchy of status, for example, with its attendant "privileged access to scarce resources," cannot long remain among these objectives.[43] The likely effect of the second has been to bring the party more firmly within the consensual framework of competitive politics: to make it partner with virtually every other political organization to the discrete negotiation of particularistic demands on the material resources of government. Thus, the party's organizational strategy has probably grown less innovative, less guided by ideology, having moved closer to a "survival orientation," a situation which Myron Weiner argues has reached full flower in the Congress organization, and which this chapter has contended is beginning to bud in the Jana Sangh.[44]

---

[43]Harold Gould's comment in "Religion and Politics in a U.P. Constituency," in *South Asian Politics and Religion*, p. 53.

[44]A basic theoretical assumption of Weiner's study of the Congress organi-

This is no more than what Rajni Kothari has been urging with respect to the national Jana Sangh party. A new federal consensus is emerging in India, he writes, more firmly and distinctly left of center than ever before, pushing *all* parties willy-nilly before it. In recent years, he declares,

> both the fact that the only national parties that have been consistently growing in strength are the two Communist parties and the fact that the various regional parties have a 'non-position' on so many national issues are likely to strengthen the hands of the new generation in the Congress keen to revive a left of center consensus in the country.... The 'rightist' parties are ceasing to press an alternative ideological position: the Jana Sangh, in its search for a national and secular identity, is shedding a great many of its earlier extremist positions on issues like language and religion (e.g. the holy cow)....

"In a society so ridden with basic developmental problems and in which government plays such a dominant role," he adds, "a left of center consensus is the only natural one to be articulated and institutionalized."[45]

With or without the consent of its militant RSS cadre, the Jana Sangh in Nagpur is rapidly making peace with the prevailing system,

---

zation concerned the importance of a "survival orientation" among its leaders, by which he meant that "leaders give a higher priority to maintaining the organization than to any external goals. By looking at the response of party leaders to proposals to change the structure of the organization or to adopt new policies, we can not only see why some proposals are rejected and others accepted but also, and more fundamentally, discover what the party leadership views as essential to the survival of the organization." The leading theme of his study was "that Congress party leaders, in order to succeed politically, are concerned, first and foremost, with doing whatever is necessary to adapt the party to its environment.... Congress is primarily concerned with recruiting members and winning support. It does not mobilize; it aggregates. It does not seek to innovate; it seeks to adapt. Though a few Congressmen dream of transforming the countryside, in practice most Congressmen are concerned simply with winning elections." *Party Building in a New Nation: The Indian National Congress*, pp. 8, 14-15.

[45]*Politics in India*, pp. 197-198. Angela Burger, who conducted her research in 1963, found evidence even then that the BJS was ideologically ambivalent. "In choice of words," she wrote, "the Jana Sangh has emphasized the Indian (Hindu) stream, but the substantive content of many policy statements is almost indistinguishable from that of other parties." *Opposition in a Dominant-Party System*, p. 278.

whose unexalted and pragmatic code of political behavior is fast be-coming the Jana Sangh's own. To say this is not to exonerate the BJS of the radical, sometimes fanatic, brand of politics which it has definitely played from time to time. Nor is it meant to imply that the change will operate necessarily to the benefit of the party or its constituents. It is to assert, in line with a number of other observers, that the party is un-dergoing a fundamental transformation away from a goal of cultural revitalization and towards one of cultural accommodation. The Jana Sangh has given clear notice that for all *practical* purposes the sacred cow has been moved off center stage, its place taken by the profane lure of developmental resources.

7

Voluntary Associations and Political Strategy

In the preceding discussions of political leadership, factional and party organization, reference has been made repeatedly to the strategic utility of voluntary associations. As we have seen, local politicians are investing enormous time and energy into the management of these associations; and control of them is now clearly a staple of local organizational goals. Surely, the calculation of political benefits to be gained from such intense associational activity includes anticipation of enhanced personal or organizational appeal to voters. Precisely how voter support is obtained through the associational medium has yet to be separately treated. Indeed, we must reserve our judgment of the strategic utility of voluntary associations until we have dealt more adequately with voter response to associational managers. It remains, then, for this chapter to make explicit the way in which voluntary associations provide a point of contact between politicians and voters and, more specifically, to elucidate the nature of the electoral obligations incurred by the political managers of voluntary associations in their quest for voter support.

This chapter focuses, therefore, on the *campaign* strategies employed by candidates in the 1969 municipal contest, since these involve consideration of voter demands and expectations in the most immediate sense. It attempts to determine the *actual* linkages between associational activity and the mechanics of soliciting voter support by tracing the integration of voluntary associations into political campaign organizations, by examining the influence of voluntary associations on campaign tactics, and by assessing the impact of associational entrepreneurship on electoral outcome.

As in previous chapters, we will encounter again the important question of the role played by ascriptive identities in the summoning of political support and, also, that of programatic party appeals. But we will meet here more directly than before the question of the basis upon which the accountability of politicians to voters is measured locally. While our survey thus far would suggest strongly that voluntary associations are attractive to politicians to a significant extent because they command fluid resources for use in responding to popular demands, are politicians *in fact* using their control of associations to obligate voters to themselves? Do the kinds of obligation thus produced transcend or replace other bonds between politicians and voters? To complement our new class of political entrepreneurs, are we now confronting a new class of voters, with new expectations and (potentially) with new means for obtaining effective response to their demands?

CAMPAIGN STRATEGY

In considering the influence of voluntary associations on campaign strategy, it is necessary to bear in mind that local politicians are by no means restricted to associational devices in charting their electoral course. An election campaign in Nagpur is a no-holds barred contest in which cunning and ingenuity in outwitting opponents count far more than scrupulous observance of the rules. Virtually every stratagem is tolerated—and tried. Exploiting voluntary associational ties, while exceedingly important, is but one of these. Let us begin by briefly surveying the alternatives, for an awareness of the variety of election practices currently in use is essential to a realistic and fair judgment of the specific role of voluntary associations.[1]

Political strategists naturally take into account the social and economic status of their constituents in plotting campaign approaches. Strategy appropriate for one group may have little effect on another. In Nagpur, the numerous and economically impoverished slumdwellers are often

---

[1]For a more detailed examination of election practices in Nagpur, see my essay, "Strategies of Political Bargaining in Indian City Politics," in *The City in Indian Politics*, Donald B. Rosenthal, editor (New Delhi: Thomson Press Limited, 1976), pp. 192-212. I have relied heavily on this essay in preparing portions of this chapter.

subjected to some of the more unsavory products of the strategists' imaginations. The poor are wined and dined, wooed with gifts and bribed with cash. There are free haircuts, free saris, free mutton dinners, free entertainment, and plenty of free intoxicants. [2] That many of the poor take advantage of the moment in these ways is an indisputable fact.[3] Precisely how many of them do so is far from certain. Estimates vary widely and few commentators do more than hazard a guess. A reasonably neutral estimate by a prominent Congress leader put the proportion of the electorate that is "purchased" in short-term negotiations immediately preceding local elections at twenty-five per cent. In his opinion, most of this was not in the form of direct gifts of cash or other material inducements, but more in the form of indirect donations to various local associations and groups. The more direct sorts of gift giving seem more prevalent in the worst slum areas, where any kind of indirection might seem the equivalent of deprivation, of whose characteristics slumdwellers are only too well aware.[4]

With respect to such short-term investments by candidates, there is simply no way to directly correlate the amount of rupees spent with the

[2]Though prohibition was then in force, bootleg liquor (in the form of so-called "tonic" and "tincture") constituted a large local industry. So freely flowed the liquor in one ward that a reveller was reliably reported to have dropped dead of overconsumption on election day. The informant noted dryly that the unfortunate individual had managed to cast his vote.

[3]So do some of the middle class. An acquaintance (a middle-aged professor of language and an experienced political organizer) related a revealing account of his voting decision in 1969. He had no particular interest in the election in his ward, and was unfamiliar with the candidates. One of the candidates, in the course of canvassing, stumbled on a formula that won my informant's support. The candidate, a successful contractor, offered to rebuild a small backyard shrine, used for religious purposes in the neighborhood, in return for voting support. Agreement was obtained. The candidate ultimately won the election. Shortly thereafter, to assure that the "deal" had not been forgotten, the professor sent his young son to remind the newly-installed corporator of his obligation.

[4]One lady candidate, matron of a rich landowning family, attributed her loss in the 1969 contest to a misjudgment of voter expectations. She boasted that she and her husband were well known for their large donations to charitable institutions in the city, and they were not prepared to acquiesce to the less dignified demands of the "backward class" voters in her ward. On the last night of the campaign, she related, their leaders came to her home requesting "negotiations." Though she had repeatedly promised suitable *post*-election rewards for their support, she refused to make any tangible *pre*-election show of her good faith. Her attachment to principle, she confessed, was apparently not appreciated.

number of votes each candidate secured. Since candidates often spend among the same people, the utility of what can only be called bribery is open to considerable question. The leader of one *zopada* (hutment) colony reported that Rs 2,000 were funneled into his locality by several candidates, without any benefit to any of them. The same group that posed as the "Jana Sangh workers" on behalf of the Jana Sangh candidate doubled as workers of any other candidate with money to spend. The Jana Sangh candidate paid the group Rs 1,000 for their assistance, he indicated, but tallied less than twenty votes in the colony. In this case, at least, the material cost of support clearly exceeded the political value of votes obtained.

Every effort is made, of course, to keep the compensated persons "honest" on election day—that is, to assure that they vote for the correct benefactor; but there is no perfect system for doing so. Very common throughout the city is the practice of insisting that the recipient individual take a vow of loyalty to the donor in front of his peers.[5] The device undoubtedly works in some cases, but the only *certain* beneficiaries, indeed, are the urban poor, who appear to exploit the situation for all it is worth.[6]

Since such conditions place considerable demands on the personal resources of politicians, they quite naturally seek to economize on their expenditures by introducing tactical contrivances designed to baffle the system. These range from outright kidnaping (of voters or political rivals) to the spreading of false rumors, character defamation, intimidation of voters by strongarmed henchmen, paid withdrawals of opposing candidates and the setting up of bogus candidacies. Particularly for those politicians lacking in personal wealth or popularity, or bearing unattractive ethnolinguistic, communal or lineage credentials among certain sectors of the electorate, these techniques are especially alluring.

---

[5]A side-benefit of the "loyalty oath" procedure is that it publishes the act of gift giving to at least a small circle of associates, among whom there is often a "spy" acting on behalf of an opposing candidate. Planting such individuals in rival campaign organizations is a frequently acknowledged and obviously useful part of strategy. By the end of the campaign, of course, few shady dealings remain in the shade.

[6]Precisely how much of the campaign windfall actually "trickles down" to individual voters is a matter of conjecture. Respondents throughout the city generally described cash gifts to individual voters of from five to ten rupees, and such non-cash items as intoxicants, free haircuts, free food and so on would have little effect unless widely distributed. My impression is that local influentials get a disproportionate share of the benefits, but that the bulk of them are distributed rather thinly among the voters.

In effect they substitute artificial for natural bonds of accountability, weakening voter bargaining power by undermining their capacity to freely choose.

Pre-election withdrawals and bogus candidacies are especially common and were reported in virtually every ward contest in the city. Bogus candidacies may be arranged for two related reasons: either to bottle up voting groups which a contestant feels he cannot obtain in any event, or to siphon off support from a leading rival. The first (the sealing off of voting groups) is intended to make voter support non-transferable due to previous commitment; that is, with its votes committed to an unpromising candidate, the target group is guarded from interfering otherwise with the election outcome. The second (siphoning support from a leading rival) constitutes a more direct attack on the rival's support base; it is an effort to split the base by inserting an alternative candidacy (other than one's own) attractive to the opponent's presumed supporters. In both cases, the intent is to manipulate voter choice through the formation of collusive coalitions among candidates who contest ostensibly as antagonists.[7]

Pre-election withdrawals are an alternative means to manipulate voter choice simply by decreasing the number of candidates. They are much easier to document than bogus candidacies since they must usually be given extraordinary publication to have any effect. Whereas the bogus candidate can rely on the official publication of his candidacy to announce the fact that he is in the race, a withdrawal has to be given special acknowledgment (usually in the form of a printed notice) in order to inform the voters that the reverse is true.[8]

The actual machinations of bogus candidacies and withdrawals provide an interesting sideshow to the mainstream of election campaigning; they not infrequently achieve rather bizarre effects. In many cases an

---

[7]Verification of bogus candidacies in any but a limited way is naturally not feasible, since these alliances are privately arranged and take their effect from this privacy. Recognition of the practice is extremely widespread, however, and a sufficient number of concrete cases were unearthed to indicate that it is widespread in fact.

[8]Withdrawals are technically not permitted after a certain cut-off date weeks before the election, so the withdrawing candidate's name will necessarily appear on the ballot in any event. Most withdrawals are therefore announced through the circulation of printed leaflets. Several such withdrawal circulars are reproduced in my essay, "Strategies of Political Bargaining in Indian City Politics," in *The City in Indian Politics,* cited above.

exchange of funds does take place, suggesting that cooperation in such arrangements may be a lucrative enterprise. Candidates and political leaders reported in interviews that they had sometimes paid or been paid substantial sums for complicity in the arrangements. In some instances a market atmosphere seems to have completely overtaken election planning, and economic motives to have replaced political ones. Some candidates were alleged to have made a commercial enterprise of contesting elections, regularly withdrawing when the price was right.

Such tactics as described above occur whether or not candidates in a particular contest are all, or mainly, of one community or of many different communities. Where candidates are of different communities, voters no doubt discriminate among them in part on this basis; but they are often unable to do so since the community identifications of contestants are rarely a perfect reflection of community distribution in the ward. The politician's problem of decreasing voter options would of course be vastly simplified if the community in every case could be depended upon to deliver voting groups; ascriptive identity is certainly among the cheapest political resources. The prevalence of such tactics as have been examined here is an indication that the task is a lot more complicated.

This is not to say that group voting is uncommon, or that ascriptive affiliations play no part in local elections. "Vote banks" are frequently mentioned by candidates, and they are organized often, no doubt, on the basis of community affiliation. But the identification of a politician with any particular community does not assure that that group's votes will be transferred to him without hard bargaining, much less that the votes of other communities needed to achieve a winning coalition will be provided at little or no cost.

THE LIMITS OF COERCION

Virtually the whole range of tactical contrivances alternative to voluntary associations showed up in the carefully designed campaign strategy of a candidate in one of the city's westside wards. In this particular case circumstances led the Congress candidate, Govindrao—, to more systematically exploit artificial devices for establishing his relationship with the voters than was true in most wards. Here was a candidate with ample personal resources but with little record of political activity in the ward, few contacts with the voters, virtually no involvement in voluntary associations, and affiliation to a minority community.[9] To establish his credentials with the voters, he and his supporters were led to compress endeavors ordinarily consuming years of patient labor into the few weeks of the campaign period. Heavy reliance on last minute tactics inevitably gave a rather crude and aggressive edge to his campaign, but at the same time magnified an aspect of local politics which otherwise would be blurred by its diffusion over time. Govindrao's strategy hinged on his ability to quickly obligate electoral support, to take extraordinary precautions to guard his likely supporters from his opponents' blandishments (in part by reducing the number of his opponents), and finally to deliver his supporters intact to the polls. We examine it in some detail, both for the illumination it casts on the craftsmanship of local political strategists as for the contrast it offers to the association-centered strategies we will shortly consider.

Govindrao, a socially prominent Brahman and lawyer, was fortunate in having as his campaign manager Premnath—, also a Brahman and lawyer, but with his background enriched with long political experience. Premnath organized their activities according to a strict itinerary and on the basis of careful pre-planning of each step, a procedure he credits to his lengthy association with the Nagpur branch of a Western firm.

Premnath's initial step was to secure large-scale maps of the ward, on which he chalked out zones in which his workers were to concentrate. Doubting the reliability of the voter lists supplied by the municipal authorities, he hired four persons to conduct a census of the electorate. They tabulated the number of listed voters who had moved, where they had moved, the names and ages of new residents, and the community identities of all voters. House numbers were plotted one by one on the maps, and the resident voters listed by house number and community affiliation to facilitate rapid and efficient contact. Premnath used over one hundred campaign workers—unemployed persons, students and government employees—drawn almost entirely from among his own associates.

The private census revealed that officially listed figures of voter registration were much exaggerated; there appeared to be almost eight hundred fewer voters in residence than was officially claimed. Since the ward is settled by a large number of government employees and well-

[9]This account is based largely on interviews with the three leading candidates and with the campaign manager of the winning candidate.

to-do families, often having little interest in local elections, it has a reputation for light voter turnout. Armed with an accurate census, Govindrao
and Premnath reckoned that no more than sixty per cent of the qualified
electorate would actually go to the polls; their estimate came within
twenty votes of the ultimate tally which, in accord with expectations,
was one of the lowest in the city. Since eight candidates planned to share
in the meager total, cautious maneuver was essential.

In contrast to some of the other candidates, neither Govindrao nor
Premnath had an established relationship with the voters or local leadership in the ward. To overcome their handicap, they chose a two-pronged
approach, working on the one hand through strategically positioned
government bureaucrats and on the other hand through local community
leaders. The first was contingent on the vulnerability of hundreds of
low-ranking government employees (peons, bearers, sweepers, washermen) attached to the numerous government departments and agencies
in the ward; the second was an acknowledgment of the need to oblige
voters in a more personal and positive manner.

According to the candidate, Govindrao, the threat of deprivation
against vulnerable employees was the key to victory in his ward. From
a notebook he provided a brief sketch of some of the government personnel who were able to exert leverage on his behalf (stating explicitly,
in each case, the type of leverage available):

1) An executive engineer in the public works department; controls
allocation of housing quarters for large numbers of government
employees; may threaten removal of housing privileges.

2) An executive in education department of zilla parishad; exerts
influence over heads of schools in the ward who are dependent for
financial support on the government; heads of schools, in turn,
carry weight with school staffs.

3) An assistant commissioner in the police department; exerts influence among police families in terms of employment, housing,
and so on.

4) A manager of a government rest house; exercises influence among
rest house staff (cooks, bearers, sweepers) dependent for housing
and employment.

5) A manager of the government milk scheme centers in the ward;
influential among milk distributors dependent for employment.

Premnath, while conceding the utility of such pressures, emphasized
the alternative approach, insisting that a cooperative relationship
between candidate and voter rooted in mutual obligation was by far the

more valuable in local elections. It was necessary, apart from coercive gestures, to convince the voters that Govindrao's candidacy was synonymous with effective intercession. Premnath went to great lengths to show courtesy and respect to voters normally ignored in the course of events. To further secure their confidence, it was necessary to repeatedly contact and woo their leaders. In this effort, Premnath made it a rule to use go-betweens of the voters' caste or religious community. As he put it, "I moved a Madrasi amongst Madrasis, a Muslim amongst Muslims, a Kunbi amongst Kunbis." These intermediaries were given voter lists broken down by community affiliation and they, rather than Govindrao and Premnath, made the initial contacts.

Thus, both friendly and coercive forms of inducement were brought to bear on the electorate.[10] Since similar tactics were being utilized by opposing candidates, however, strategy was adapted to further constrain voter choice through the simple expedient of eliminating rivals. Govindrao admitted having sought the withdrawal of at least three candidates; but he was successful in only one case, in which the candidate pulled out late in the campaign, according to Govindrao, for an amount of money equivalent to his expenditures up to that point in the race. In a second case, that of a tribal candidate, Govindrao was reasonably contented when assured that the individual would not withdraw for any *other* candidate, thus sealing off the tribal voters behind a man with no likelihood of victory. The tribal admitted to Govindrao that his candidacy was bogus, but insisted that he was already too heavily obligated to his "sponsor" to withdraw without reprisal. In the third case, when it became known that Govindrao was anxious to negotiate the candidate's withdrawal, the candidate was "kidnaped," according to Govindrao, and held incommunicado until the election was over.

In spite of such bold machinations, voters can still slip from the candidate's grasp unless the most thorough precautions are taken to keep them in tow. This is especially true among the poorer class of voters, who are so economically dependent and so vulnerable to reprisals that it is difficult for any single candidate to outbid his rivals. Total dependence is almost an advantage, in this respect, for the poor can then demand more lavish inducements.

This fact shows up most clearly in the last few days and nights of

[10]While admitting having used other kinds of material inducements in the campaign, Govindrao and Premnath denied having made any cash bribes to the voters.

the campaign. The notorious "nocturnal negotiations" of this period are frequently of critical importance. Candidates at this point make extraordinary last minute efforts to outwit their opponents, using whatever methods seem necessary and pushing the boundaries of permissible action to the limit. For instance, Premnath operated six automobiles[11] during these last nights; his workers continuously cruised the ward in an effort to keep under observation Govindrao's known supporters as well as his opponents. Key voters among the poorer groups in the ward had constantly to be entertained, wined and dined in these last days; if left alone, they were liable to be lost. One of Govindrao's rivals, a member of a particularly wealthy family, sent out his own mobilized squads late at night laden, according to Premnath, with bootleg liquor and other enticements. To baffle his plans Premnath devised a system of automobile surveillance designed to give his rival's emissaries not a moment of privacy with their target groups of voters. Premnath's drivers were instructed to blink their headlights once, in passing near one another, to signal their identity; any other vehicle operating in late night hours was likely to be that of a political rival. If one was encountered, it was relentlessly pursued, making private negotiations difficult to conduct. Premnath's workers were equipped with cameras, an additional device for thwarting illicit transactions.

In any democratic polity the voter is prized; on election day the value of a vote can be judged to some extent by the lengths to which opponents go in mustering voters to the polling booth. In Nagpur the value of the vote apparently approaches its maximum. Few serious candidates leave anything to chance on election day, taking every precaution to assure that their supporters actually do arrive at the polls. Premnath utilized nine automobiles and several cycle rikshas, for example, to convey his voters to the polling booths.[12] At each of several booths, lists of Govindrao's known supporters were retained; teams of workers checked off names as voters were delivered to cast their votes. Six to eight workers were assigned from each polling station as foot

---

[11]The number would be unimpressive in the United States; in Nagpur, where automobiles remain a rare luxury possession, it constitutes an almost unparalleled mechanized unit of political warfare. In 1966, in all of Nagpur district, there were only 5,041 registered motor cars. Bureau of economics and statistics, government of Maharashtra, *Socio Economic Review and District Statistical Abstract of NagpurDistrict (1965-66)*, p. 97.

[12]Their use is technically illegal, but the rule is observed most often in the breach.

workers to individually contact voters at their homes, while two other workers manned autos assigned to each polling station, picking up groups of voters from pre-planned locations.

Quickwittedness and vigilance were vital because even at this late stage competition for votes remained intense. Premnath, with his talent for organization, was particularly astute in devising election day strategy. He arranged, for example, for certain locality leaders to stand innocently at streetside at some point during the day; their presence would serve to attract others for conversation, regardless of political commitments. Coincidentally, one of Premnath's election vehicles would pull up and the whole group would be taken to the polls—now "obliged" to Govindrao, even in this small way.[13]

Another tactic used by Premnath was to have some of his workers lounge about a locality, ostentatiously displaying badges of their political affiliation in an attempt to convey the impression that Govindrao's forces were not operating very strongly. Discreetly, three or four locally unknown workers would be sent scurrying through the area hustling out the voters, undisturbed by the opposition. When such a group of voters was finally gathered together, it would be carried to the polls via a circuitous route; Premnath feared that to do otherwise would invite his rivals to attempt to involve his vehicle in an accident or even to shoot out the tires with revolvers.

Premnath displayed particular genius in delivering one group of voters. Over a dozen of Govindrao's known supporters were incarcerated just before the election, according to Premnath at the instigation of an opponent. Premnath, having useful contacts among the police, managed to have the prisoners temporarily bound over to his custody on election day and marched them to the polls.

He was not always so successful in outwitting his antagonists. A prominent Communist party leader, according to Premnath, had apparently persuaded election officials long before the campaign was well

[13]Upon arriving, such voters are of course free, in the privacy of the polling booth, to vote for whomsoever they choose. However, there is presumably some psychological value in having as many voters as possible pass through one's own election booth (mandap) traditionally set up at the polling stations by each candidate. Voters must secure their voter registration number from any one of these booths in order to cast a ballot. Cases were reported in which voters—sometimes *en masse*—betrayed their patrons once behind the polling curtain; but candidates appear to feel that the publicity of political alignment which the present registration system fosters has the worthwhile effect on many voters of psychological reinforcement.

underway to position the polling booths inconveniently for Govindrao's known groups of supporters. Since the ward is quite large, the resulting long trek to the polling station could be expected to dampen the motivation of the more disinterested among Govindrao's constituents. Since Premnath joined the campaign at a relatively late date, the maneuver was impossible to undo.

Govindrao received less than fifty per cent of the votes cast; yet the contrivances which he and his manager used helped to give him a tally over twice as high as that received by his nearest rival. The antidote to the candidate's apparent weakness in the ward was, on the one hand, to give a reasonably convincing demonstration of his ability to materially affect the wellbeing of the poorer class of voters and, on the other hand, to trim voter capacity to choose among competitors by resorting to a variety of baffling techniques including, but not restricted to, the paid withdrawal of opposing candidates.

That coercion was an important part of both of these was freely admitted. One may doubt, in fact, whether voter effectiveness was a reality at all in this case where a candidacy was foisted arbitrarily and suddenly on highly dependent voters with little option in some instances but to accept the patronage of a self-appointed and influential political leader.

But the conditions which provided the candidate leverage of this sort are not so abundant in most other wards; and even in this case were not sufficient to dissuade the candidate and his manager from employing virtually every other technique for assuring voter support.

THE POLITICAL HISTORY OF CENTRAL AVENUE

We turn now to consider several cases in which voluntary associations figured prominently in the campaign strategies of candidates. While admitting that the tactics already described are in wide use throughout the city, it will be contended that those candidates possessed of associational talents have an added resource upon which to draw in designing campaign strategy. The importance of this added resource lies not only in its capacity to supplement whatever other assets a candidate may bring to bear in wooing the electorate, but in its ability to arouse positive voter reaction in lieu of such coercive measures as have been examined. This is especially clear in the campaign strategies of those candidates contesting for office in the wards neighboring Central Avenue, the political history of which we now examine.

Central Avenue is a modern, four-lane concrete road running west to east through some of the most congested areas of central Nagpur. Its slightly less than three miles' length cuts across the heart of the city's older eastern half, beginning near the busy bridge crossing the railway yards near Nagpur's major rail terminal and ending in the open fields of Garoba Maidan. Here, at the eastern edge of the city, it connects with the older highway leading the fifty miles or so to neighboring Bhandara district. It is one of the few lengthy strips of modern road in the entire city, and is the only major road traversing the crowded central wards.

Central Avenue is a development scheme of the Nagpur Improvement Trust (NIT).[14] It is the Trust's only major inner-city road building project. It was first proposed in 1939; construction of it began in the middle 'forties.[15] After three decades Central Avenue was still an unfinished road in early 1970, its midsection blemished with a rough, unpaved stretch of less than half a mile. At this point in the road, the so-called Part IIB, demolition had been halted, leaving some structures standing like cutaway dollhouses, mute testimonials to the limitations on eminent domain and to the talents of local political strategists.

This discussion will center on the recent consequences of the Central Avenue improvement project on the municipal electoral contest in a single ward whose boundaries straddle the road. It will consider the perspective of the planning agency responsible for the road's development and the opportunities which its construction afforded for the growth of local voluntary associations. Further, it will describe the manner in which these associations tended to cut across otherwise impenetrable community barriers by functioning as pressure groups for the extraction of material concessions from the government. Lastly and most importantly, it will detail the particular consequences of the road's construction on the organization and conduct of a political campaign, pointing out the opportunities for the political opposition to negotiate advantages out of the confrontation between the public and the government.

[14]Unless otherwise indicated, the material on the construction of Central Avenue is drawn from interviews with several executive officers of the Nagpur Improvement Trust in November 1969. For the Trust's role in connection with cooperative housing societies, see Chapter 3, above.

[15]A brief history of the road and the Improvement Trust is contained in Padmakar L. Joshi *et al., Nagpur City Centennial Volume,* pp. 51-55. For a penetrating discussion of the politics of town planning in another Indian city (Indore), see Rodney W. Jones, *Urban Politics in India,* pp. 229-262.

The Improvement Trust is a formidable opponent.[16] Formed in 1937, it has grown gradually into the city's most important and powerful town planning agency, presiding over large assets and a substantial budget, and making decisions crucial for the city's future.[17] Since its inception it has obtained state government sanction for thirty-five schemes, falling under such headings as canalization, industrial area improvement, drainage and sewage disposal, road building and widening, housing accommodation and new subdivisional layout constructions. Five of these broad schemes were completed by 1969, including the first and third sections of the Central Avenue Road Scheme. Over the years, the Trust has grown into a mature and amazingly self-sufficient institution.[18] Paradoxically, it has never outgrown its early and sustained lack of popularity.[19]

[16]Although the discussion here will relate mainly to that type of leverage exerted by the local, ward-level politician on the urban planning agency, at least at two other points the Trust would appear highly vulnerable to various sorts of political pressures. One of these is the NIT's board of trustees, which consists of nine persons representative of several urban agencies and interests. Its composition has changed from time to time, but has typically included both elected politicians and administrative officials, whose influence is felt at the level of policy formation. The other point of vulnerability is among the NIT's employees; and here the Bharatiya Jana Sangh seems to have almost a monopoly. Ramjiwan Choudhari, member of the state legislative council (Vidhan Parishad) and president of the district Jana Sangh (1969-70), is also president of the Improvement Trust Workers Union. This union is an affiliate of the Bharatiya Mazdur Sangh (BMS), widely recognized as the labor front of the Jana Sangh. According to Advocate G. K. Athawale, general secretary of the Vidarbha branch of the BMS, the Trust union is the oldest Nagpur union affiliated with the BMS, having been organized in 1958. It is the only well-established union among NIT employees, of whose total of 1,200, from 900 to 1,000 are members. Athawale was interviewed on 20 December 1969.

[17]For the year closing 31 March 1968, the NIT's total capital expenditure was Rs 17,067,023. Nagpur Improvement Trust, *Annual Report, 1967-68*, p. 32.

[18]Over the years, the Trust has increased its financial autonomy, giving it some degree of latitude in its relations both with the state and with local government. For the year ending 31 March 1968, capital and revenue receipts of premia for the lease of building sites alone amounted to over Rs 3,200,000. Loans from the state, in contrast, showed a steady decline during the 1960s. The balance on loan on 1 April 1961, was over Rs 9,000,000; by the end of March 1968, the figure was reduced to a little more than Rs 6,300,000. Nagpur Improvement Trust, *Annual Report* (years 1961 through 1968).

[19]The NIT came into being in the 1930s under the sponsorship of the British commissioner over the opposition of some members of the municipal government and without even the support of the newly-elected provincial Congress

Central Avenue was planned in three major stages, the second stage having two sections, IIA and IIB. Each stage involved the acquisition of well over 1,000 built-up properties, and the implementation of each has faced stiff political opposition. Although construction of Part I was begun in the middle 'forties, it was not finally completed until 1966. Part IIA, though sanctioned for development in 1948, was only reaching completion in 1969. And Part III, sanctioned in 1945, was finally completed only in 1969. As these parts have all (politically) passed into history, only the construction of Part IIB will be examined more closely here.

This last redoubt of the road's antagonists runs about one-third of a mile between Adam Shah Chowk and a point slightly beyond Santi Road. Late in 1969, thirty years after the date of the road's original proposal, this stretch was temporarily paved, permitting use for the first time of the entire length of the road. Part IIB included about seven hundred mainly sturdy (pakka) structures, of which only about a hundred had been acquired by the date of the corporation election in 1969. And of these, about fifty had already been restored to their owners after satisfactory adjustments were made to their property. The plan for this section was originally framed in 1958 and sanctioned by the state in 1962. The involved plots, which the Trust had been seeking to acquire for about two rupees per square foot, form part of the areas of Itwari, Santi Road, Gurudkhamb and Mangalwari.

The NIT's procedures in acquiring land for the road have provided useful ammunition for its opponents' activities on behalf of the affected homeowners. At the start of a scheme notification of acquisition is given to every householder after careful determination of houseownership in the locality and an evaluation of property values. The scheme is then published in the government gazette and in the local press, and objections are solicited. Public meetings are then held to hear complaints,

---

ministry. A few projects, including the Central Avenue Scheme, were proposed in 1939, but World War II interfered and little was implemented until the mid-1940s when an influential chairman plunged into acquisition of land for the road. His enthusiasm for demolition was answered, upon the resumption of power by the post-war provincial Congress government, with his early transfer and the emasculation of the Trust's budget. A Trust enquiry commission was appointed in 1946, and while it deliberated the Trust was inactive, for it was then heavily dependent on government loans for financing its works. The commission submitted its report in 1948 and, after an organizational shuffle, the NIT resumed its development—and that of the Central Avenue Road—in an independent India. Padmakar L. Joshi *et al.*, *Nagpur City Centennial Volume*, pp. 52-53.

after which the proposed scheme, together with the objections, is submitted to the board of trustees for their consideration. If approved by the board, the scheme is submitted to the state government, complete with full details, cost estimates, use analyses, and so forth. Upon receiving the sanction of the state government for the project, acquisition proceedings are initiated by the local district collector through the action of local courts in accord with regulations laid down in the Land Acquisition Act, a locally-amended central government law specifying the conditions of acquisition and compensation. In adjudicating the value of the condemned plots, the court is obliged to consider the value of the land as of the date on which the scheme was originally published for objections. In the case of Part I of the Central Avenue Road Scheme, this meant that official valuation was to be based on 1939 land values; in the case of Part IIB, on 1958 values. Furthermore, the court is obliged by law to fix compensatory rates in accord with *land use* rather than *potential market* values.

Much of the opposition to the NIT's *modus operandi* takes the form of court litigation and derives from objection to this current use-value basis of compensation. The homeowners' defenders argue that compensation should be based on the marketable value of the property, particularly in light of the economic injustice imposed on homeowners by the lengthy delays in implementing the scheme. In the case of Part IIB, almost a dozen years elapsed between notification and construction. After a lower court awarded the plaintiffs market values in two cases in 1967, the Trust carried the issue to the state high court. By the end of 1969, in fact, there were a total of about fifty cases lying before the courts stemming from implementation of Part IIB alone.

Another major objection to the NIT's procedure has had to do with its insistence, in the case of Central Avenue, on a big road having easement rights extending to fifty feet on either side of the road. Opponents point out that the Trust purchases the land at extremely low rates (less than a rupee per square foot) and then resells the developed frontage plots for commercial use at as high as thirty rupees per square foot. The NIT replies that its rate of compensation has increased in recent years and, further, that resale at rates as high as thirty rupees has been exceptional. According to the Trust, developed plots naturally increase their value; and from such increased values the Trust must obtain its operating capital. It has no other major source of income. Moreover, regardless of the NIT's profit, evictees are well-compensated; even when they include in their number outright encroachers owning nothing but a shrewd sense of timing, they generally obtain developed plots at concessional rates in resettlement areas. [20] And finally, the Trust argues that it is bound by law to acquire *all* the property coming under its scheme to enable it to compel property owners to accept whatever adjustments are necessary in constructing such things as access roads. A large percentage of the condemned plots is ultimately restored to the original owners. In Part IIB, for instance, about seventy per cent of the properties were to be restored to the plotholders after necessary adjustments were made.

Regardless of where justice lies, there are obviously ample grounds for litigation as much as for the political mobilization of the affected homeowners. As was the case with the older sections of the road, political opportunities are highly transient. There is strong evidence in this case that the opportunity was not missed, and in fact was successfully seized by the Jana Sangh candidate in Nikalas Mandir ward. His overwhelming victory can be explained only in terms of a substantial transfer of normally non-Jana Sangh voters to the Jana Sangh, in some part due to his and his party's effective exploitation of the Trust's rather acid relationship with the constituents of that ward.

Such an assertion is admittedly impossible to support from electoral statistics alone, and their utility is even less in this case, thanks to the reapportionment carried out in 1968, which carved seventy-five out of the former forty-two wards. Nonetheless, a comparison of voting returns in the municipal elections of 1962 and 1969 between the pre-reapportionment Ayachit Mandir ward and the present truncated Nikalas Mandir ward is still persuasive. [21] The 1969 Jana Sangh candidate in Nikalas Mandir ward, the same who contested in Ayachit Mandir ward in 1962, increased his percentage of the total vote by 22.7 per cent over 1962. [22] His new ward contained only four of the six census tracts which comprised the older ward, but his increased share of the vote is not easily explained away as the result of his oppo-

[20]Concessional rates were abandoned in 1968 due to the Trust's finding that about fifty per cent of the resettled evictees of Parts I and IIA had already sold their compensatory plots.

[21]Less than ward-level voting figures were not made availabe for any of the municipal elections, preventing comparison of returns by census tract or polling booth.

[22]He received 26.8 per cent in 1962 and 49.5 per cent in 1969, as compared to 24.9 and 31.5 per cent for Congress, and 37.9 and 6.3 per cent for the NVAS in the same years. Independent candidates received only 10.2 per cent of the vote in 1962 and 12.6 per cent in 1969. NMC election returns.

nents having lost their normal supporters to reapportionment: in *both* sections of the reapportioned Ayachit Mandir ward the results show equally impressive advances for the Jana Sangh.[23]

The Jana Sangh candidate in Nikalas Mandir ward in the 1969 contest was Madhaorao M. Khule, a Marathi-speaker of the tiny Kasar (cutler) caste.[24] His systematic efforts to attract non-Jana Sangh voters to his support, undertaken deliberately in the wake of his defeat in 1962, are a striking illustration of the sort of political leverage made opportune by the Central Avenue Road Scheme. Born in Wardha district (adjacent to Nagpur district on the south) in 1918, and educated two years beyond high school matriculation in a teacher training college, he is today a frank, forceful and energetic shopkeeper, a dedicated member of the Rashtriya Swayamsewak Sangh (RSS), and an important figure in the city Jana Sangh. After completing college in 1942, he entered government service and worked up to 1948 as a clerk in the district court at Chanda (in Chanda district), in what was then Central Provinces. He joined the RSS in 1932; in those pre-independence years he was an RSS organizer for Chanda district. In the wake of Gandhi's assassination in 1948, Khule was obliged to leave government service owing to his RSS affiliation. He came to Nagpur in 1949, entered the stationery business, and has remained in it ever since. He has been a member of the Jana Sangh since the party's founding in 1951, and is now secretary of the east zonal committee (mandal samiti) of the party's city organization, responsible for nineteen of the city's seventy-five wards. Since 1952 he has been the Jana Sangh's chief organizer in his sector of the city.

Khule's numerous activities are a firm indication of his long-range strategy to enlist the support of the socially heterogeneous and politically fragmented constituents of Nikalas Mandir ward. The margin of his personal stationery lists, in addition to his political positions, ten associations of which he is currently president. All were founded under his

[23]Nikalas Mandir ward overlies Part IIB of the Central Avenue Road Scheme in about equal measure with the Ayachit Mandir ward. Together, the boundaries of these two new wards mark roughly the old boundaries of the former Ayachit Mandir ward, in which the Jana Sangh failed to elect in any of the three previous municipal elections. In the middle of the area comprising these wards stands a national headquarters building of the RSS. Data on reapportionment was obtained from the central records department, Nagpur municipal corporation.

[24]Interviewed on 10, 11 September 1969.

tutelage in the period since 1962, most of them in the years 1964-1966. Over half are "unions" organized among various categories of transport workers, retailers and retail employees, while the rest are "neighborhood" groups formed to air particular grievances. All are strictly local (Nagpur) associations. All have as their objectives the hindrance, alteration or more energetic enforcement of government legislation. Their names are indicative of the types of groups organized:

1) Nagpur Improvement Trust Injustice Opposition Association
2) Weekly Market Retail Shopkeepers Union
3) Farmers Safeguarding Campaign
4) Bharatiya Cartsmen Union
5) Bharatiya Shopkeepers Conduct Act Committee
6) Tonga Owners Association
7) Bharatiya Riksha Laborers Council
8) Santi Locality Citizens Society
9) Dirty and Unkempt Locality Movement Association
10) Auto Riksha Owners and Drivers Union

The only one of these associations which proved of considerable value in the 1969 campaign, according to Khule, was the first listed—the Nagpur Improvement Trust Injustice Opposition Association. In the new Nikalas Mandir ward, 424 households were directly affected by the road project, a number of potential supporters far greater than Khule could rely upon from his other associations. [25] Unlike most of the other groups, the NIT opposition association took its membership almost exclusively from Khule's own ward, even in its truncated state. Furthermore, this particular association was tied to a highly specific and spatially narrow set of grievances. Founded in 1965, its objective was very simply to stall implementation of the NIT's projected Part IIB of the road scheme until compensation more advantageous to the affected residents had first been obtained. In company with some of the top leaders of the city Jana Sangh, Khule led the demand for re-evaluation of the plots, with success obvious in the prolonged stalemate. [26] Accord-

[25] It is difficult to estimate exactly how many *voters* would thus be affected. According to NIT calculations, one household structure, even those of hutment (zopada) quality, typically holds about ten persons. A scheme involving the acquisition of 500 household structures could affect as many as 5,000 persons, of whom perhaps twenty-five per cent would be adults.

[26] While plans for this sector of the road were first announced in 1958, the first steps toward implementation were not taken until 1963 upon receipt of state government sanction. The legal dispute dates from that point.

ing to Khule, the Trust took possession of the condemned right-of-way at very low rates fixed years earlier, compensating at a rate less than one rupee per square foot while selling the same land to commercial developers at an average rate of twenty rupees per square foot—or over twenty times the compensatory rate.

Khule's 1969 campaign strategy was heavily reliant on his capacity to link together his various associational interests. His strategy lacked both exclusivistic communal and partisan programatic appeals to the electorate. It consisted largely of recruiting local influentials into his associational network where a regularized process of discrete negotiations could be conducted using such devices as the Trust's obligation to compensate for acquired properties as the principal resource.

The most durable base of support upon which Khule built his electoral organization consisted of the 400 to 500 Brahman voters who constitute the "Jana Sangh-minded" of his ward.[27] Of these, about 100 are active members of the RSS, and they, as might be expected in a ward within walking distance of RSS headquarters, worked hard for Khule.

Otherwise, Khule followed a strategy of arranging private meetings with locality leaders of each community group in the ward. Thereafter, with the locality leaders in tow, he canvassed house to house, both in order to systematically check voter registration as well as to exhibit to the voters his support by local leadership. Closer to election day, small locality meetings were arranged again in order to reinforce whatever bonds had been forged already. Individual contact, though as complete as he could make it, was not for the purpose of "convincing" voters, but rather for enabling a precise tally of deliverable support. Khule declares without hesitation that the bloc delivery of votes is far more important than the number obtained through individual volition. And they were delivered to him, in his judgment, owing to his varied efforts to solve the grievances of discrete locality groups, and particularly of those affected by the Trust's Central Avenue Road Scheme.

[27]Khule's ward is small and congested, consisting mainly of five old residential localities (mohallas): Bapurao Gully, Gurudkhamb, Santi Road, Adam Shah Chowk, and Koshtipura. It has an official registered voting population of 4,646. It is a mixed-caste population, the larger groups being Koshti, Brahman, and Sonar, with substantial numbers of Muslim, Gujarati, Marwadi, Mehtar, Mang, Dhobi, Teli and Kunbi voters. Khule's own Kasar community numbers only a few in the ward. There are no large factories or big commercial houses in the ward. Occupationally, the bulk of the population consists of shopkeepers and small businessmen, large numbers of government employees, handloom weavers, goldsmiths and laborers of various trades.

Khule's specific campaign techniques coincided remarkably with his concept of the local political process. Since electoral support, in his judgment, is earned over time largely through the negotiated exchange of political intercession in return for votes, he views mass contacts, big election meetings and campaign hoopla as useless for enlisting voters. He held no formal public meetings whatsoever, took out no processions, put up no posters, distributed no handbills, engaged no loudspeakers, opened no campaign offices, and in general violated every local convention of political campaigning. Practically the only visible signs of his campaign were the wall slogans painted by his workers. However, household canvassing, the only certain procedure for accurately tallying the quantities of negotiable votes, was extremely thorough: 273 new voters were enrolled due to the care taken in checking registration door to door, and voters registered in Nikalas Mandir ward but living elsewhere were also systematically contacted if still in Nagpur, and on election day were brought to the polling stations in conveyances provided by the candidate. Two days prior to the polling, twenty-five of his workers were assigned to tour the ward creating a "win" atmosphere in all localities; on polling day itself twenty workers were assigned to each sector of several hundred households to recontact known supporters.

We would expect to find that Khule's leadership of the opposition to the Central Avenue Road Scheme would pay extra dividends in that section of his ward immediately adjacent to and most directly affected by the road's construction. And this appears to have been the case. Of the four voting booths in his ward, Khule received his highest tally—468 votes—from the Adam Shah akhada booth, from which in 1962 he had rung up only thirty-two votes. [28] Among other groups in the vicinity of the Adam Shah akhada, whose red-earthed wrestling ring lies exposed by an NIT bulldozer to passersby on Central Avenue, lives a Muslim community with about 130 voters. In spite of his RSS background, Khule claimed overwhelming voting support from this group, as from other Muslim groups in the ward. He gave the names of two Muslim leaders in the locality whose backing had been influential in securing their community's support for his candidacy. [29] Both were interviewed and substantially confirmed his claim. One, a former wrestler and pre-

[28]Polling booth figures were provided by Khule himself. They could not be verified from official results.

[29]Khule listed a total of six key supporters from some of the groups, including Muslims, not ordinarily enrolled in his otherwise heavily Brahman and RSS campaign organization. All were interviewed in January/February 1970; and

sently the owner of a tiny cloth shop, is an ex-Congress worker, expelled in 1969 for his disloyalty to the party. The second, a sixty-five year old wrestling master (ustad) and metal craftsman, is a lifelong resident of Adam Shah Chowk. His own home falls within the Central Avenue Scheme and is doomed to demolition. Formerly a Congress worker, he was president of the Adam Shah akhada, demolished in late 1969 by the Trust. He serves today as treasurer of the Masjid Committee of Adam Shah Chowk, a registered public trust managing, he claims, local property worth Rs 150,000, including three mosques, a crematorium and graveyard. Possessing obvious material interest in the road's development, he supported Khule, in part, because he felt aggrieved that the NIT offered inadequate compensation for acquired properties. He is himself a plaintiff in legal action against the Trust. Both of these Muslim supporters credited Khule with effective leadership against the NIT, and applauded his energetic leadership of local associations.[30]

Khule's concept of the political process and his campaign strategy testify to the electoral value of the Central Avenue Road Scheme. His concept is by no means exceptional: the electoral value in providing

---

collectively they lend credence to his claim of a highly diversified electoral coalition. In addition to the two Muslims, they included one tribal, one Koshti, one Jain, and one Mehtar (sweeper). On closer examination, one revealed that he had in fact supported one of Khule's opponents. Another was named as a key supporter by *two* candidates, a not uncommon phenomenon in the sometimes bizarre atmosphere of local politics. A third conceded that he had supported Khule, but insisted that he had delivered no other vote to the polls than his own and hardly deserved the title of "key worker." The other three were, however, both "men of influence" and outspoken supporters of Khule. None of the six claimed to have had any prior association with the BJS. It is noteworthy, too, that Khule's thumbnail sketches of these men, despite his partial exaggeration of the fullness of their support, were astonishingly frank. Far from depicting them as all men of high scruple and lofty character, he portrayed one as a "goonda chieftain who has seen the inside of all the jails of India"—a man prominent in extortion rackets and the bootleg liquor business; and another as a goonda leader "immune from the prosecution of police." In Nagpur politics, it seems one cannot be too finicky about the caste *or* occupational pedigree of one's political associates.

[30]Both also credited Khule with having defended local Muslim residents against the attacks of Buddhists at the time of the communal riots between these two groups in the summer of 1968. Though the riots did not directly affect this ward, these two local Muslim leaders confirmed Khule's claim that he had actually changed his residence to the Muslim locality for the duration of the riots, and had been its most active protector.

leadership to urban renewal-affected homeowners is well recognized by others in his party.[31] In this connection Khule's chief opponent, Govind-rao M. Khode, a Congressman, prominent trade union organizer, and an apparently formidable foe, adds an illuminating perspective.[32]

Khode, a Brahman and since 1967 a member of the working commit-tee of the Nagpur city district Congress committee, attributes a major share of the cause of his defeat to the effects of the Central Avenue Scheme and the calculated exploitation of it by the Jana Sangh and its candi-date Khule. Khode acknowledges that Khule and his party have been actively defending the interests of the plotholders, and that their efforts have resulted in legal action which has successfully stalled demolition and further acquisition. In 1967, Khode notes, the BJS appointed the influential lawyer N. M. Belekar, the party's unsuccessful standard-bearer in the Lok Sabha contest of that year, to fight the NIT on behalf of the evictees and threatened homeowners.[33] Khode feels, however, that Khule and the Jana Sangh have used unfair means in "negotiating" the support of the road's victims. Shortly after his defeat in the election, Khode lodged a petition with the election commission charging the vic-tor with foul play. Specifically, Khode alleged that the resettled and dis-gruntled voters of over 600 homes demolished by the Trust about one year earlier had been conveyed by Khule's workers to the polling stations of Nikalas Mandir ward where they were still registered, in Khode's opi-nion, incorrectly. Furthermore, he alleged, the Trust sent notification of acquisition to 500 or 600 additional residents whose homes were yet undemolished *only eight days prior to the election*. Since the Jana Sangh is especially well represented among the Trust's employees, the untimely mailing, in Khode's view, was probably premeditated.

The Central Avenue road is a very long road, politically, and the fore-going case does not exhaust its capacity for influencing local political outcomes. It should be clear by now, however, that candidates, their local supporters, and certainly the Trust itself are not blind to the road's political potentialities. That the road helped to swing the votes of a group

[31]BSJ organizational strategy in the city is discussed at length in Chapter 6, above.
[32]Interviewed on 19 November 1969. One of four secretaries of the Maha-rashtra state Indian National Trade Union Congress (INTUC), responsible for the eight districts of Vidarbha, Khode was one of five INTUC-connected Congress candidates in the city. Nikalas Mandir ward has few resident members of INTUC, a fact which may have been related to his defeat.
[33]For Belekar's role in connection with weaver production cooperatives, see Chapter 6, above.

of Muslims to the Jana Sangh candidate—to an RSS activist within the very precinct where that militant Hindu group was born in 1925—is itself a fact of considerable significance. But if it helped to goad not only Muslims, but Brahmans and sweepers, washermen and weavers, shop-keepers and bootleggers, into a coalition of calculated self-interest, then the primordial loyalties of caste and kin, not to mention partisan loyalties to political organizations, will have to move over and make room for the pragmatic loyalties engendered by Central Avenue.

CAMPAIGNING IN SAKKARDARA

Political campaigners gamble on their talent to sort through and piece together the multiplicity of group interests ordinarily found in any constituency. In this, there are no rules or procedures to mecha-nically define appropriate strategy, much less to guarantee victory at the polls. The extraordinarily varied tactical approaches alone of the seventy-five winners in Nagpur's 1969 municipal election, had we the time to explore them all, would testify to this. But there is little doubt that a candidate's ability to personally construct a network of influential contacts and loyal campaign workers is a key component of most win-ning strategies, especially so where local political party organizations are weak and factionalized, and where candidates are frequently left to their own devices.

We have already seen (in Khule's campaign, for instance) how the patient and determined cultivation of associational ties can be used to mobilize voters behind a candidate with no other visible attraction for them. We look now at a contest which emphasizes perhaps even more dramatically the way in which voluntary associations, when fully integrated into campaign organizations, pay handsome dividends at the polls. These dividends include the ability to span community cleavages. And for some they include victory. But, as this section will attempt to establish, they include also the fostering of new kinds of durable group loyalty to political leaders having little or nothing to do with the expectation of electoral victory. We focus here on the election contest in Sakkardara ward, where cooperative housing societies have come to play a particularly prominent role.

The largest in area, Sakkardara is also one of the largest in population of Nagpur's seventy-five wards (with 8,076 registered voters). Its newly elected corporator, Bhausaheb Surve, is a lifelong resident and one of its most prominent and active politicians.[34] The head of four housing societies, he considers the provision of adequate housing as the single most critical problem facing the corporation; he ranks it as his own most important interest. It was also, as the pages to follow will demonstrate, an important factor in his campaign strategy and ultimate victory.

Surve's political background is in no way an exception to the rule that political party identification is a subsidiary concern to Indian politicians, at least at the local level. His political career began in the middle 1950s in the form of various associational activities, but he did not then profess any particular party affiliation. He joined the Congress party, in fact, only a few months prior to the March election of 1969, having had with it no prior formal connection. His first election experience was in 1957 when he unsuccessfully contested the corporation election *against* Congress as a member of the Maharashtra Nagrik Samiti.[35] In 1962 he stood in the municipal election again, this time under the banner of the Republican Party of India. He defeated his nearest rival, the Congress candidate, by over a thousand votes.[36] In 1964-65 he served as mayor, elected to the post by a non-Congress coalition then controlling the corporation.[37] In 1967 he fought the legislative assembly election from the Nagpur central constituency on the ticket of a splinter party—the Jana Congress—born at the time of the general election. He fell third, well behind the Congress and Republican party candidates.[38]

[34]Interviewed on 12/15 October 1969. Born in 1931, Surve is occupationally a landowner and self-styled social worker. Maratha by caste, his family is related to the royal Bhonsale family which ruled in Nagpur before the British brought it to ruin in the 1850s. His home lies inside the walls of what remains of one of the former royal palaces.

[35]The MNS was the local branch of the Samyukta Maharashtra Samiti, at the time promoting the cause of a united Maharashtra. Surve won 825 votes in that contest, placing third behind a Bhonsale prince and Ramjiwan Choudhari, local BJS leader. In that election he stood in the former Mahal ward lying to the north of Sakkardara.

[36]He contested on this occasion from Siraspeth ward lying adjacent to Sakkardara on the west.

[37]Padmakar L. Joshi *et al.*, *Nagpur City Centennial Volume*, p. 188.

[38]The Congress candidate was Madan Gopal Agarwal, one of the city's most prominent political leaders, also a former mayor, and in 1969 state deputy minister for urban development, public health and housing. The RPI candidate, Dr D.P. Meshram, another former mayor, is one of Nagpur's most colorful politicians. His background is related in Chapter 4, above.

During these same politically highly active years, Surve was increasingly becoming involved in the cooperative housing movement. He founded two and took over management of two other housing societies. They enrolled differing social groups—textile millworkers, printing press and other tradesmen, middle-income "white collar" workers and government employees. And they were directed at solving different types of problems—acquisition of land, approval of unauthorized settlement on government land, sanction of permanent public housing privileges for terminated public employees or, more simply, improved roads, water and electricity supply.

As leader of these societies, Surve had ample opportunity to play the role of intermediary with the city corporation, the NIT, the Vidarbha Housing Board, or with the various agencies of state government. But the political support of these few societies, presuming their members to have been more or less politically obliged, at best could not account for more than a modest portion of the whopping vote he secured— 1,853 votes (34.8 per cent of the total)—almost twice again as large as that obtained by his nearest rival.[39]

The problem is partially resolved by bearing in mind that the candidate's linkage with the electorate is not and need not be completely direct. In a ward as sprawling and populous as Sakkardara, the maintenance of effective direct association with the majority would be difficult indeed; in a society fragmented socially into a multitude of discrete ascriptive groups, it becomes almost an impossibility. What the politician can do, and what Bhausaheb Surve has done, is to construct a loose network of local and autonomous voluntary associations at the apex of which he occupies the role of patron-in-chief. In this way, while clearly burdening himself with the need to satisfy many highly diverse demands, he shifts much of the responsibility for political organizational work to local influentials or link leaders, the key workers in locality associations.

The resulting electoral organization is one of the more impressive in Nagpur city, capable of mounting a massive election campaign.[40]

---

[39]Surve is of course active in fields other than housing. He is well known, for instance, for his leadership of the Maratha Lancers, for twenty-five years one of the region's most prominent sports associations. In addition, he is a more or less nominal member of several temple societies, joining them (not unlike his American counterpart) in each area of the ward, occasionally making financial contributions and participating in their festival celebrations.

[40]Like Madhaorao Khule's campaign, Surve's was thorough and systematic.

Surve claims an independent workers organization of more than 500 persons drawn from half the city of Nagpur. He considers them his permanent supporters, associated with him for reasons other than party.[41] He acknowledges that among these workers in the recent election were members of his sports club—the Maratha Lancers—as well as members of the several housing societies and tenants associations in which he is himself an executive. However, in his own view, the core of his political organization is built out of a coalition of locality leaders spread throughout his vast ward and beyond, each having his *own* organized network of support in his own locality.

Surve gave a by no means exhaustive list of thirteen such personalities, all of them leaders or members of such associations as housing cooperatives, locality development and civic action committees, religious and temple societies, sport and wrestling societies, festival, singing and drama groups, and so on. Of the thirteen, nine were interviewed. Their caste, religious community and linguistic identities support the contention that Surve's network is held together not by primordial affection but by a continuous exchange of material for political benefits. It is a cosmopolitan group, often drawing its members from communities having only small representations in the ward.[42] Known for ten

---

Virtually every household was contacted and registration checked for new voters and for those transferred out of the ward. On polling day, almost all likely supporters were recontacted and numerous vehicles were available to convey voters to the polling booths. In striking contrast to Khule's campaign, however, Surve's was one of the most colorful and amply financed in the city. Twenty public meetings were staged, and nearly twenty campaign offices (one for each mohalla) were opened. Three or four large public processions were organized, and many smaller ones. Loudspeaker vans moved through the ward mornings and evenings trumpeting his candidacy for ten days prior to the election.

[41]Local Congress workers did aid his campaign, but having only recently joined the Congress, he could count on no backlog of party support. Numerous prestigious Congress leaders made campaign appearances on his behalf, nonetheless, and five other Congress candidates (all winners in their own wards) made joint appearances and shared workers with him.

[42]Sakkardara ward consists mainly of newer housing developments spreading southward from the inner city, plus about seven older villages dotting its sprawling "rural" landscape. The two leading candidates, Surve and Onkarrao Deshmukh, though disagreeing on specific figures, listed substantially the same castes as predominating among the voters: Kunbi, Teli, Mahar and Maratha. The first is Deshmukh's caste and the last, the smallest of the four,

of them, community affiliations included Marathi-, Hindi- and Urdu-speakers; Hindu, Muslim and Jain religious membership; and Rangari, Kunbi, Kumbhar, Kshatriya, Sonar, Sutar and Maratha caste membership. They are not representative of all the communities in the ward, but Surve (a Maratha) does not have a monopoly on political organization in Sakkardara. In this election he faced ten other candidates, some of them with impressive records of associational activity in their own localities or among particular communities, a point which will be illustrated further on.[43]

Of those interviewed, five of Surve's locality leaders were active in local housing associations of one sort or another, all of which would likely be benefited if linked to a politician of Surve's stature. A closer examination of these five local personalities and their associations will reveal the more precise structure of Surve's organizational network, in particular the heterogeneity of the groups involved and the material concerns that hold them together.[44]

Madhaorao S—, Rangari (dye-maker) in caste and Jain in religion, has for ten years been a friend and political supporter of Surve. A government employee for two decades, he has no formal political party affiliation. A resident of Bhande Plot locality in Sakkardara ward, he has been since 1966 secretary of the Nagrik Vikas Cooperative Housing Society, of which all 106 plotholders of Bhande Plot are members. The land on which the development rests was purchased by individual settlers around 1960 from a local landowner-agriculturist. The society was formed a few years later, and in October 1968 the Trust finally sanctioned its layout. Surve has had no direct personal connection with the society, but since the middle of 1968 has been instrumental in obtaining benefits for the plotholders. Bhande Plot has about 600 voters, mainly millworkers of mixed caste background,

---

is Surve's. There is also a substantial group of Muslims, resident mainly in Tajbag locality.

[43]Surve's nearest rival, Onkarrao Deshmukh, a Kunbi, is himself a prominent political figure. He had four campaigns under his belt prior to 1969. In the 1957 corporation election, contesting on a Congress ticket, he polled the highest vote of any candidate in the entire city (2,911 of 4,717 votes) in old Sakkardara ward. He was injured in a scooter accident shortly before the 1969 election, affecting his mobility and perhaps the election's outcome. Deshmukh was interviewed on 28 July 1969.

[44]Surve's network of supporters involves more than those interested in housing problems, but since housing is his principal interest the others will not be considered here.

predominantly Kunbi and Teli. According to the respondent's estimate, Surve won about half the locality's votes.

Gangaram P—, who identified himself as a Hindu Kshatriya, is headmaster of a municipal primary school, a government employee and member of no political party. A resident of Shivnagar locality in Sakkardara, he has known Surve well since about 1962, when he was a primary school teacher and Surve was chairman of the corporation education committee. The respondent has long been active in teachers' organizations, having thrice been secretary of the Mahanagar Prathmik Shiksa Sangh (corporation primary teachers society), whose membership embraces all of the public primary teachers in the city. He is presently working president of the Nandanwan Layout Society, which in 1968 secured twenty-five acres of land adjacent to Shivnagar from the NIT on which to settle corporation teachers. He is also a member of the nine-man working committee of the Shivnagar Housing Society, to which belong 80 of the locality's plotholders. The residents of Shivnagar, of whose 332 plotholders 60 are corporation teachers, presently occupy their homes on a rental basis from the corporation. The society demands immediate ownership of these plots. Up to the 1969 election, Gangaram was also a member of the Utkarsha Mandal (uplift committee), a locality development organization in Shivnagar. But when its president, Anant Dhage, decided to contest the election against Surve, the respondent was obliged to terminate his membership. In his opinion, most of Shivnagar's voters supported Dhage.

A third supporter, Anandrao D—, Sutar (carpenter) in caste, is a government postal employee and therefore also has no formal party affiliation. He is a resident of the newly established (1961) Nehrunagar colony which forms part of the Mirchy Bazar sector of Sakkardara ward. For the last few years, Anandrao has been the honorary secretary of the Nehrunagar Vikas Samiti (development committee), with about 200 members drawn from the locality's plotholders. Nehrunagar plots were originally granted as part of a slum clearance program. The land is leased from the government at very low rates, but the leases are due to expire after thirty years. The plotholders want full ownership now. Anandrao is also honorary secretary since 1967 of the Nagpur Slum Clearance Scheme Federation, which unites the members of five locality associations scattered about the city, including those of Shivnagar and Nehrunagar in Sakkardara. Under the presidentship of Anant Dhage, Surve's rival in Shivnagar, it now has about 1,125 claimed members. Its principal objective is to secure ownership of plots presently given on a rental basis by the NIT. According to Anandrao's estimate, Surve received the majority of Nehrunagar's votes, while Dhage, not well known outside his own locality, obtained about ten per cent.

A fourth supporter, Balaji T—, Kunbi in caste and a building contractor by occupation, is a former member of the Maratha Lancers and an old friend of Surve. An active Congress worker for thirty years, Balaji is a resident of Telipura locality, consisting mainly of the hut-ment dwellings of laboring class people, in the Old Shukravari area of Sakkardara ward. He is secretary of the Sakkardara branch of the Nagrik Sudhar Samiti (citizens development committee), having locally about 190 houseowners (makanwallahs) and 150 tenants (kirayawal-lahs) enrolled, virtually the whole of Telipura. The locality is contained in the NIT's Industrial Colony Scheme in the northern part of the ward; its residents have been living for years under the threat of ex-pulsion. The residents, claiming to have been on the site for over a century, demand legitimate title to their plots. Some adjacent plots have been obtained for resettlement purposes, but the situation remains essentially unresolved. Balaji estimates that Surve received the support of over 400 of the locality's approximately 800 registered voters, a mixed-caste group of Teli, Kunbi, Mahar and other communities.

The fifth and last of the group, Karim S—, is a Muslim hakim or practitioner of the *unani* (traditional) system of medicine. He is a resident of the Tajbag locality of Sakkardara ward. Karim has been chairman since 1950 of the Tajabad Prakashan Samiti (Tajbag memo-rial committee), formed decades ago to manage the maintenance, finan-cing, and organizing of religious functions and anniversary celebrations at a highly popular religious shrine.

An almost entirely Muslim area, Tajbag is a unique settlement lying on the outskirts of the ward and the city. Its adult population of about 400 consists to a considerable extent of concessionaires, riksha-pullers, laborers and beggars drawn to the site ever since 1925, due to its fame as a shrine holy to both Hindu and Muslim. There they have found employment in transporting the hordes of pilgrims who visit the shrine every year, or in selling them pictures, statues and trinkets, or simply begging from them. At Tajbag in the early years of this century lived Sant Baba Tajudin Auliya, one of central India's most famous and beloved spiritual leaders. To his shrine each year come about half a million pilgrims to pay reverence to his memory. As their numbers have grown, so has the material value of the shrine and the land on which it rests. The area falls under the NIT's Sakkardara Street Scheme;

negotiations have been underway for some time between the NIT and the shrine's own trustees who claim the surrounding eighty-five acres as shrine property.

With respect to each of the above five cases, there was at the time of the municipal election a serious local grievance in differing stages of resolution, having to do with housing and affecting large numbers of voters. A few months prior to the election, the settlers of Bhande Plot had obtained the Trust's sanction for their unauthorized layout; the residents of Shivnagar were then in the process of seeking termination of the corporation's leasehold on their plots; the residents of Nehrunagar were demanding an end to their tenancy under the NIT; the hutment-dwellers of Telipura were threatened with demolition; and the livelihoods of the hundreds of Muslims of Tajbag depend very directly on the status of the shrine. These were clearly not the *sole* grievances, and in some cases, as in Tajbag,[45] may have been quite secondary. But housing problems are fundamental and are hardly likely to have achieved the obvious importance they have to Surve and to many of his key supporters were they not also of considerable significance to the voters.[46]

SHIVNAGAR AND ITS ASSOCIATIONAL PATRON

Candidates vary greatly amongst themselves in terms of the assets (in men, resources and ideas) they have available in developing a political campaign. Those possessed of considerable personal wealth, numerous followers, influential positions of leadership, experience and versatility (like Surve), are likely to pursue strategies differing in magnitude if not in substance from those (clearly in the majority) less well endowed. Pertinent to our inquiry is the question whether possession of at least quantitatively superior assets is an essential element in successfully appealing to voters. Stated simply, is the shrewd, talented but poor

[45]According to Surve's own estimate, he obtained few if any Muslim votes in this election due to the previous summer's riots between the Muslims and Buddhists. The riots directly affected Tajbag, and the Muslim community there could well have been alienated from Surve by his party's alliance with the mainly Buddhist Republican party.

[46]Many of Surve's supporters, like Surve, are equipped to handle demands other than those relating to housing. Three of the five described above are additionally leaders in credit, educational or similar associations.

politician necessarily at a disadvantage in mounting a campaign strategy? Events in Sakkardara ward are particularly revealing in this respect.

Anant Dhage, a tailor and palmist of very modest means, was one of eleven candidates contesting the election in Sakkardara. He was clearly a loser in the election, receiving 393 votes (7.3 per cent of the total) and placing fifth; but this was no surprise to him or to anyone else.[47] What is a surprise is that he received as large a vote as he did with fewer visible assets than virtually any candidate in the field. His victory of sorts cannot be explained away by resort to a theory of fragmented communal loyalties, for the locality in which he lives and which gave him almost its entire vote is a new settlement and a hodgepodge of castes.[48] Nor is it likely that he bought his way to local success, an event made even more unlikely in a competition headed by a candidate as well provisioned as Bhausaheb Surve. Moreover, he was without the support of an organized political party. Dhage does have a long record of political activity with the Congress party, but left it over a decade ago because he was dissatisfied. He contested the election of 1969 against the Congress knowing full well, he states, that he could not win.

In 1963 Dhage founded the Shivnagar Utkarsha Mandal (uplift committee), a neighborhood development association. The Mandal, with about 200 members drawn entirely from the locality's 332 plot-holders, is concerned with such problems as water supply, electricity, roads and land tenure. In meeting the water supply problem, for instance, the Mandal dug a common well for the residents, while at the same time pressing the municipal government to provide water through the existing, but inoperative, taps.

In 1967 Dhage convened a mandal-affiliated housing society (the Shivnagar Housing Society), an association having eighty shareholders in the locality. The society's grievance is a familiar one. All of Shivnagar's plots presently belong to the municipal government and are leased by their tenants. The locality was settled mainly beginning around 1962, and has been used principally to relocate families moved from

---

[47]Interviewed on 12 August 1969. Material on the contest in this ward is based on interviews with six candidates and nine campaign workers.

[48]Dhage did not reveal his caste identity. He was described by other candidates as a Shimpi (tailor), but some interviewees considered Shimpi to be a purely occupational designation. In any case, none of his opponents considered him guilty of using "casteism" in his electioneering.

more congested areas of the city as a result of urban development projects. Dhage served as the society's intermediary with city officials, soliciting their approval for sale of the plots to their present leaseholders. In this connection he has taken the lead in the formation of the Nagpur Slum Clearance Scheme Federation, an alliance of five groups with the same grievance.

That the voters of Shivnagar had made up their minds about Dhage before the campaign seems most probable, for he appears not to have had either the means or the motivation to compete on the same grounds with the slick organizations of his major rivals. Dhage's campaign was a low-keyed, simple affair costing, or so he claims, only Rs 275. He had only about a half dozen campaign workers to help him, all residents of Shivnagar, all members of the Utkarsha Mandal. He ran his campaign entirely independent of any other candidates, group or party. He did no house to house canvassing, and contacted virtually no one in the ward outside of Shivnagar. He did not systematically check voter registration, did not distribute voter registration cards,[49] and did not print any handbills advertizing his candidacy until three days prior to election day, and then only to counter the rumor that he had withdrawn from the contest. Dhage opened only one campaign office, took out no processions, and hired a mobile loudspeaker unit for two days only. He held three small public meetings during the campaign, and on election day waited stoically for the voters' decision, neither recontacting them nor providing them conveyance to the polls. He received about seventy-five per cent of his votes (about 300 of the total 393) from Shivnagar, a clear majority of the votes cast in that locality.[50]

Dhage's personal achievement would appear to be a defeat for his supporters, who have clearly failed to oblige the new ward representative. Since there is likely to be a clamor of demands from every part of Sakkardara for Surve's attention, Shivnagar's voters may have to pay for their decision. On the other hand, though Shivnagar's voters lost the election, they did not lose their own local patron, whom they *have* obliged for his attention and his intercession.

---

[49]Dhage is the sole candidate in the city known to me not to have taken this precautionary measure, which has much the same function as the pre-marked sample ballot commonly distributed in American elections.

[50]He and his rivals are in agreement on this point.

SUMMARY

In devising campaign strategy, local politicians have clearly stretched the boundaries of permissible activity to the limit. Democratic institutions have been perverted, and voters are exploited, manipulated and, in some cases, defrauded in their attempt to exercise choice in electoral competition. Some politicians appear to be motivated by little else, indeed, than personal opportunism. At the same time, there is ample evidence that political leaders, irrespective of their personal motivations, perceive the necessity for responding to the demands of large numbers of voters—voters of every socio-economic category. Competition for votes is intense and voting support is apparently not cheaply acquired. Though coercion and every form of electoral machination are to be found, they occur within an environment suffused with a spirit of accommodation and in which the interdependence of candidates and voters is a pronounced trait.

Local political campaigning involves only the most limited consideration of broad public issues. To be sure, campaign manifestos are couched in lofty rhetoric; but in actually soliciting support politicians most typically seize upon the essentially discrete demands of voters or voter groups. Poverty clearly makes a large class of voters responsive to this type of campaign appeal. But the question whether such voters are adequately rewarded for their pragmatism is difficult to answer. The access of voters to at least low-level political leadership is definitely considerable: slum colonies literally abound with politicians during election periods—and not only then. Rare, indeed, is the settlement that does not have its own corps of fulltime and industrious "social workers," involved in every sort of welfare and developmental activity. Moreover, the extreme competition for the voting support of the city's poor (who are, if anything, numerous) is an indication that their capacity to influence results is substantial. The poor can and do extort some distribution of resources from their political patrons. The result may be corruption, but not of the innocents.

This chapter has given further indication that a guiding principle in the relationship between politicians and their constituents in Nagpur is that political support be given to the most responsive patron, regardless of community or party affiliation. With respect to community, the cases of Surve, Dhage and Khule are persuasive evidence that a base of electoral support is not necessarily constructed from the ranks merely of one's own or a single community group. This is especially so in wards or localities heterogeneous in composition, largely true of both Sakkardara and Nikalas Mandir wards. It is even more the case where the ambitions of the political leader transcend the immediate locality, very much the case with Surve.

Voters appear to be, in addition, rather "party-blind." There are no doubt pockets of dependable "Congress-minded" or "Jana Sangh-minded" voters in every ward; but their numbers are rarely claimed to be more than a few hundred strong in any ward. The contingent of Brahman/RSS loyalists in Nikalas Mandir ward may have been instrumental in promoting Khule's candidacy; but it was not a sufficient cause of his victory. Voters would have a difficult time, in any event, in selecting the "real" Congressman from among candidates (as in Sakkardara ward) whose chameleon-like change of party apparel makes readily visible their own autonomy of party organization. Perhaps most convincing of all is the behavior of the Muslims of Adam Shah Chowk who, in the shadow of RSS headquarters and in spite of decades of India-wide communal hostility of the most lethal variety, did give their support to an acknowledged and well known RSS activist and Jana Sangh leader.

We have seen, too, that anticipation of victory is not a necessary condition for voter support. It is certainly an asset (and was explicitly recognized as such by Khule in his deliberate effort to create a "winning" atmosphere), for the winner's capability to satisfy voter needs is beyond a doubt enhanced by occupancy of official position. But it is not a necessity because voters are apparently as concerned with the *immediate* accountability of local leaders as they are with the politician's stature in the city. Surve was easily the best bet in Sakkardara; Dhage among the poorest. Surve is definitely a responsive leader; but in a ward of such dimensions, with so many discrete demands arising from so many localities, with so many natural barriers of class, caste and kinship, and with so many rivals for the role of intermediary, it is quite understandable why Anant Dhage held the edge in Shivnagar locality. In return for his conscientious and continuous intercession on their behalf, Dhage requested and the settlers of Shivnagar gave their political support.

Thus the pattern of obligation between politician and voters has little to do with the voters' expectations of the politician's *future* performance in some remote legislative arena; the politician is held accountable (if at all) rather for the more immediate transactions he undertakes with local administrative agencies on behalf of his constituents.

He can be effective in this type of activity (e.g., interceding with the police, with municipal authorities, with heads of schools) regardless of his electoral record: victory at the polls is often the politician's personal reward; it does not necessarily represent his constituents' successful bid for influence on the public decision making process. The formal credentials of an elected legislator are an aid to but not a criterion of participation in the political management of popular demands.

In particular, this chapter has sought to make clear that voluntary associations, enrolling vast numbers of the electorate and catering to specific and concrete needs, do provide an enormous resource for political campaigners. Whether confined to a single locality (as in Shivnagar) or spread in a network throughout the ward (true of Surve's pyramidal organization), voluntary associations provide influential contacts, campaign workers and—most critically—bonds of loyalty transcending community and party affiliation. Few of Nagpur's politicians would gamble their electoral fate on associational entrepreneurship as thoroughly as did Anant Dhage. Denied opportunity in the Congress organization and possessed of few other tangible assets, perhaps he had no other choice. Most of them (including many with outstanding records of associational activity) apply whatever techniques seem permissible and profitable (and, of these, coercive manipulation is not the least common). But there is good reason to believe that local strategists, aware both of the uses *and the limitations* of coercive and exploitative tactics, find now in associational management an alternative and, certainly for the voters, more constructive political opportunity.

8

Conclusion

Hundreds of voluntary associations have been spawned in Nagpur in the few decades since independence was granted India in 1947. Many of them are the offspring of deliberate government policy. Others have appeared spontaneously in response to popular needs and expectations. They affect the lives of virtually all of the city's inhabitants, often in ways that their founders did not anticipate. Few have a history longer than a decade or two; and about their future little can be said with certainty. But what is certain is that they deserve far more than passing reference in the study of Indian urban politics.

Whatever the intent of their designers, voluntary associations have proven enormously attractive to local politicians. In virtually every mohalla sprout education and credit societies, neighborhood development committees, athletic and cooperative associations, more often than not under the guardianship of political patrons. For the most powerful party leader as for the lowliest campaign worker, associational management is now a principal ingredient of the workaday world of local politics and a major determinant of successful political careers. Faction leaders recruit energetic associational entrepreneurs, and reward them with tickets to contest elections. Party leaders fashion organizational goals in the new language of associational politics—of credit societies, marketing and producers' cooperatives infiltrated and controlled. And campaign strategists, with an eye on deeply ingrained traditions of communal loyalty, mobilize electoral coalitions pieced together from the material interests of far-flung networks of voluntary associations. In a major way, local politicians now appeal to the electorate with the resources of these associations—cash credit, production rebates, title to land, educational opportunities, health services, and benefits of many other kinds.

The associations have been made attractive to local politicians above all else by their command of such resources. Naturally, there are other resources available—ideological and community attachments, and personal wealth are among them. But only the most impercipient politician could fail to see the political potential extruding from the increasingly bulging assets of voluntary associations. The discretion available to associational managers in disposing of these assets was obvious enough: government regulation and supervision are notoriously relaxed. That this discretion might apply to the distribution of handsome public subsidies channeled through many of these associations could not have made plainer the opportunity for productive political management of the process. After all, what could subsidize local developmental programs could equally well support the career ambitions of local political leaders.

Voluntary associations are not, of course, uniformly attractive to politicians. For one thing, material assets vary considerably. The trivial resources of most temple associations, for example, hardly stand comparison with the often imposing physical holdings of many education societies. For another, governmental subsidy is not evenly or impartially distributed. The award of government grants depends as much on the government's own developmental priorities as on the needs of associational groups. Without a large voting constituency to buttress its claims, the archaic handloom weaving industry, for instance, would almost certainly have been left to die a natural death. It is no mystery that government assistance to the weaver associations waxes with the onset of each election, and wanes thereafter. But there is little to prevent virtually any association from *becoming* politically attractive as a result of a change in its fortunes. This was the fate, for example, of Nagpur's traditional wrestling societies upon receipt of a government grant for the construction of a stadium.

Direct government subsidy is not absolutely essential to arouse political interest in voluntary associations. To the contrary, it may be the exclusion of particular groups from public benefits which invites political intercession. This was certainly the case with respect to the Jana Sangh-sponsored neighborhood action groups formed to extract higher rates of compensation for land acquired by urban renewal authorities. Far from being subsidized, these associations obtained government concessions only after prolonged litigation in the courts.

What the evidence suggests, however, is that the political value of associational management is most emphatically present when the association functions *primarily* as active intermediary agent between government developmental administration and affected groups in the population—in brief, when it is commissioned as local patron of public resources. Virtually any association can perform this function: civic and social service associations (such as the Congress Sewa Dal or Bharat Sewak Samaj), athletic organizations, or even literary and cultural groups,[1] are involved in development programs and from time to time are given charge of government subsidies. Since in Nagpur the co-operatives and education societies are the most thoroughly subsidized voluntary associations, they provide the most vivid and unambiguous evidence of the thesis. The argument gains strength from the fact that many other types of association are just as liable to political penetration when and if they cross the thin line that divides private from public agencies in India.

Perhaps the principal advantage implicit in associational access to the public trough is that it endows the political managers of associations with a resource that is both highly attractive and secular. No other source of patronage provides a more ample supply of benefits to meet the material wants and needs of the mass public. No other source is better equipped to cut across traditional social barriers of caste, linguistic and religious community. Campaign strategists may yet draft their plans on the basis of ascriptively organized vote banks; but they do so in full knowledge of the fact that votes (singly or in batches) are often delivered in anticipation of material reward.[2]

[1]The great importance of government planning resources even to literary associations is made strikingly apparent in Jyotirindra Das Gupta's perceptive study of linguistic group politics and national policy. According to the author, the acceptance by the central and state governments of responsibility for the promotion and development of regional languages has caused the flow of substantial funds to voluntary literary associations for the preparation of dictionaries, encyclopedias, coinage of terms, translation, teaching and propagation. *Language Conflict and National Development: Group Politics and National Language Policy in India* (Berkeley: University of California Press, 1970), especially pp. 169-175, 213-217.

[2]According to one recent study, "*en bloc* caste vote and political homogeneity are rapidly disappearing in the contemporary Indian political culture. Instead, electoral diversity within castes is growing in the face of tireless effort on the part of certain 'caste associations' and the adroit nomination of caste candidates to attract caste votes." A. H. Somjee, "Caste and the Decline of Political Homogeneity," *American Political Science Review*, LXVII, 806.

There is no doubt that local Congressmen enjoy preferred access to public subsidy. In a state ruled without interruption by the Congress party, it could hardly be otherwise. But since each association constitutes a separate arena in which parties, factions, and independent entrepreneurs are free to contest for control of the vital intermediary function, there is opportunity for virtually every group in the city, regardless of political attachment, traditional social status, or even numbers, to claim a share of executive authority. Indeed, elections of the managing committees of these associations are contested as vigorously as the municipal election itself.[3] Congress does not monopolize the voluntary associations of Nagpur.

Nor are voluntary associations the exclusive preserve of well-heeled politicians. In several cases, it was apparent that candidates with limited personal resources were able to trade successfully upon the public works performed by voluntary associations, at times parlaying associational entrepreneurship into electoral victory at the expense of opponents far better endowed in personal wealth or other assets. While poverty is clearly a handicap in local election contests, associational resources augment the political resources of both the poor and rich political leader.

It should be clear by now why voluntary associations are attractive to local politicians. But what about the voters? Do voluntary associations safeguard *their* interests?

It is true that the associations tend to foster a discrete and intermittent pattern of political demands; and it requires little imagination to realize that programatic developmental objectives in the areas of education, housing, welfare, cooperativism or urban planning may be partially or even wholly prostituted in the service of private political objectives. Evidence indicates that Nagpur's numerous weaver cooperatives, for example, have been not merely politicized but organizationally greatly weakened by the rather complete erosion of their economic goals. Active membership is meager, enthusiasm for the cooperative concept virtually nil, public confidence at a low ebb, and economic cooperation only scantily practiced. More government resources channeled into the move-

[3]One director of a prominent cooperative housing society stated that the "election to the housing society is like the corporation election. You really should see it!" In the last election of its managing board, thirty persons contested for fourteen seats, and about 3,600 of 6,600 shareholders actually voted. Another informant, president for over a decade of a major cooperative bank, reported that elections to its managing committee were fought with all the regalia of a regular public election, including systematic canvassing and the use of cars to convey voters to polling stations.

ment may induce greater participation, but such an event will just as
surely add to the annoyance of those who do not share in the limited
and necessarily discriminatory distribution of benefits which discrete
political negotiation naturally engenders. Political deprivation has created an army of dissident weavers; and cooperative voluntary association
is the victim. For when governmental inputs are sidetracked to meet
competitive political objectives, the losers in that competition are unlikely to sacrifice anything on behalf of economic cooperativism. If they
sacrifice at all, it will be to overcome their immediate political opponents
and not their long-term economic problems. Without the wholehearted
support of the weavers, cooperativism cannot succeed. Ironically, the
very instrument created to bring about such cooperation has made it
less likely than ever.

In speaking of weaver societies, however, we are dealing with an industry facing obstacles which no amount of cooperative association
could wash away. Economically highly vulnerable, the weaving industry
simply cannot fend off enough political intervention to permit reasonably
unhampered pursuit of its own goals. It was a poor place, in other words,
in which to expect the cooperative seedling to grow.

The adulteration of associational goals is probably more the rule than
the exception; few of Nagpur's better endowed associations are un-
touched by scandal. But the rule does not apply equally to all associations; few others have been so gravely undermined as the weaver
societies. While they serve *homo politicus* as well as Saraswati,[4] Nagpur's
hundreds of education societies, for example, are clearly providing an
education to many children. If politics were absent from schools, resources and entrepreneurial talent to exploit them might also be absent.[5]

[4]Saraswati is the Hindu goddess of learning.

[5]Nagpur is full of examples of schools that died, not for want of students but
for lack of political acumen commensurate with the need for financial support.
There is always the argument, of course, that the quality of the schools would
be far greater *without* the meddling of politicians. "It may seem surprising, in
the circumstances," writes Gunnar Myrdal, "that the nationalization of school
systems has aroused so little interest in South Asia, the more so when we recall
that many of these countries profess a socialist orientation, which might be expected to make them less indulgent toward the disruptive effects of private
enterprise in the educational field. From a modern Western point of view the
strengthening of the public school system and the discontinuance of state subsidies to private schools—particularly the denominational ones—unless they are
firmly incorporated in the public school system, would seem a logical decision."
Asian Drama, III pp. 1707-1708.

It is, frankly, very difficult to judge whether voter interests are served well by associational enterprise. We know that voluntary associations provide an environment in which popular claims on governmental resources may be lodged. We know, too, that the intensity of competition for votes (even in a contest as humble as the municipal election) is great, and that associational resources are extensively employed in this competition. But are significant numbers of voters making use of this opportunity, extracting material concessions in exchange for voting support? Or are they, indeed, politically dependent, apathetic and naive, essentially incapable of holding their own against the politicians whose stakes allegedly "are not opportunities to advance the national interest but power, personal advantage, patronage, and graft"?[6] The prevalence of manipulative tactics, not infrequently coercive in form, and the fact that political responsibility is limited in many cases to the concession of rewards that can have only the slightest impact on the general well-being of constituents are indications, to be sure, that what there is of political accountability is in constant jeopardy. And whatever success voters have in obtaining satisfaction of their demands in associational arenas, the fact remains that such success applies only to a single range of local political relationships—the personal encounter between politician and supporter—and not to the exercise of public authority in distant executive and legislative institutions. But are there not other, more positive, indications?

I believe there are. The political perversions of voluntary associations, as well as the regrettable excesses in campaign strategy, which we have examined, appear to me to be a reaction by politicians to a rising tide of popular awareness of the reciprocal nature of political bargaining and of the considerable benefits to be gained from it. If politicians are obliged to go to extremes in attempts to harness the decisions of voters, the suggestion is implicit that voters possess political ingenuity of their own counterbalancing the chicanery of politicians. Unless we make the questionable assumption that voting behavior has little or nothing to do with the material interests of individuals or groups, the amazing display of enterprise by political candidates, faction leaders and party organizations is difficult to explain. What results is, indeed, a coarse and untidy style of politics. There are ample signs, however, that voters are learning to play the bargaining game well enough to assure themselves some share in the allocation of public goods. This falls far short of an iron-

[6] *Ibid.*, II, p. 776.

clad guarantee that equity will prevail in the process of distribution. Even less does it warrant the belief that progress toward vital public goals will not be retarded by the indulgence of private wants and the squandering of public assets. But if one of those goals is to give greater depth and meaning to political participation by holding political leaders accountable for their effectiveness in responding to popular demands, then progress—at least at the local level—may already have been substantial.

This brings us directly to the matter of virtue. For here an inescapable dilemma appears: Can impoverished India *afford* the luxury of meaningful popular political participation?

In Gabriel Almond and Sidney Verba's seminal study of political culture in five nations, the authors' sketched a paradigm of the democratic polity in which the system's ability to *limit* political participation was singled out as a key parameter. In comparison with the other nations in their study, they found that the "civic cultures" of Britain and America had struck the best balance between active political participation and passivity. "This is not to say," they wrote,

> that politics is unimportant in Britain and America. Respondents report that it plays a significant role in their lives, it is of interest to the populace, it is a topic of conversation. It is all these things frequently—more frequently, in fact, than in the other three nations. Yet politics is "kept in its place." The values associated with it are subordinate in significant respects to more general social values, and these more general social values act to temper political controversy within the two nations. In this way, again, we have a "managed" or "balanced" involvement in politics: an involvement that is kept from challenging the integration and stability of the political system.[7]

If "balanced" involvement is held to be crucial to democratic stability in the prospering industrial goliaths of the West, one can readily see the logic in arguing for a guarded popular participation in politics in the frail democracies of the Third World. In those countries, the argument runs, the pace and scope of social change simply have to be met by resolute decision making: irreversible socio-economic changes have dramatically heightened the need for coordinated and controlled social action at the

---

[7]*The Civic Culture: Political Attitudes and Democracy in Five Nations* (Boston: Little, Brown and Company, 1965), pp. 241-242.

same time that increased political participation is burdening political systems with mammoth quantities of new demands.[8]

The burden of political participation is incontestably great in India and, if the preceding account of local voluntary associations in Nagpur is not misleading, is growing ever greater. Anxiety over this development is not without justification: the public decision making process at all levels is clearly threatened with inundation by seemingly insatiable demands. And yet, there is something unprecedented and, hence, unpredictable about the evolving pattern of Indian democracy. "The point about Indian development," writes the eminent Indian political scientist Rajni Kothari,

> which gives it the character of an unprecedented undertaking is that while economic and social change is in important respects planned and directed from above, it is nonetheless carried on within the framework of an open and undirected polity. This means that manipulation of change in the image of a few dominant ideas gets conditioned by an accelerated pace of political competition, a changing structure of power and influence, and a widening base of political consultation and persuasion. The model is based less on coercing individuals and groups into new directions of action than on indulging them towards their own growth, albeit within a framework enacted from above. It is based less on the transcendence of individual self-interest by reference to 'reasons of state' than on reconciling such self-interest with the common good as interpreted by a legitimized elite in an idiom of persuasion.[9]

Kothari's "open" and "indulgent" polity, developing almost planlessly through the barely contained confrontation between traditional and modern sectors, is an obvious candidate for Gunnar Myrdal's class of socially undisciplined "soft states." Kothari himself readily admits that the early economic goals of India's leaders (rapid and sustained economic development directed by central bureaucratic planners) have proved noticeably incongruent with the political structures (parliamentary institutions based on universal suffrage and a widening electoral base) adopted to achieve them.[10] But the convergence of such institutional

[8]Gabriel Almond and G. Bingham Powell, Jr., *Comparative Politics: A Developmental Approach* (Boston: Little, Brown and Company, 1966), pp. 91–97.
[9]*Politics in India*, pp. 8–9.
[10]*Ibid.*, pp. 14–15.

structures with such goals would have required, according to him, de-emphasized political participation (as opposed to tactical mobilization) and a reduction in political competition. Social justice and equality would have had to have been delayed. And long-range national growth and material prosperity would have had to have been given precedence over the philosophy of the welfare state and the politics of mass consumption. India's actual strategy, to the contrary, has been one of simultaneous goal pursuit "rather than any sequential ordering through suppression of competitive goals."[11] Preoccupation with the dynamics of power—the ineluctable consequence of its commitment to political integration and mass democratic institutions—has forced the leadership "to compromise one after another the simple-minded canons of sacrifice and austerity it preached during the years following independence." It now gives precedence "to the complex and difficult task of mobilizing intermediate and peripheral structures through a simultaneous pursuit of both aggregative and participatory goals, rather than simply to re-map its institutions for the primary purpose of extracting from the people a growing economic surplus for the state."[12]

If India's ruling elites intend to strive for their own goals by bartering political power piecemeal for popular assent to modernization, the "modernity" ultimately achieved will likely conform to no image currently held either by Indians or outsiders. India's indulgent brand of politics inevitably generates plural valuations of social desiderata, of "the good life," and of the appropriate ends of development. If political competition is to be deliberately planted in an ongoing cultural and social dialectic among these discrepant valuations, as Kothari suggests, the actual as opposed to ideal direction of Indian development cannot be programed for delivery in sequential stages. The ultimate *uniformity* and *predictability* of development would be contingent, in the last analysis, upon the prior *deflation* of politics. Simply stated, the "free enterprise" politics which we have seen rampant in Nagpur would have to give way to the grand developmental vision of a much more austere "socialist" society.

The surprising turn of events in the summer of 1975 may already have set in motion the deflation of free enterprise politics. The non-communist political opposition has suffered a severe setback in the arrest and detention of thousands of its leaders; and Prime Minister

[11] *Ibid.*, p. 16.
[12] *Ibid.*

Gandhi seems determined, as never before in her ten years of rule, to place curbs on the open and indulgent style of politics that has characterized India since independence was gained. The atmosphere of drift and indecision of preceding years has been replaced, at least temporarily, by one of discipline and purpose. Not yet can the full impact of these developments on the institutional foundations of Indian political life be discerned; but there is little question that the survival of democracy is itself now at stake.

Is Indian democracy worth salvaging? This study of voluntary associations does not provide an unambiguous answer. We have seen indications that democracy "works" at the local level in one of the world's most socially segmented, hierarchically stratified, and impoverished societies. Most of the politicians encountered in the course of this study earned whatever electoral support they had essentially by responding to voter demands. Most of them labored hard at this task, seizing upon virtually every available resource to attract support, negating in their behavior those assumptions about Hindu fatalism or blind casteism so common among Indian democracy's critics. Most of them displayed at least grudging respect for the people whose votes they so earnestly coveted. The voters of Nagpur do not seem to be mere passive objects or abject spectators of the political process. Indeed, in its stout affirmation of participatory values, Indian democracy has endowed millions of citizens with political dignity of a sort that is rare on this planet.

There is, of course, a less roseate dimension of Indian politics. Adequate defenses against the most sordid varieties of political corruption have yet to be discovered; and some of the world's worst forms of social inequity persist in spite of (perhaps even *because* of) decades of democracy. Like it or not, we are forced to confront the unpleasant irony that in its democratic achievements may lie the seeds of India's economic failure. Nothing is more certain than that the existing system has lent itself to the steady wasting of India's exceedingly scarce resources. The common public interest has often been sacrificed to private political efficacy. Confidence in voluntarism in the domain of public developmental policy may well have been misplaced.

It would be unwise, however, to lay on democracy's doorstep sole blame for India's economic and social afflictions. Many of India's problems are beyond immediate solution; for some of them there may be no *political* remedy at all. Scrapping democracy may transfer power without rendering it any more capable, just, or effective. Are we to believe that the interests of Nagpur's voters would be better protected *without* the opportunity for meaningful political participation? Political power can be wielded to the advantage of the few under virtually any system; oligarchies are not more certain vehicles of economic advancement than are liberal democracies. Perhaps it has not been democracy as such, but its deliberate distortion by those whose privileges are most threatened by it, that has thwarted realization of the lofty objectives repeated year after year in the manifestos of the ruling Congress party. Are the privileged now to be stripped of their power and influence? Or, in the deflation of free enterprise politics, will they be made more secure than ever?

We began this study by acknowledging that stability and persistence could not fairly be reckoned political virtues if they resulted in nothing more than that. We have argued that there are, indeed, other virtues in Indian democracy, some of them growing with the consent of the ruling elite, some without it. These other virtues have been growing to the point where stability itself could not endure. In the year immediately preceding the emergency decree of 1975, Congress regimes in several states (most notably in Gujarat and Bihar) were severely shaken or even toppled from power in outbursts of popular resentment. Congress control of Nagpur itself was lost in the spring of 1975.[13] Repressive government action may restore stability, but much more than that is required to overcome India's problems. The worst mistake of all may be to victimize democracy, for there are other and far more dangerous villains. Among these are national leaders—in and out of the Congress —who seem not to know what must be done to cure their country's malaise, or possess the will to do it. The question now may really be whether the promise of a more *responsible* political leadership germinating in the voluntary associations of Nagpur can survive and spread *together* with political stability.

[13]In the city's fifth post-independence municipal election held in January 1975, Congress managed to win only fifteen of the seventy-five seats. With its RPI ally faring even worse (winning only two seats), this represented the party's worst setback in the city since independence. *Hitavada*, 1 February 1975.

Bibliography

PUBLIC DOCUMENTS

Government of India. *Census of India, 1961.* Vol. X: *Maharashtra.* Pt X: *Cities of Maharashtra (Nagpur).* New Delhi: Manager of Publications, 1968. Pp. 582-650.

————. *Report on the Fourth General Elections in India, 1967.* 2 vols. New Delhi: Government of India Press, 1968.

Government of India, Ministry of Information and Broadcasting. *Fourth General Elections: An Analysis.* New Delhi: Publications Division, 1967.

Government of Maharashtra, Bureau of Economics and Statistics. *Handbook of Basic Statistics of Maharashtra State 1968.* Bombay: Government Central Press, 1969.

————. *Socio Economic Review and District Statistical Abstract of Nagpur District, 1965-66.* Bombay: Government Printing and Stationery (1967?).

————. *Statistical Abstract of Maharashtra State: 1963-64, 1964-65 and 1965-66.* Bombay: Government Printing and Stationery, 1969.

Government of Maharashtra, Census Office. *Nagpur District Census Handbook.* Bombay: Government Printing and Stationery, 1965.

Government of Maharashtra, Commissioner for Cooperation and Registrar of Cooperative Societies (Poona). "Industrial Cooperatives." Leaflet. Bombay: Government Central Press (1968?).

Government of Maharashtra, Cooperative Department. *Cooperative Societies in Maharashtra State: Government Annual Report (1966-67)* (Marathi). Bombay: Government Central Press, 1968.

Government of Maharashtra. *Maharashtra State Gazetteers, Nagpur District.* Revised edition. Bombay: Government Printing and Stationery, 1966.

Joshi, Padmakar L. *et al. Nagpur City Centennial Volume* (Marathi). Nagpur: Nagpur Municipal Corporation, 1964.

Lewy, Guenter. *Militant Hindu Nationalism: The Early Phase.* Report prepared for the United States Department of Defense, Advanced Research Projects Agency. Washington: 1967.

Record of Proceedings, Panjabrao vs. D. P. Meshram and Others. 2 pts. Civil Appeal No. 19 in the Supreme Court of India, on appeal from the High Court of Maharashtra (Nagpur Bench). New Delhi: 1964.

BOOKS

Almond, Gabriel and Powell, Jr., G. Bingham. *Comparative Politics: A Developmental Approach*. Boston: Little, Brown and Company, 1966.

Almond, Gabriel and Verba, Sidney. *The Civic Culture: Political Attitudes and Democracy in Five Nations*. Princeton: Princeton University Press, 1963.

Bailey, F. G. *Politics and Social Change: Orissa in 1959*. Berkeley: University of California Press, 1963.

Baxter, Craig. *The Jana Sangh: A Biography of an Indian Political Party*. Philadelphia: University of Pennsylvania Press, 1969.

Béteille, André. *Caste, Class, and Power*. Berkeley: University of California Press, 1965.

Brass, Paul R. *Factional Politics in an Indian State: The Congress Party in Uttar Pradesh*. Berkeley: University of California Press, 1965.

————. *Language, Religion and Politics in North India*. London: Cambridge University Press, 1974.

Brecher, Michael. *Nehru: A Political Biography*. Boston: Beacon Press, 1962.

Burger, Angela S. *Opposition in a Dominant-Party System*. Berkeley: University of California Press, 1969.

Carras, Mary C. *The Dynamics of Indian Political Factions*. London: Cambridge University Press, 1972.

Curran, Jr., Jean A. *Militant Hinduism in Indian Politics: A Study of the R.S.S.* New York: International Secretariat, Institute of Pacific Relations, 1951.

Das Gupta, Jyotirindra. *Language Conflict and National Development: Group Politics and National Language Policy in India*. Berkeley: University of California Press, 1970.

Dumont, Louis. *Homo Hierarchicus: The Caste System and Its Implications*. Chicago: The University of Chicago Press, 1970.

Enloe, Cynthia H. *Ethnic Conflict and Political Development*. Boston: Little, Brown and Company, 1973.

Erdman, Howard L. *The Swatantra Party and Indian Conservatism*. London: Cambridge University Press, 1967.

Harrison, Selig. *India The Most Dangerous Decades*. Princeton: Princeton University Press, 1960.

Ilchman, Warren F., Ilchman, Alice Stone, and Hastings, Philip K. *The New Men of Knowledge and the Developing Nations*. Studies in Comparative Administration, No. 1. Berkeley: Institute of Governmental Studies, University of California, 1968.

Isaacs, Harold. *India's Ex-Untouchables*. New York: John Day Company, 1964.

Jones, Rodney, W. *Urban Politics in India: Area, Power, and Policy in a Penetrated System*. Berkeley: University of California Press, 1974.

Kochanek, Stanley A. *The Congress Party of India: The Dynamics of One-Party Democracy*. Princeton: Princeton University Press, 1968.

Kothari, Rajni. *Politics in India*. Boston: Little, Brown and Company, 1970.
————, editor. *Caste in Indian Politics*. New Delhi: Orient Longman Ltd., 1970.
Mahar, Michael J., editor. *The Untouchables in Contemporary India*. Tucson: The University of Arizona Press, 1972.
Mamoria, C. B. and Saksena, R. D. *Co-operation in India*. Allahabad: Kitab Mahal, 1967.
Morris-Jones, W. H. *The Government and Politics of India*. London: Hutchinson University Library, 1971.
Myrdal, Gunnar. *Asian Drama: An Inquiry into the Poverty of Nations*. 3 vols. Middlesex, England: The Penguin Press, 1968.
Nanekar, K. R. *Handloom Industry in Madhya Pradesh*. Nagpur: Nagpur University Press, 1968.
Nelson, Joan M. *Migrants, Urban Poverty, and Instability in Developing Nations*. Occasional Papers in International Affairs, No. 22. Cambridge: Center for International Affairs, Harvard University, 1969.
Palmer, Monte. *Dilemmas of Political Development*. Itasca, Illinois: F. F. Peacock Publishers, Inc., 1973.
Purohit, B. R. *Hindu Revivalism and Indian Nationalism*. Sagar, Madhya Pradesh: Sathi Prakashan, 1965.
Pye, Lucian W. *Aspects of Political Development*. Boston: Little, Brown and Company, 1966.
Rabushka, Alvin and Shepsle, Kenneth A. *Politics in Plural Societies: A Theory of Democratic Instability*. Columbus: Charles E. Merrill Publishing Company, 1972.
Rosenthal, Donald B. *The Limited Elite: Politics and Government in Two Indian Cities*. Chicago: The University of Chicago Press, 1970.
Rudolph, Lloyd I. and Rudolph, Susanne H. *The Modernity of Tradition: Political Development in India*. Chicago: The University of Chicago Press, 1967.
Sharma, B. A. V. and Jangam, R. T. *The Bombay Municipal Corporation: An Election Study*. Bombay: Popular Book Depot, 1962.
Singh, G. S. *Maratha Geopolitics and the Indian Nation*. Bombay: Manaktalas, 1966.
Sirsikar, V. M. *Political Behavior in India: A Case Study of the 1962 General Elections*. Bombay: Manaktalas, 1965.
Sisson, Richard. *The Congress Party in Rajasthan*. Berkeley: University of California Press, 1972.
Smith, Donald E. *India as a Secular State*. Princeton: Princeton University Press, 1963.
Sterling, Richard W. *Macropolitics: International Relations in a Global Society*. New York: Alfred A. Knopf, 1974.
Venkatarangaiya, M. and Pattabhiram, M., editors. *Local Government in India*. Bombay: Allied Publishers, 1969.
Verma, S. P. and Bhambhri, C. P., editors. *Elections and Political Consciousness in India*. Meerut: Meenakshi Prakashan, 1967.
Wallace, Anthony F. C. *Culture and Personality*. New York: Random House, 1961.
Weiner, Myron. *Party Building in a New Nation: The Indian National Congress*. Chicago: The University of Chicago Press, 1967.

————. *Party Politics in India: The Development of a Multi-Party System*. Princeton: Princeton University Press, 1957.

————. *The Politics of Scarcity: Public Pressure and Political Response in India*. Chicago: The University of Chicago Press, 1962.

Weiner, Myron and Kothari, Rajni, editors. *Indian Voting Behavior*. Calcutta: Firma K. L. Mukhopadhyay, 1965.

ARTICLES AND PERIODICALS

Arora, Phyllis. "Patterns of Political Response in Indian Peasant Society," *Asian Political Processes*, Henry S. Albinski, editor. Boston: Allyn and Bacon, Inc., 1971. Pp. 33–47.

Baxter, Craig. "The Jana Sangh: A Brief History," *South Asian Politics and Religion*, Donald E. Smith, editor. Princeton: Princeton University Press, 1966. Pp. 74–101.

Brass, Paul. "Uttar Pradesh," *State Politics in India*, Myron Weiner, editor. Princeton: Princeton University Press, 1968. Pp. 61–124.

Church, Roderick. "Authority and Influence in Indian Municipal Politics: Administrators and Councillors in Lucknow," *Asian Survey*, XIII (April 1973), 421–438.

Connor, Walker. "Ethnology and the Peace of South Asia," *World Politics*, XXII (October 1969), 51–85.

Eisenstadt, Samuel N. "Breakdowns of Modernization," *Economic Development and Cultural Change*, XII (July 1964), 345–367.

Geertz, Clifford. "The Integrative Revolution: Primordial Sentiments and Civil Politics in the New States," *Old Societies and New States: The Quest for Modernity in Asia and Africa*, Clifford Geertz, editor. New York: The Free Press of Glencoe, 1963. Pp. 105–157.

Gould, Harold. "Educational Structures and Political Processes in Faizabad District, Uttar Pradesh," *Education and Politics in India*, Susanne H. Rudolph and Lloyd I. Rudolph, editors. Cambridge: Harvard University Press, 1972. Pp. 94–120.

————. "Religion and Politics in a U.P. Constituency," *South Asian Politics and Religion*, Donald E. Smith, editor. Princeton: Princeton University Press, 1966. Pp. 51–73.

Graham, Bruce D. "Syama Prasad Mookerjee and the Communalist Alternative," *Soundings in Modern Asian History*, D. A. Low, editor. Berkeley: University of California Press, 1968. Pp. 330–374.

Hart, Henry C. "Bombay Politics: Pluralism or Polarization?" *Journal of Asian Studies*, XX (May 1961), 267–274.

Hirschman, Albert O. "The Search for Paradigms as a Hindrance to Understanding," *World Politics*, XXII (April 1970), 329–343.

Hitavada. Daily. Nagpur. January 1969 to March 1970.

Huntington, Samuel P. "Political Development and Political Decay," *World Politics*, XVII (April 1965), 386–430.

The Indian Express. Daily. New Delhi. January 1969 to March 1970.

Joshi, Ram. "India 1974: Growing Political Crisis," *Asian Survey*, XV (February 1975), 85-95.

————. "Maharashtra," *State Politics in India*, Myron Weiner, editor. Princeton: Princeton University Press, 1968. Pp. 177-212.

Katzenstein, Mary F. "Origins of Nativism: The Emergence of Shiv Sena in Bombay," *Asian Survey*, XIII (April 1973), 386-399.

Kini, N.G.S. "Caste as a Factor in State Politics," *State Politics in India*, Iqbal Narain, editor. Meerut: Meenakshi Prakashan, 1967. Pp. 562-574.

Lambert, Richard D. "Hindu Communal Groups in Indian Politics," *Leadership and Political Institutions in India*, Richard L. Park and Irene Tinker, editors. Princeton: Princeton University Press, 1959. Pp. 211-224.

La Palombara, Joseph and Weiner, Myron. "The Origin and Development of Political Parties," *Political Parties and Political Development*, Joseph La Palombara and Myron Weiner, editors. Princeton: Princeton University Press, 1966. Pp. 3-42.

Maharashtra Law Journal, 1965.

Mayer, Peter. "Patterns of Urban Political Culture in India," *Asian Survey*, XIII (April 1973), 400-407.

Morris-Jones, W. H. "Political Recruitment and Political Development," *Politics and Change in Developing Countries*, Colin Leys, editor. London: Cambridge University Press, 1969. Pp. 113-134.

Morrison, Barrie M. "Asian Drama, Act II: Development Prospects in South Asia," *Pacific Affairs*, 48 (Spring 1975), 5-26.

Nagpur Diary. Weekly. 21 December 1968.

Nagpur Times. Daily. January 1969 to March 1970.

Nair, Kusum. "Asian Drama—A Critique," *Economic Development and Cultural Change*, XVII (July 1969), 449-459.

Narain, Iqbal. "Rural Local Politics and Primary School Management," *Education and Politics in India*, Susanne H. Rudolph and Lloyd I. Rudolph, editors. Cambridge: Harvard University Press, 1972. Pp. 148-164.

Navbharat. Daily. Nagpur. January 1969 to March 1970.

Palmer, Norman. "India's Fourth General Election," *Asian Survey*, VII (May 1967), 275-291.

Pye, Lucian. "The Non-Western Political Process," *The Dynamics of Modernization and Social Change: A Reader*, George S. Masannat, editor. Pacific Palisades: Goodyear Publishing Company, Inc., 1973. Pp. 30-32.

Riggs, Fred W. "Comparative Politics and the Study of Political Parties: A Structural Approach," *Approaches to the Study of Party Organization*, William J. Crotty, editor. Boston: Allyn and Bacon, Inc., 1968. Pp. 45-104.

Rosenthal, Donald B. "Administrative Politics in Two Indian Cities," *Asian Survey*, VI (April 1966), 201-215.

————. "Deurbanization, Elite Displacement, and Political Change in India," *Comparative Politics*, II (January 1970), 169-201.

————. "Educational Politics and Public Policymaking in Maharashtra, India," *Comparative Education Review*, 18 (February 1974), 79-95.

————. "Factions and Alliances in Indian City Politics," *Midwest Journal of Political Science*, X (August 1966), 320-349.

————. "Friendship and Deference Patterns in Two Indian Municipal Councils," *Social Forces*, XLV (December 1966), 178-192.

———. "Functions of Urban Political Systems: Comparative Analysis and the Indian Case," *Community Structure and Decision-Making: Comparative Analyses*, Terry N. Clark, editor. San Francisco: Chandler Publishing Company, 1968. Pp. 269-303.

———. " 'Making It' in Maharashtra," *Journal of Politics*, 36 (May 1974), 409-437.

———. "Sources of District Congress Factionalism in Maharashtra," *Economic and Political Weekly*, VII (19 August 1972), 1725-1746.

Scott, James C. "Corruption, Machine Politics, and Political Change," *American Political Science Review*, LXIII (December 1969), 1142-1158.

Somjee, A. H. "Caste and the Decline of Political Homogeneity," *American Political Science Review*, LXVII (September 1973), 799-816.

Srinivasan, R. and Sharma, B. A. V. "Politics in Urban India: A Study of Four Corporations," *Studies in Indian Democracy*, S. P. Aiyar and R. Srinivasan, editors. Bombay: Allied Publishers, 1965. Pp. 467-514.

Tarun Bharat. Daily. Nagpur. January 1969 to March 1970.

Tinker, Hugh. "South Asia: The Colonial Backlash," *The Study of International Affairs*, Roger Morgan, editor. New York: Oxford University Press, for The Royal Institute of International Affairs, 1972. Pp. 249-270.

Weiner, Myron. "Political Integration and Political Development," *Political Development and Social Change*, Jason L. Finkle and Richard W. Gable, editors. New York: John Wiley and Sons, Inc., 1966. Pp. 551-562.

Wirsing, Robert G. "Associational 'Micro-Arenas' in Indian Urban Politics," *Asian Survey*, XIII (April 1973), 408-420.

———. "Strategies of Political Bargaining in Indian City Politics," *The City in Indian Politics*, Donald B. Rosenthal, editor. New Delhi: Thomson Press Limited, 1976. Pp. 192-212.

Wood, Glynn. "National Planning and Public Demand in Indian Higher Education," *Minerva*, X (January 1972), 83-106.

Zelliot, Eleanor. "Buddhism and Politics in Maharashtra," *South Asian Politics and Religion*, Donald E. Smith, editor. Princeton: Princeton University Press, 1966. Pp. 191-212.

Unpublished Materials

Fontera, Richard M. "Cultural Pluralism and Communalism: The Development of the Government of India Act of 1935." Unpublished Ph.D. dissertation, New York University, 1964.

Jones, Rodney. "Towards Comparative Urban Studies: A Linkage Model of Urban Politics in India." Paper prepared for delivery at the Annual Meeting of the International Studies Association, Pittsburg, 3-5 April 1970. Mimeographed.

Norman, Robert T. "Urban Political Development: India." Paper prepared for delivery at the Annual Meeting of the American Political Science Association, Chicago, 7-11 September 1971. Mimeographed.

Odenburg, Philip K. "Indian Urban Politics: Citizen, Administrator, and Councilor in Delhi." Paper prepared for delivery at the Annual Meeting of the American Political Science Association, Chicago, 7-11 September 1971. Mimeographed.

———. "Indian Urban Politics, With Particular Reference to the Nagpur Corporation." Unpublished Master's thesis, Department of Political Science, University of Chicago, 1968.

Rosenthal, Donald B. "Local Power and Comparative Politics: Notes Toward the Study of Comparative Local Politics." Paper prepared for delivery at the Annual Meeting of the American Political Science Association, Washington, D.C., 5-9 September 1972. Mimeographed.

Watson, Vincent. "Communal Politics in India and the United States: A Comparative Analysis." Research Paper No. 10. Atlanta: School of Arts and Sciences, Georgia State College, 1965. Mimeographed.

OTHER SOURCES

Applications submitted to Nagpur City District Congress Committee for party nominations to contest in Nagpur Municipal Corporation Election, 16 March 1969 (in the files of the Committee).

Citizens Education Society. *Citizens Education Society, Nagpur—Objectives and Operation.* Nagpur: Privately printed (1969?). Leaflet.

Minutes of executive meeting, 27 July 1969, and general meetings, 14 September and 25 October 1969, Nagpur City Akhada Federation Committee, Nagpur (in the files of the Committee). Typewritten.

Nagpur Improvement Trust. Annual reports, 1961 through 1968. Printed brochures.

Nagpur University. *Annual Report* (year ending 30 June 1969). Nagpur: Nagpur University Press, 1969.

"A Note on the Cooperative Movement in Nagpur District." Memorandum prepared for Shri P. P. Dharmadhikari, District Deputy Registrar Cooperative Societies, Gandhi Sagar, Nagpur, November 1969 (in the files of the Registrar). Typewritten.

People's Welfare Society. "Proposed Residential College." Promotional bulletin of the Society. Nagpur: Privately printed (1968?).

Samarth, Ramkrishna P. "Candidature of Shri R. P. Samarth for the Nagpur Parliamentary Constituency No. 21 Along with Brief Review of His Social and Public Work Since Last 30 Years." Publicity folder (1967). Mimeographed.

———. "Ward Public Institutions and Workers Record." Questionnaire (1970). Mimeographed.

Shri Shivaji Education Society. *Amended Constitution.* Amravati: Privately printed, 1967.

———. *Annual Report (1967-68).* Amravati: Privately printed, 1968.

Index

Agarwal, Madan Gopal, 28, 177n
Ahuja, Ramprakash S., 137-138, 139n, 143
Aiyar, S. P., 4n
Akhadas. *See* Athletic associations
Albinski, Henry S., 6n
All-India Congress Committee (AICC), 82n, 114
Almond, Gabriel, 195, 196n
Ambedkar, B. R., 86-96 *passim*
Ambedkar Memorial Committee, 93
Arora, Phyllis, 6
Arya Samaj, 132
Athawale, G. K., 143n, 166n
Athletic associations, 40, 107-108; factional dispute over, 115-122
Auliya, Sant Baba Tajudin, 182
Awode, Haridas, 25n, 89n, 91

Bailey, F. G., 17n, 75n, 129n
Bajarang Dal, 110-112. *See also* Colonelbag faction
Banfield, Edward C., 104n
Barakes. *See* Mahars
Bawanes. *See* Mahars
Baxter, Craig, 18n, 24n, 134n
Belekar, N. M., 146-147, 149n, 175
Beteille, Andre, 44
Bhambhri, C. P., 4n
Bharatiya Jana Sangh (BJS), in Buldhana district, 135; caste com-
position of, 136-141; and Hindu revivalism, 131-135; and Koshtis, 146-149; in Maharashtra, 136n; and Mochis, 145-146; in Nagpur district, 136; and Nagpur party system, 20-44 *passim*; and Nagpur Improvement Trust, 166n, 169-176; organizational strategy of, 135-152; and Rashtriya Swayamsevak Sangh, 134-135; in Uttar Pradesh, 142n; in Vidarbha division, 135; and voluntary associations, 141-149; in Yeotmal district, 136
Bharatiya Kranti Dal, 22n
Bhartiya Mazdur Sangh (BMS), 143n, 166n
Bharat Sewak Samaj (BSS), 95, 191
Bhonsale ruling family, 108, 177n
Bhoyar, B. D., 118n
Bombay, 27n; cotton textile industry of, 49-50
Borkar, A. M., 92
Brahmans, 25, 32n, 33n; and Jana Sangh party, 136-141 *passim*; party identification of, 34-39 *passim*
Brahmo Samaj, 132
Brass, Paul R., 8n, 17n, 24n, 104-105, 122, 124, 128n, 134, 142n
Brecher, Michael, 1n
Buddhists. *See* Mahars
Burger, Angela S., 18n, 33n, 142n, 151n